AN INTRODU
MARXIST ECONOMICS

AN INTRODUCTION TO MARXIST ECONOMICS

George Catephores

M
MACMILLAN
EDUCATION

First published 1989

Published by
MACMILLAN EDUCATION LTD
Houndmills, Basingstoke, Hampshire RG21 2XS
and London
Companies and representatives
throughout the world

Typeset by Wessex Typesetters
(Division of The Eastern Press Ltd)
Frome, Somerset

Printed in Hong Kong

British Library Cataloguing in Publication Data
Catephores, George
An introduction to Marxist economics.
1. Marxian economics
I. Title
335.4   HB97.5
ISBN 0–333–46101–0 (hardcover)
ISBN 0–333–46102–9 (paperback)

Contents

Preface

Lecturers in Marxist economics may have sometimes experienced the feeling that their subject-matter falls into two distinct parts: an early and easy, followed by a late and difficult one.

The early part covers things like the labour theory of value, surplus-value and the fundamentals of an analysis of exploitation. For a lecturer prepared to relegate discussion of more controversial issues (the transformation problem, homogeneous versus heterogeneous labour) to a separate section of the course, the task here is both manageable and quite enjoyable. The relevant theory has been left by its original author in a highly finished state. It is coherent, well-argued, often quite plainly written, almost tailor-made for textbook presentation.

In addition – given the stubborn resistance of mainstream economics to allowing a niche for the idea which, after Marx, appears to many as plain commonsense: that in a capitalist market economy exploitation of labour is fully consistent with general competitive equilibrium – Marxist economics with its emphasis on exploitation retains, despite its age, an air of freshness and originality that takes the audience by surprise.

The effect is heightened by the strong appeal of this part of Marxism to the ordinary person's sense of elementary justice. What could be fairer than to base an economic theory of value and distribution on the premise that, under ideal conditions, only productive labour should confer a title of ownership (hence the basis of purchasing power) to the product. Clarity, originality plus a sense of moral commitment, all combine to make this first part of a course on Marxist economics a lecturer's and an audience's paradise.

In the second part, things take a very different turn. Here it is the intricacies of the mechanism of the capitalist mode of production in its macroeconomic consequences that have to be confronted. How to relate the labour theory of value to them is neither obvious nor easy. Thorny issues, like unemployment, monopolies, crises, technical change, capital accumulation, credit, money, enrichment or impoverishment of whole social classes, growth versus stagnation and economic decline, these are the matters which must be placed on the agenda. On topics like these the original sources of Marxist economics are not nearly as helpful as on the topic of exploitation. Not that the sources suffer from any deficiency of ideas. On the contrary, ideas abound; sometimes one wonders if there might not be a surfeit of them. But clarity, logical order, continuity in development, the traditional qualities of a good textbook (and, perhaps, of a bad book) are often painfully missing. What was a lecturer's paradise has turned into his (let alone the audience's) nightmare. What is one to do?

The traditional response to this question has been an attempt to set aside a lot of side issues and go for the 'grand structure' of Marx's analysis. The chase for that structure among Marx's prolific writings can be frustrating but also fascinating. One often feels lost in the midst of unresolvable complications when, all of a sudden, the way is illuminated by one of Marx's flashes of genius that pierce through the darkness. One feels worn down by the unspeakable tedium of far-too-long, far-too-repetitive passages, until one's spirits are mercifully lifted by some unexpected outburst of Marx's sardonic humour. In fact, the chase can become so engrossing that some never have the heart to bring it to a conclusion and emerge from the woods, holding for display whatever game they were able to capture.

In a broader sense Marx himself was, to a certain extent, such an enchanted huntsman. The chase, in the unpublished manuscripts he kept piling up on top of one another interminably, was much vaster in comparison to the results he allowed himself, or was allowed by circumstances, to publish, during his lifetime. For example, in the *Preface* to the first German edition of *Capital*, Vol. I, he wrote that 'the ultimate aim of this work is to lay bare the economic law of motion of modern society'. But, despite the enormous analytical material he contributed towards this aim, he never explicitly pointed the finger to one of his various formulations, selecting it as the definitive version of some such law.

It was inevitable that others would attempt to do it for him. Propagation of ideas, whether in academic life or in politics, requires something more definable, more capable of being intellectually appropriated, domesticated even, than the tempestuous, often baffling, open-endedness of Marx's explosive thinking. The outburst of a scientific revolution has to be followed by normal science.[1] It is the province of the latter to systematise, to state in a methodical, cut-and-dried manner, laws and models often left in their urgency incomplete, only indistinctly discernible, by those who were pressed to achieve some great original breakthrough.

Shouldn't we all be grateful to the 'normal scientists', for their pedestrian spadework? They are the ones who make our job possible. They bring the task of lecturing, teaching, preaching, scribbling, listening to, learning and even taking political action down to dimensions commensurate with the average limitations of most people. The present author, at least, is certainly grateful, regarding the problem of the gap between the two successive areas of Marxist economics, to one such 'normal scientist' who made the author's lecturing work at all possible. Long years ago a paper by Ronald Meek[2] alerted him to the existence of a concise statement of what might be regarded as coming close to Marx's promised 'law of motion' of capitalism. Meek had not written the statement himself. He found it ready-made in the book by the American Marxist Joseph Gillman,[3] *The Falling Rate of Profit*, and used it without alteration and (of course) with full acknowledgement.

Gillman himself cannot really be said to have extracted from Marx's writings one unique statement summarising the whole central tendency of the capitalist system. Rather, he proposed a complex of four 'laws of motion' of capitalism: (i) the law of the falling rate of profit, (ii) the law of the increasing severity of the cyclical crisis, (iii) the law of concentration and centralisation of capital and (iv) the law of the increasing misery of the working class. Four though they are, these 'laws' are sufficiently integrated to be treated as a coherent model, representing the more narrowly economic side of the capitalist mode of production.

From the point of view of the gap mentioned earlier, between the labour theory of value and the macroeconomic analysis of the capitalist economy, Gillman's summary of the four 'laws' does manage to create a bridge. The law of the falling rate of profit, the centrepiece of the model implicit in Gillman's statement, can be seen as a direct derivation from the labour theory of value and surplus-value. Crises also must be analysed within the framework of a theory of the accumulation process, itself described in value terms. Given such linkages, the transition from value theory to Marxist macroeconomics becomes possible, while the succinct statement of the four 'laws' offers a comprehensive framework for the orderly presentation of the rather less well organised parts of Marx's argument. Finally, the emphasis on the evolutionary trends of capitalist development, expressed particularly in the law of increasing concentration and centralisation of capital, links up the more narrowly economic model with the wider vistas of change in and succession of modes of production, opened up by the general theory of historical materialism.

This last point does raise some additional difficulties. If the capitalist system evolves during the period of its existence, is it possible to understand its workings with the help of just one single model or is a sequence of models necessary? Marx, in some way, had anticipated that difficulty when he wrote, again in the *Preface* to the first edition of *Capital*, Vol. I: 'The country that is more developed industrially only shows, to the less developed, the image of its own future'. It should, therefore, be possible for the theorist to take the standpoint of that 'future', to position himself at the level of the most developed capitalist economy in existence, and give a comprehensive view both of the highest stage of capitalist development and of the road towards it with the help of one single theoretical instrument, the analytical model applicable primarily to advanced capitalism.

Historical materialism, the labour theory of value, Marxist macroeconomics and economic development can in this way form one cluster round the nucleus of the four 'laws of motion' assembled by Gillman. The benefits of this approach are not exhausted by the advantages of presentation. The fullness, the strong internal cohesiveness of Marxist theory it brings out are, in themselves, an important step towards establishing the truth of the theory. Many followers of Marx have been won over to his teaching by the perception of its integrative power praised by probably the greatest among them, Lenin, in the following glowing terms:[4]

> The Marxist doctrine is omnipotent because it is true. It is comprehensive and harmonious, and provides men with an integral world outlook irreconcilable with any form of superstition, reaction or defence of bourgeois oppression.

The present author believes that until relatively recently a model broadly similar to the one described at the beginning of the previous paragraph commanded, in some version or other, the loyalties of most practitioners of Marxism, whether in academic teaching or in political life. He would name it 'the early Marxist model', which, together with very many other Marxist 'normal scientists', he also adopted for his teaching and tried to defend by his research.

The main problem of all 'normal scientists', convinced as they are by some impressive successes of their paradigm into believing in its basic validity, is how to deal with contrary evidence. Collecting more evidence, clarifying and interpreting the existing one or reconciling it with their paradigm by introducing into the latter minor modifications are all strategies that have to be applied on one occasion or another. What is not permitted by the rules of the game is that they abandon a tried basic interpretative scheme as soon as a slight frown appears on the face of empirical evidence. If they did this they would be guilty of 'naïve falsificationism', which not even Popper would condone.[5] And often 'normal scientists' have to dismiss, as irrelevant, clashes of their theories with the data which are far more serious than a mere frown on the face of empirical evidence. Not even practitioners of Newton's paradigm escaped that fate,[6] let alone followers of disciplines far less exact than classical physics.

Practitioners of the 'early Marxist model', though unsupported by the prestige or the successes of physics, did not fall much behind Newtonians in stubbornness, in the defence of their paradigm. Gradually, however, anomalies and counter-evidence piled up to the point where some of them realised the need for drastic revisions. These would usually take the following form: one of the four 'laws' of Gillman's summary would be abandoned first, in view of what was seen as overwhelming evidence against it. But in a system of thought as tightly knit as the early Marxist model it would prove impossible to let go of just one part. A general and far-reaching overhaul of the total structure was sooner or later called for.

The case of P. M. Sweezy is instructive in this respect. Himself an outstanding practitioner of the early model and author of a classic textbook on the subject (his *Theory of Capitalist Development*), he proposed a critique of the law of the falling rate of profit, while still defending the basic model in its totality. In his textbook he went only part of the way, by formulating certain qualifications to the 'law'. But he soon perceived that the other aspects of the model had to be modified accordingly, and eventually a radically new model to be proposed.

This he did, together with P. A. Baran in their *Monopoly Capital*, where the law of the tendency of the rate of profit to fall was replaced by the new law, proposed by the authors, of the tendency of the surplus to rise. Sweezy and Baran – fully cognisant of the strong cohesion between the various parts of Marxist analysis, and in particular between the labour theory of value and the law of the falling rate of profit – did not fail to point out that, in their new approach, the labour theory of value was no longer directly applicable. They justified this by arguing that under monopoly capitalism (the currently relevant phase of the capitalist mode of production which they were intent on analysing), market structure led to a kind of pricing inconsistent with the competitive assumptions of the labour theory of value. They then proceeded to define the absorption of surplus as the new, main economic problem of capitalism in its monopoly phase.

Baran and Sweezy's work provides one example of a genuinely far-reaching attempt at replacing the early Marxist model by one intended to account better for the changed circumstances of the capitalist economy. Their work, or other work along the same lines as theirs, does not render the early Marxist model totally obsolete. As Sweezy has recently said,[7] analysis dependent on the labour theory of value is indispensable to an understanding of the basic structure which pervades all phases of the capitalist mode of production.

While subscribing to this view, as far as the labour theory of value is concerned, the present author would maintain that the early Marxist model, seen as a cluster of ideas around the four 'laws of motion' collected by Gillman, is no longer tenable. Too much empirical evidence against certain of its aspects, too much theoretical criticism against certain of its concepts has accumulated. These can no longer be brushed aside, no matter how strong be the instincts of 'normal Marxist scientists' in defence of their basic paradigm.

On the other hand, in the opinion of the present author, what has become imperative is not the total rejection and replacement but rather the construction of a modified version of the early model. Without anticipating any part of this book, the author may say that he has bent his effort towards presenting basic Marxist economics in the form of a transition from the early to what he would call the 'modified Marxist model'. The law of increasing misery has been lost in the transition and the law of the falling rate of profit has lost its central place, but the modified Marxist model, defended in the book (particularly in the last chapters) is quite recognisably a member of the same family as the early one.

Where the modified Marxist model departs drastically from its predecessors is not so much in its economics but in its sociopolitical implications. By incorporating a law of increasing misery, the early Marxist model made the maturing of a working class revolution to all intents and purposes inevitable. Without such a law, the revolutionary prediction is much less obvious. Under the modified Marxist model it remains true that capitalism gradually builds up the objective conditions of a socialist transformation of society and that it is itself a very unpleasant, exploitative system. But it no longer deteriorates sufficiently to compel the emergence of the subjective conditions, the formation of revolutionary consciousness among the majority of the population. Such consciousness has to be developed via the alternative process of political self-education of the disadvantaged class, the content of consciousness becoming the positive approval and choice in favour of socialist institutions rather than the merely negative rejection of capitalist institutions. In democratic regimes, persuasion rather than violent confrontation of social classes may ultimately prove sufficient for the formation among the majority of those attitudes needed for socialist change. Whether such 'non-revolutionary' implications will prevail on a global, or even local, scale, the present author does not presume to know. They seem to fit the conditions of advanced capitalist societies of our epoch. It is from underdeveloped capitalist countries that all revolutionary tempests have started in our century. The revolutionary implications of the early Marxist model, inspired in Marx's days by the experiences of the then most advanced of capitalist societies, that of Britain, are probably much more relevant nowadays in some of the underdeveloped parts of the world, going through the labour of their industrial revolutions. What is, probably, even more relevant for them, from the point of view of their revolutionary potential, is a brief but extremely perceptive remark, addressed by Marx, in the *Preface* to the first edition of *Capital*, Vol I, to his native Germany – in 1867 still an underdeveloped, by the then British standards – country. Marx wrote:[8]

> In all . . . spheres, we, like all the rest of Continental Western Europe, suffer not only from the development of capitalist production, but also from the incompleteness of that development. Alongside of modern evils, a whole series of inherited evils oppress us, arising from the passive survival of antiquated modes of production, with their inevitable train of social and political anachronisms.

This confluence of old and new evils may be the best explanation of the revolutionary turmoil observed in the third world today (or in earlier epochs in the history of what now are advanced capitalist countries). If so, revolutionary potential reaches its maximum in early rather than in late capitalism.

The majority of Marxist theorists hold the view that in the modern monopolistic phase of world capitalism underdeveloped countries cannot look forward to ever graduating to advanced capitalist status. If so, 'the country that is more developed industrially' no longer shows to the less developed 'the image of its own future'. The analysis relevant to advanced capitalism – the modified Marxist model – can no longer be treated as broadly valid for underdeveloped countries also. To these the early Marxist model may still apply. In view of the drastically different socio-political implications of the two models, this separation opens up a serious rift in Marxist theory.

It is not the only one. The relaxation of the links between economics and politics, consequent upon the transition from the early to the modified Marxist model, must be seen as equally serious. Separate theoretical treatment of developed and underdeveloped capitalism, separate economic and political trends in advanced capitalism, all this is rather distant from the 'comprehensive and harmonious' doctrine that had fascinated Lenin. Yet, in the greater, sometimes confusing, multiplicity of models or approaches, which nowadays claim to derive their inspiration from Marx (or actually derive it therefrom, without claiming it), the vigour and versatility of the original source is attested. Whether and to what extent modifications to Marx's analysis, introduced with the intention of bringing his insights up to date with regard to developments since his times, do serve his vast project is something current practitioners cannot say with any certainty. Only a new synthesis, as bold and as comprehensive as that of Marx could resolve this question, by measuring the worth of each partial contribution or criticism against the totality of a new composition. Until then Samuelson's admonition (who would have himself a lot to answer for on a day of judgment such as he imagined) issued on the occasion of the centenary commemoration of *Capital*, Vol I, by the American Economic Association, will haunt practitioners, friendly or unfriendly, of Marxist theory.[9]

Let me conclude by wishing that, like Tom Sawyer attending his own funeral, Karl Marx could be present at his own centennial. When 'the Moor' rose to speak how we would all pay for our presumptuousness.

Acknowledgements

The author would like to thank Professor Meghnad Desai, who gave part of his time generously to read and thoroughly discuss an earlier draft of this book. The final version has greatly benefited, both in substance and in style, from his suggestions, as indeed from those of Dr John King, who refereed the book for Macmillan. Professor G. H. Cohen has kindly read the first chapter of the book, where he made various useful remarks, and Dr Malcolm Pemberton has checked some of the mathematics. Professor M. Morishima has checked the section which refers to the Fundamental Marxian Theorem and suggested an essential improvement of presentation. None of the above is, of course, responsible for opinions expressed or errors still remaining, despite their massive weeding-out operations. Such responsibility rests exclusively with the author.

In the person of Jennifer Pegg, the author was blessed with a helpful and most encouraging editor, while in Pam Doolin he discovered the typist of his dreams. The sheer professionalism of both of them was such as to make one almost forget the ills of capitalism.

GEORGE CATEPHORES

CHAPTER 1

Economics and historical materialism

Marxist economics and socialism

People who lead their lives in societies of mixed economies, dominated by private capitalism, find themselves confronted by a rather paradoxical situation. Their economic practices, the whole pervasive ethos of their society, rest on the assumption of individualism, of personal gain. Yet, the abstract individualism of their living conditions often turns out to be a hindrance rather than a help to the achievement of individual aims. To take just one example among many, there is probably nothing more individualistic than the private motor car. Yet, its use in the centre of cities notoriously destroys the presumed objective of individuals, fast, independent and comfortable travel.

Contradictions of this kind, which turn an apparently preordained order of things in society upside down, naturally prompt the question: What if the social order were intentionally inverted? Instead of starting with individualism to end up with the frustration of personal aspirations, individuals might try starting with socialism in order to achieve better fulfilment of their needs. The persistence with which the temptation of the socialist alternative recurs in people's minds (has, in fact recurred in people's minds for centuries) justifies the closer study of the possibilities of socialist economic organisation.

In Marxist economics, the central theme of the subject is exactly the transition from a capitalist to a socialist economy. The main object of systematic study, on the other hand, is not so much this transition itself or socialism, its supposed outcome. Rather it is the maturation, on the inside of capitalist structures, of conditions conducive to a socialist transformation of society. This makes Marxist economics the study of capitalism from the vantage point of socialist change.

The idea of socialism did not originate in the context of Marxist thought. It was adopted by Marx from pre-existing theories of social philosophy as well as from the objectives of nineteenth-century European working-class movements. The British Chartists provided one of the more potent early influences. This historical and practical antecedence of the idea of socialism removes from Marxism all trace of dogmatic arbitrariness. Before becoming a theoretical field of study socialism has been – it still is – a living idea. Had there been no spontaneous socialist movement in capitalist society, Marxist theory would have lost most of its interest and influence long ago.

Marxist thought has adopted socialism and proclaimed it to be the proper aim of the working class. In doing so, however, Marxism has striven to provide a new element, which Marx perceived as missing from the theories of socialist thinkers prior to him. This is a scientific prediction of socialism, as the type of society to which development under capitalism is inherently tending. If true, the existence of such a tendency guarantees the feasibility of a socialist organisation of human affairs; it redeems socialism from the utopian aspects of early social reform schemes. A rigorous proof of the feasibility of socialist aspirations is one of the main constituents of Marxist economics which, in addition, purports to establish the necessity (or, in some extreme versions, the inevitability) of a socialist transformation.

This proof represents the positive part of Marxist economic theory. It is based on an objective analysis of the mechanics of the day-to-day operation, as well as of the long-term evolutionary trends of the capitalist economy. From this analysis, recommendations on the concrete measures for bringing about a socialist transformation under specific conditions may follow. They would constitute the prescriptive (or even normative) part of this kind of economics. Marx himself attached uppermost importance to the prescriptive part, as can be inferred from his early maxim:[1]

> The philosophers have only *interpreted* the world in various ways; the point, however, is to *change* it.

The scientific character of Marxist economic theory appears both in its effort at objective explanation, in the positive part, and in the framing of recommendations on means of action – consistently with the analysis – in the prescriptive part. It may be argued that the chief recommendation of Marxist theory is socialism itself, which is not a means but an end. Hence any asseverations of scientific objectivity on the part of Marxists, merely serve the purpose of attempting spuriously to invest the prestige of science on a preselected set of value judgements.

Socialism, however, is not just an end; it is both a means and an end. It is a means of resolving a number of economic difficulties which beset capitalism; it is an end, in so far as it is deemed, by its supporters, to offer a desirable way of life, more satisfying than that under capitalism. Those who, unlike the author, subscribe to the philosophical position of the impossibility of deriving an *ought* from an *is* may deny the scientific character of socialism as an end; by the mere methodological argument they cannot challenge the scientific character of socialism as a means.

Marxist economics and historical materialism

Marxism as a whole constitutes a theoretical endeavour much broader than
Marxist economics; the latter, however, occupies a decisively central place in
the Marxist construction. This did not come about by accident but by
theoretical design. Marx selected the economy as the main area of study
because he considered economic causation of social phenomena as relatively
more dominant than political, religious, ethnic etc. causes, without denying
that they also were at work in the shaping of social affairs.

Marx and his followers (not even all of those, nowadays) stand alone in
subscribing to an explicit, thorough, well-organised theory of historical
evolution of society placing human economic (or rather productive) activity
at the centre of the stage. But in a looser, less committed way, the dominant
character of economic causation has been accepted, often without any
reference to and even in ignorance of the Marxist way of thinking, by a whole
host of economists, historians and sociologists. Keynes is a good case in point.
In his *Treatise on Money* he wrote:[2]

Shakespeare, like Newton and Darwin, died rich . . . But whether or not Pope is
right that Shakespeare

'For gain not glory winged his roving flight
And grew immortal in his own despite'

his active career chanced to fall at the date of dates, when any level-headed person
in England disposed to make money could hardly help doing so. 1575 to 1620 were
the palmy days of profit – one of the greatest 'bull' movements ever known until
modern days in the United States . . . – Shakespeare being eleven years old in 1575
and dying in 1616. I offer it as a thesis for examination by those who like rash
generalisations, that by far the larger proportion of the world's greatest writers and
artists have flourished in the atmosphere of buoyancy, exhilaration and the freedom
from economic cares felt by the governing class, which is engendered by profit
inflations.

Whether such generalisations are rash or not is an issue which philosophers
of history have been discussing for a long time and will no doubt continue to
discuss. (Keynes's direct linkage between poetry and profit inflation would
lift many an eyebrow among sophisticated Marxists, who would accuse him
of 'reductionism'). To the extent that a resolution of the issue may be
advanced by rigorous formulation, Marx has offered a very tightly-knit
hypothesis in his 1859 *Preface to the Contribution to the Critique of Political
Economy*. Although the contents of this text are by now famous, known
almost to the point of tedium by anyone acquainted with Marxist thought, it
still remains one of the best ways of introducing it to those newly interested.
For this reason and also for its intrinsic value its relevant part is reproduced
here in full:[3]

The general result at which I arrived and which once won, served as a guiding thread for my studies, can be briefly formulated as follows: In the social production of their life, men enter into definite relations that are indispensable and independent of their will, relations of production which correspond to a definite stage of development of their material productive forces. The sum total of these relations of production constitutes the economic structure of society, the real foundation, on which rises a legal and political superstructure and to which correspond definite forms of social consciousness. The mode of production of material life conditions the social, political and intellectual life process in general. It is not the consciousness of men that determines their being, but, on the contrary, their social being that determines their consciousness. At a certain stage of their development, the material productive forces of society come in conflict with the existing relations of production, or – what is but a legal expression for the same thing – with the property relations within which they have been at work hitherto. From forms of development of the productive forces these relations turn into their fetters. Then begins an epoch of social revolution. With the change of the economic foundation the entire immense superstructure is more or less rapidly transformed. In considering such transformations a distinction should always be made between the material transformation of the economic conditions of production, which can be determined with the precision of natural science, and the legal, political, religious, aesthetic or philosophic – in short, ideological forms in which men become conscious of this conflict and fight it out. Just as our opinion of an individual is not based on what he thinks of himself, so can we not judge of such a period of transformation by its own consciousness; on the contrary, this consciousness must be explained rather from the contradictions of material life, from the existing conflict between the social productive forces and the relations of production. No social order ever perishes before all the productive forces for which there is room in it have developed; and new, higher relations of production never appear before the material conditions of their existence have matured in the womb of the old society itself. Therefore mankind always sets itself only such tasks as it can solve; since, looking at the matter more closely, it will always be found that the task itself arises, only when the material conditions for its solution already exist or are at least in the process of formation. In broad outlines Asiatic, ancient, feudal and modern bourgeois modes of production can be designated as progressive epochs in the economic formation of society. The bourgeois relations of production are the last antagonistic forms of the social process of production – antagonistic not in the sense of individual antagonism, but of one arising from the social conditions of life of the individuals; at the same time the productive forces developing in the womb of bourgeois society create the material conditions for the solution of that antagonism. This social formation brings, therefore, the prehistory of human society to a close.

The text shows why economics (or Political Economy, as the subject was known in the nineteenth century) came to the centre of Marx's attention. More than that, it can be seen as a programme of research bringing together economics, law, history, philosophy, politics, in fact all social sciences into one gigantic explanatory synthesis which does not neglect the achievements of natural science. This major research programme contains, as its main component, a research subprogramme for economics. It is the intention of the present book to present Marxist economics as the implementation of that subprogramme, the main points of which are the following:

(1)   Production is the most crucial aspect of economic activity. It is more fundamental than exchange, because society can subsist and has, in fact, subsisted for long periods without much exchange, but it could not carry on for any length of time without production. Also, production is basic in the sense that most people spend most of their time employed in it.

(2)   The bourgeois mode of production is the area of main interest. The reason for that is again obvious. Marx, like ourselves, lived in bourgeois society. He constructed his economic analysis as a means of influencing his own contemporary life.

(3)   In the bourgeois, as in every mode of production, two epochs succeed each other: an early one, during which relations of production act on production forces positively; and a late one, during which they act on them negatively, bringing about a crisis in society. The means of resolution of that crisis consist of the socialist transformation of the relations of production. On the other hand, socialism, from being a utopian moral doctrine in precapitalist conditions, finds a realistic foundation in the level of material productivity achieved despite the harsh, antagonistic production relations of this system.

The task here outlined for Marxist economics is to discover and explain how capitalistic relations of production (relations of ownership, management and exploitation) promote the growth of the forces of production, how they fetter this growth at a later stage and in what way socialist relations can give new scope to the development of production forces. The historical materialist hypothesis of the 1859 *Preface* can serve as a guiding thread through Marxist economic analysis. By no means, however, does this imply any automatic superiority of economic theory, based on Marxist principles, over any other kind of economic theory. A school of scientific thought may or may not need philosophical underpinnings, but if it has such, it cannot invoke them as a proof of the validity of its discoveries. This it has to demonstrate in solving scientific problems on an equal basis with other schools, whether explicitly associated with some fundamental philosophy or not. Scientific success may reflect favourably on an underlying philosophy but not vice versa. If, on the other hand, the philosophy is, on general grounds, flawed, any scientific research programme it may have inspired will also probably suffer from serious shortcomings. For this, if for no other reason, some acquaintance with the criticisms addressed to historical materialism from philosophical quarters is useful to students of Marxist economics.

The critical Right and the critical Left

Controversy has raged around the historical materialist hypothesis of the 1859 *Preface*, focusing mainly on two points: the determinants of the historical evolution of social institutions, and the determinants of human intellectual activity (the base-superstructure problem). Some overlap between the two critical discourses does exist. If ideas can be shown to develop independently of material, practical considerations and conditions, the presumption is created that they also lead forward in historical development. Economics, however, has to neglect most aspects of the base-superstructure problem. Any intelligent discussion of it ought to involve not only law and politics, subjects somewhat contiguous to economics, but also philosophy, aesthetics, religion, and psychology – disciplines which the economist cannot say very much about.

Unquestionably, greater affinity exists between economics and the study of the historical evolution of social institutions. The topic has often preoccupied outstanding economists, not necessarily Marxist (e.g. Schumpeter, Keynes, Galbraith). They have on the whole been able to assert a strong link between the development of the economy and that of society. Marxists, while not opposed to such contributions, add to them the specific claim of the primacy of production in economic and, by extension, in social life. From that basis, they make global predictions, not about single institutions or sets of institutions but about the likely future course of society, as an integrated whole. This is where the Marxist theory comes up against serious criticisms both from the Left and from the Right.

On the Right, the Austro-British philosopher Sir Karl Popper has concentrated his fire on the impossibility of making scientific predictions about global historical developments, such as the drastic transformation of one social regime into another. Historical materialism does claim that such predictions are possible, that they constitute, in fact, the main task of the science of history. It follows in Popper's view that historical materialism is an unsound philosophy, which saddles science with a patently unscientific task.

Popper's criticism is presented by its author as an argument addressed not specifically against historical materialism but rather against historicism, a term which allegedly covers a whole family of related doctrines, Marxism being just one of them. The criticism is cast in methodological form although it does involve many points of substance on the question of causality in history.

The criticism from the Left, on the other hand, is directly substantive. It challenges the historical materialism of the 1859 *Preface* in the name of using, as a primary explanatory principle of historical evolution, not the growth of the forces of production but the development of the class struggle. Marx himself opens the main text of the Communist Manifesto with the sentence 'The history of all hitherto existing society is the history of class struggles'.

Therefore, in arguing in favour of the primacy of the class struggle, critics from the Left do not reject Marx; they choose to give pride of place to one aspect of Marx's teaching rather than another. In the following paragraphs, these two lines of criticism will be examined in succession.

The predictability of social change

Popper insists that global revolutions, even if they can be identified among the mercurial multitude of historical changes, are, in their specificity, unique, non-recurrent events. They are controlled by processes, the idiosyncratic character of which makes scientific prediction, of the kind successfully practised in natural science, impossible. Scientific laws, on the basis of which predictions are made, cannot be inferred from single instances, from historical events unique in character. There can be no such thing as laws of history. Even if historical laws were not to be inductively drawn from experience but were derived by pure logic, they would not merit to be called scientific, unless their predictions could be tested against factual evidence. Prediction takes the form of the statement 'if A then B'. For the possibility of random coincidence to be avoided, testing of such propositions must be repeated a number of times before one can talk of verification. (Strictly speaking, one can never talk of verification; by Popper's criterion, a scientific hypothesis is held to be true, until testing throws up one instance of falsification.) But in the changing, ever-flowing, circumstances of history no prediction of the form 'if A is present then B follows' can ever be tested more than once, since by the time of the second testing either A is no longer there or its influence on B has ceased. From the present position of the sun, the moon and the earth scientists, armed with Kepler's and Newton's laws, can very accurately predict a sequence of solar eclipses, stretching far into the future. But from the present policies of the Conservative, Labour and Alliance parties only a very rash person would venture to predict the outcome of a sequence of general elections.

Many explanations of the changeableness of human affairs can be imagined. Popper ultimately came to focus on one of them: the importance of knowledge as a factor determining the course of human history. Knowledge progresses by making original discoveries; to the extent that these are translated to social developments, they produce original, non-repetitive historical patterns. This has obvious implications for the predictability of historical events. The future development of knowledge cannot be scientifically predicted. To claim the opposite would lead to a logical contradiction. If a person can predict the future contents of knowledge, he already possesses that knowledge; therefore he is not predicting anything. Taken to its logical conclusion any claim about the predictability of new knowledge should end up with the admission of the possibility of omniscience (since on the basis of a first prediction one could formulate a second, a third, and so on *ad infinitum*). But if future knowledge cannot be predicted and if the development of society depends on the development of knowledge, the course of human history cannot be predicted. By extension, no worthwhile testable hypothesis about the course of history can be formulated. What cannot be predicted can obviously not be tested. Prediction of global social change would require that the predictor know the contents not only of single items of future knowledge but also the way they would come together to form a global pattern. This would make predictions of global social change doubly impossible.

A Marxist restatement of Popper

No Marxist would think of contesting the point that knowledge exercises a very potent, even a decisive influence on historical development. The meaning of Marx's polemic against idealistic explanations of historical evolution was not that human thought played no role whatsoever, or even a secondary one, in social life. He insisted that arbitrary abstract theorising about man and society was impotent and irrelevant. Knowledge, on the other hand, particularly scientific knowledge combined with man's practice of changing, of dominating his material environment, he considered as one of the most basic social forces. To the extent that scientific knowledge became an immediate force of production, as it increasingly did, it had to be accepted as a major determinant of the course of history. In that way, Popper's insistence on its importance could be made fully consistent with historical materialism. In stressing the importance of knowledge in history, Popper did not, of course, specify that it must operate as a force of production. However, here the form of his argument, modified in the stated sense, will be pursued for a while, before the original form is considered again.

Treating knowledge as a force of production does not imply that its future growth becomes scientifically predictable. On the contrary, the possibility now emerges that the course of development of the forces of production itself cannot be predicted.

How much does the validity of the hypothesis in the 1859 *Preface* require the predictability of the development of society's productive capacities? To answer this question the various levels of generality of Marx's argument must be carefully distinguished. At the highest level, historical materialism is just an assertion of a necessary correspondence between forces and relations of production. This correspondence is an empirical relationship. It can only be challenged by direct reference to observation, not indirectly, by some methodological denial of the predictability of knowledge.

Is the correspondence principle a testable hypothesis in Popper's sense? Can it be falsified? By a planned controlled experiment, certainly not. Societies do not change their institutions merely to test the correctness of alternative theories. Could it be falsified by observation? This is not to be excluded, but it is hard to imagine what kind of observed case would be both conclusive and non-trivial. It might be said that if a tribe of primitive hunters who had organised themselves into corporations and set up a kind of stock exchange were discovered before capitalism had come into being anywhere else in the world, Marx's principle would have suffered a decisive defeat. The *recherché* character of the example testifies, perhaps, to the dubious value of falsifiability established by such means. It might be more reasonable to see the correspondence principle as one so basic that its testing could not be conducted in isolation from the rest of the main body of Marxist theory. Marxism as a whole can, of course, provide a large number of falsifiable specific hypotheses. The cumulative weight of success or failure would eventually consolidate or sweep away even fundamental principles, that of correspondence not excluded.[4]

Correspondence is never perfect. At times it turns to almost its opposite, a discrepancy between forces and relations that may assume the acute form of a contradiction. This raises two questions: (a) what is it that mainly determines the disturbance of any initial harmony: a change in the forces or a change in the relations of production? (b) Given that acute discrepancy is an anomalous and damaging state of things which cannot last for ever, how is it resolved: by the relations adapting to the forces or vice versa? The problem which (a) and (b) jointly raise is described as that of the primacy of the forces (or of the relations) of production. It is more relevant to the criticism of the 1859 *Preface* from the Left, but the reply to (a) is also important for Popper's predictability argument.

The answer to (a) must rest on the acknowledgement of the antagonistic character of society. A different answer would be correct for non-antagonistic societies, but we are not much concerned with them. This narrows down the range of the correspondence thesis, which for the rest of this section is studied in one subset of possible modes of production only, those which have an antagonistic character.

What kind of society is the one described in the Preface as 'antagonistic'? The text merely suggests that it is not referring to 'individual antagonism, but of one arising from the social conditions of life of the individuals'. Taking into account Marx's approach as a whole, it is not, perhaps, too arbitrary to suggest that, despite the lack of any explicit reference to classes and the possible existence of antagonisms of other kinds (e.g. between sexes, between nationalities), the antagonism he has in mind in the *Preface* is class antagonism.

All modes of production listed by Marx (Asiatic, ancient, feudal, modern bourgeois) (with the possible exception of Asiatic, an imperfectly analysed society, presenting the strange features of exploitation by the State, combined with classlessness) have been described as class-antagonistic. The material of history is admittedly very idiosyncratic, but in the case of the class phenomenon, what must be considered, by the standards of historical study, a fairly wide sample of similar cases does exist. This permits the tracing of certain repetitive patterns which lie at the basis of scientific prediction. Let it be noted here that Popper does admit the possibility of prediction of historical events, if they can be shown to belong to a repetitive pattern known from the past, but he treats any such cases as trivial. This is again a matter of substance, not resolvable by reference to the scientific unpredictability of scientific knowledge.

Under class antagonism Marx observes that the split in society culminates in a sequence of class dictatorships, with the ruling classes appropriating the surplus product of the economy, while the dominated classes are made to perform unrewarded labour for the benefit of the rulers. It is in the obvious interest of ruling classes to maintain and defend the exploitative relations (of production) described. Their vested interests impose on the relations of production the characteristic of rigidity, of resistance to change, while the development of productive forces is, in the nature of the matter, allowed much wider scope. The prediction follows that, in class-antagonistic modes of production, discrepancies between forces and relations of production are likely to arise, as a result of changes in the character of the production process. When they do, they cause the mechanism of the economy to work with hitches and breakdowns, that culminate in generalised social *malaise*. A hitherto non-ruling class may perceive its opportunity in this situation – particularly if the mutation in the production process places it in a position of some strength – and may challenge the power of the ruling class, that is ultimately the existing relations of production. The ruling class will defend its domination, a revolutionary crisis in society resulting as the climax of the process.

This seems like the minimal prediction which can be extracted from the 1859 *Preface*, seen in the context of the rest of Marx's work. It rests on the changeability of the forces of production contrasted with the relative immobility of the relations of production caused by class antagonism. It implies an interpretation of Marx fully consistent with the decisive primacy of the forces of production, as far as the origins of the process of change (question (a) above) are concerned. It does not prejudge the answer to question (b) (the outcome of the process of social strife).

The prediction stated above can be restricted even more, if it is rephrased in a conditional manner to read: if there occurs a change in the forces of production, a discrepancy between them and the relations of production, leading to a process of social strife, will follow in all class-antagonistic societies. In this form, the prediction rests purely on historically observed social regularities, the repetition of which can reasonably be expected. It is not premised on the prediction of the future course of the forces of production, nor even on the necessity of their future growth or decline. It must, therefore, on the strictest Popperian grounds, be accepted as an admissible hypothesis, which is not at all trivial.

Against the conditional character of the prediction it might be argued that

Marx has committed himself to the inevitability of the growth of the forces of production. Most of Marx's work would indeed become irrelevant if growth in the forces of production were to be replaced by their immobility. From this, however, it does not follow that Marx predicted the inevitability of such growth. His inclusion, in the list of the 1859 *Preface*, of the Asiatic mode of production which elsewhere he had described as suffering from millenial stagnation, ought to constitute sufficient evidence that he did contemplate the possibility of a stationary economy. Could one not extend the alternatives to include the possibility of a regression in the forces of production?

Admittedly the 1859 *Preface*, strongly supported by his other writings, conveys the feeling that progress, more or less continuous, was what Marx expected. For a thinker like him, who encompassed in his vision the whole drama of human history, from the Stone Age to the nineteenth century, it is not surprising that he would treat progress as the typical overall characteristic of development. He did not ignore the possibility that progress could be arrested by long periods of stagnation (the Asiatic mode). It may further be presumed that a theorist of his broadness of vision would not have rejected the possibility of regression, had it been put to him. Even had he done so, others need not follow. To take just one example, it seems quite plausible that, by the end of the Roman Empire, production forces in Western Europe had entered a phase of actual decline, in the context of production relations which had become static. The main evidence of this is the well-documented decline of the slave-labour-force and of population in general.

The discrepancy between forces and relations of production that followed as a result of the fall in the numbers of slaves, was not of the form usually considered typical of Marxist analysis, nor was it perceived as such by Marx, despite his deep knowledge of Roman history. Forces of production were not pressing against their institutional integument, rather the opposite: they were draining away from their container. Even so, the discrepancy called forth an enormous social upheaval which prepared the ground for the collapse of the Empire under the onslaught of the invading barbarian tribes. One is tempted to conclude that Marx's prediction of social crisis in class-antagonistic societies under the impact of a discrepancy between forces and relations of production is equally valid for the case of retrogression as well as of advance of society's productive capacity. Moreover, it would seem that, at such a level of generality, the more specific character of the transformation of production forces does not have to be predicted at all. The prediction simply is: given sufficient change of production forces in a class-antagonistic society, a revolution or some upheaval of catastrophic nature is bound to erupt. Not being dependent on any specific forecast about the future character of the forces of production, the prediction remains unshaken by Popper's objection to the possibility of scientifically predicting the future course of knowledge. Moreover, it has been subjected to the testing of repeated historical crises and has not been falsified, yet.

Knowledge has, so far, been treated as a force of production. Popper would certainly object to having it limited in this manner. However, even knowledge of unspecified content, assuming it played the ultimately decisive determinant role ascribed to it by Popper, would be confronted, in class-antagonistic societies, with situations similar to those applying to production forces. Knowledge would itself have to be produced in institutions (relations of production of knowledge) dominated, in class-antagonistic societies, by the ruling class. The accumulation of knowledge in a context of rigid class relations would eventually lead to crisis, with the ruling classes defending a form of organisation consistent with their material interests even against knowledge itself. The resistance of the Medieval Church to the spread of the ideas of Copernicus (himself a cleric), is, perhaps, suggestive of the relevant type of conflict. Marx's predictions, based on the rigidity of class structure versus the versatility of human creativeness, would seem to provide the most appropriate scheme even for Popper's hypothesis of historical causality.

The current interest of Marxism would, however, be very limited if its predictions were restricted to the widely general sort of statement described above as impervious to Popper's methodological objections. Marxist claims to contemporary relevance rest on much more specific forecasts about the future course of industrial technology and organisation. Extrapolating from trends barely perceptible in the mid-nineteenth century, Marx predicted the emergence of a highly integrated production mechanism, consisting typically of large-scale units, increasingly mechanised to the point of automation and achieving unprecedentedly high levels of productivity. Market coordination of production would become increasingly dysfunctional for this kind of production process. Its technically integrated character would respond much better to the *ex ante* coordination of planning at the level of the whole of society, rather than of individual enterprises. Being an obstacle of social economic planning, private property over the means of production would be replaced by communal ownership at the level, again, of society as a whole. The guarantee of a person's living and welfare, for the sake of which individuals turned to the acquisition of private property under capitalism, would be replaced by the obligation of society to provide a decent standard of living to each one of its members. High levels of productivity achieved through mechanisation and the application of science to production, would make distribution on an egalitarian basis feasible. Universal affluence would reduce competitive tension among individuals and make the administration of the economy by consensus a realistic proposition.

This second prediction is obviously quite different and much more specific than the basic, very much broader one, discussed earlier. Still, despite Popper's strictures and despite the fact that it involves some anticipation of future knowledge (e.g. automation) it can, in its positive part, claim scientific rather than 'prophetic' status, as Popper would have it. It has been admitted above, that the prediction of future knowledge embroils the predictor in a logical contradiction. It implies possession in the present of knowledge to be acquired in the future. This, however, is true only in a very narrow sense. It precludes anticipation of fully articulated, complete future knowledge. It does not at all rule out forecasts about the general character of future knowledge, which can be derived from the extrapolation of present trends. This extrapolation is not limited to theoretical, but also encompasses practical, developments. On their basis it can build a rough sketch of a future society and, in that way, predict global historical change. What it cannot foresee is the possible emergence of situations capable of affecting, or even reversing, current trends. To that extent, therefore, Marx's, or anyone's predictions of similar kinds must be treated as tentative. This does not make them either 'prophetic' or unscientific.

Classes and the primacy of the forces of production

The critique addressed to the historical materialism of the 1859 *Preface* from the Left focuses on what it perceives as its mechanistic character. A literal – or, perhaps, too literal – reading of the *Preface* does convey the impression that conscious human action, subjective human agencies, whether individual or collective, are active on the scene of history merely as actors playing out roles assigned to them by a script, the writing of which they can have nothing to do with. The movement of social development as a whole is structured by impersonal, or rather non-subjective forces, so that history becomes a process without a subject. Critics of this interpretation of historical materialism object that the dynamics of historical development are determined by the policies of the self-constituting classes into which a class-antagonistic society finds itself split, and that the structural categories listed in the *Preface* (forces of production, relations of production, base, superstructure) are not explanatory but merely formally classificatory devices, used by the theorist to register and organise the outcome of social class conflict.

If class struggle is to be treated as the main analytical concept, then the question as to what makes classes constitute themselves and take action, and under what conditions their action becomes effective acquires importance. Not equal importance, however, at each and every stage of historical development. For Marx it becomes crucial at the second epoch of each one of his modes of production, when relations of production have begun to 'fetter' the forces. It is then that 'an epoch of social revolution begins', when men become 'conscious of the conflict' and 'fight it out'. Prior to that, although the ruling class may be presumed to display some energy in either developing the forces of production or at least maintaining the social framework that allows others to develop them, it is also likely to find itself able to act more or less unopposed. The real test comes when, after a discrepancy has developed, a hitherto non-ruling class perceives the possibilities and launches a revolutionary challenge.

In situations where the evolution of the production process has stored up new potential requiring, for it to be released, an institutional change, progress is conditional on the victory of the revolutionary class. This outcome cannot be taken as a foregone conclusion. Objective developments may favour social transformation, but the class that would benefit from them might find it impossible to mobilise the energy required for a successful onslaught. Marx contemplates this possibility in the *Manifesto* when he writes that class-struggle ends 'either in a revolutionary reconstitution of society at large, or in the common ruin of the contending classes'. Therefore, to the question about the primacy of production forces, whether, given a discrepancy, it is the relations that adapt to the forces or vice versa, the answer must be inconclusive. New relations of production are not the automatic consequence of the rise of new forces, and in that sense forces of production are not fully primary.

It appears, thus, impossible to interpret Marxist analysis as exclusively structural or exclusively subjective (in the sense of class subjectivity). The objective material situation provides undoubtedly a very potent influence on human action, both by creating possibilities and by imposing constraints. Human agents try to ascertain both possibilities and constraints and to map out a course of action. In so doing they discern alternatives among which they choose, although, in antagonistic societies, there is no guarantee that they have any clear consciousness of what their choices are ultimately about. Their action (whether they are individuals or classes) is partly objectively determined, partly entails certain degrees of freedom which may even be increased by Popperian changes in knowledge. Human action in history is neither arbitrary nor totally unpredictable. Objective conditions give rise to a whole range of options, which social classes may or may not discern, may or may not be able to take. Human creativeness is not exercised in a void. It operates under predetermined conditions which, in its turn, it helps to determine further. Historical prediction, seen as a range of possible outcomes rather than as a unique forecast, should under these circumstances be possible. It is all a problem of balance, as Marx could himself very well see and described in a striking manner:[5]

> Men make their own history, but they do not make it just as they please; they do not make it under circumstances chosen by themselves, but under circumstances directly encountered, given and transmitted from the past.

PART I

THE GROWTH OF THE
FORCES OF PRODUCTION

CHAPTER 2

Commodity production and capitalism

Towards a definition of capitalism

The range of Chapter 1 has to be narrowed down now to one of the modes of production listed by Marx in the 1859 *Preface* – the one described there as 'modern bourgeois', or as capitalism, in our current usage.

In common understanding it is doubtful whether production springs first to mind when capitalism is considered. Other characteristics like big finance, big commerce, ruthless competitiveness, the money-making obsession or economic crises take precedence. The task of the present chapter is to lay down the groundwork that will eventually make it possible to connect together, hopefully in a coherent manner, such commonsense features of the capitalistic mode of production among themselves and with their common basis in the production process.

The first, rather trite, but even so quite important thing to notice about capitalism is its character of a gigantic market economy (this is what the characteristic mainstream economic analysis concentrates on with great refinement but virtually to the exclusion of everything else). What kind of a market economy? An attempt to answer this question, and in so doing to provide the definition sought, will be made in two stages. *Simple commodity production*, a mode of production similar to capitalism in its total dependence on a market economy, will be defined first in its main aspects. *Capitalism* will, then, be introduced by the expedient of replacing two of the crucial characteristics of simple commodity production with two different ones, while leaving all others intact. Apart from the purely aesthetic advantage of elegance and economy of thought, this procedure achieves certain important results of substance. On the one hand it emphasises, by contrasting capitalism with a more elementary market economy, the futility of attempting to reduce all capitalist relations to simple replicas of ordinary acts of exchange. The exploitative character of the capitalist system as against the non-exploitative nature of exchange in simple commodity production plays here the decisive part. On the other hand, by maintaining a large number of the characteristics of simple commodity production in the definition of capitalism the procedure focuses attention upon the strong continuity that exists between a capitalist economy and ordinary exchange. The dual nature of capitalism, both close to and very distant from an economy based on non-capitalist trade, is thus brought strikingly into relief.

The concept of simple commodity production

A brief discussion of the theoretical status of the concepts associated with simple commodity production may help towards correct appreciation of the results of the method described. Simple commodity production is a semi-hypothetical, semi-realistic mode of production which, although discussed by Marx in various places, is not included in the list of the 1859 *Preface*. It must be said at the outset that all modes of production mentioned in the *Preface* are to some extent idealisations of real historical situations. From this point of view simple commodity production is no different, so that its relative lack of realism cannot be the reason for its exclusion. However, in its case there is an additional consideration. The historical situations to which, as an analytical entity, it corresponds, consist of the various instances where local, as distinct from long-distance, trade has been of main importance before the dawn of the capitalist era (set in Europe round about the middle of the 16th century). Trade of such description was supplied, and often personally conducted, by small producers (*petty commodity producers*) living in close proximity; artisans and peasant-farmers who owned their means of production and worked for themselves, independently of any master (i.e. who were neither serfs nor slaves). There is sufficient evidence of the historical existence of such groups, reinforced by direct observation since, in a number of cases, small-scale production and trade continued long after large capitalist manufacturing had conquered the field in the chief sectors of the economy. However (with the possible exception of North American colonies in the 18th century) neither under capitalism nor in previous epochs is there any evidence to suggest that small commodity production ever became anything more than an *enclave* in the midst of an economy organised according to drastically different principles (in precapitalist times the principle of self-sufficiency). This may be the reason why Marx, who sometimes treated simple commodity production as if it were a mode of production in its own right on a par with capitalism, feudalism etc., avoided including it in the list of historical modes of production in the 1859 *Preface*.

There is no denying that at the beginning of the capitalist era small commodity production had made significant inroads into the economic structure of late medieval Europe. It is arguable that, to some extent, capitalism finds its origins in the small local trading and artisanal manufacturing activity of that epoch. In constructing a theoretical model of economic development by stages, it may be justified, on those historical grounds, to introduce as one of the stages the construct of simple commodity production. From real, historically extant, petty commodity production, this construct would differ in two ways. First, it would be represented as a universally prevalent, precapitalist state of non-capitalist market production and exchange while petty commodity production is localised, spatially discontinuous, with its several centres separated by vast tracts of essentially self-sufficient subsistence agriculture. Second, it would be described as a fully-fledged exchange economy, while actual small commodity production remains undeveloped in various ways. It makes little, if any, use of money, depending to a large extent on barter. Exchange ratios between pairs of similar goods may differ widely in its various, non-communicating local markets. Producers or traders are not free to compete on equal terms in all branches of economic activity but have to stick to their traditional occupations, under the yoke of medieval regulation.

The model of simple commodity production assumes all such market imperfections away. It attributes to a supposed precapitalist market economy the commodity-exchange techniques and the freedom of trade of a fairly advanced stage of competitive capitalism. To that extent the model is artificial. On the other hand, it cannot be denied that actual, historically extant precapitalist trade could both flourish under the regime theoretically imputed to it in the simple commodity production construct and for a period remain under the control of small self-employed traders or artisans, i.e. remain non-capitalist.

If, therefore, the aim of the analytical technique employed is to bring into striking relief the most crucial specific characteristics of capitalism, by contrasting them with an idealised image of an anterior historical situation, the introduction of simple commodity production becomes legitimate. At the same time its exclusion from the list of the 1859 *Preface* also falls into place, justified by its role as an auxiliary rather than a main explanatory construct of historical evolution.

The commodity and its characteristics

The definition of commodity production presupposes the definition of a commodity. This is defined as a useful object, a product of labour, which is exchanged against other products. It does not have to be produced for the purpose of being exchanged; its original destination may have been the producer's own consumption. If so, the good becomes a commodity only through the act of exchange. If, on the other hand, it has been produced exclusively (or even mainly) with the aim of being exchanged, it is a commodity right from the production stage. It then becomes possible to talk of commodity production as a specific type of economic organisation (the Marxist argument does not exclude from the definition non-material commodities such as services, but this aspect of the theory is not pursued here).

With this broad definition in mind, the characteristics of simple commodity production, stated and understood as steps towards a definition of capitalist relations of production, will be outlined. They come in three groups: technical, economic and legal. This classification can be useful, both heuristically and analytically, provided that it is not taken as establishing rigid demarcation lines between spheres which, in the nature of the matter, constitute one coherent and interconnected whole.

(a) Technical characteristics

(a) Universal division of labour. This is assumed to be completely refined, i.e. to display a number of specialisations equal to the number of finished products. Semi-processed goods are treated as finished products if traded separately.

(b) All production is carried out on a small scale by single individual producers, each of whom specialises in just one production activity. The techniques of production are of a comparable degree of complexity for all. Historically the 'individual' is likely to be a family or a master-craftsman with his apprentices while specialisation is never total, but for present purposes such qualifications are unnecessary.

(c) All factors of production, material and human, are assumed to be fully mobile as among sectors of the economy. All produced inputs (as distinct from land and labour) are as much commodities as the final output. One is dealing with 'production of commodities by means of commodities', to recall the title of a famous book by P. Sraffa.[1]

(b) Economic characteristics

'Economic' is used here in the narrow sense of 'pertaining to the coordinating mechanism of the economy'.

(a) Every producer is self-employed. Regarding what, how much and how to produce, he is subject to nobody but his own private will. Exclusion of all extra-individual authority covers even impersonal authority like that of tradition, of pre-established social patterns of preference, of adherence to some fixed ideal type of society and also to any pre-established order deriving from a comprehensive social plan of production, if a plan were possible. Division of labour is not pre-arranged but entirely spontaneous. To use one striking formulation of Marx, *anarchy of production* prevails.

(b) There are no artificial monopolies, or none that can be sustained in the long run.

(c) Absence of *ex ante* coordination in the division of labour leads to the need for coordination *ex post*. This is achieved through the price mechanism and factor mobility. Given anarchy of production, recurrent disequilibria in the various markets, accompanied by continuous corrective movements of resources from one sector to another, are likely. As long as disequilibria do not become cumulative, however, (which, in simple commodity production, for reasons to be explained in Chapter 5, they never do) such movements of prices and quantities can be seen as simple fluctuations around more or less stable equilibrium points. General equilibrium of prices and quantities can thus be deduced as a theoretical possibility, corresponding to an (unattainable) perfect balance among all sectors in the division of labour. (An account of the price mechanism in terms of the labour theory of value is attempted in the following chapter.)

Prices quoted in the market are not necessarily money prices. For the theoretical analysis of simple commodity production a complete list of barter-ratios is sufficient, although in practice it is impossible to envisage a fully integrated market economy which makes no use of money as a medium of exchange.

It is important at this point to pause and contemplate the condition of commodity producers in pursuit of those activities by which they sustain their lives. Division of labour makes them dependent on one another so that production for them can only be a social activity. Their labour is meaningful only as work performed for one another, as *social labour*. The social character of their work is not, however, directly effective during the production process. They are interdependent but they do not cooperate directly. Each one makes his own decisions about production and performs the necessary technical acts in isolation, taking the labour of others into account only in so far as it assumes for him the form of cost which he has had to pay in order to purchase from others the necessary inputs. Labour appears in production as individual, *private labour*, while its inherently social character is held in abeyance at the stage of production, to become manifest only at the stage of exchange. Through exchange, however, which both precedes and follows production, it does exercise an indirect controlling influence on the production process.

Commodity producers have no direct social links as producers. They set up such links as traders, when they exchange their products. The market is the only remaining social relationship in an otherwise atomised society. The social character of labour asserts itself there, because in exchange only so much of everyone's labour is rewarded, by the offer of someone else's commodities, as has been performed in accordance with proportions and norms implicit in the social structure of production. If too much labour has been directed to one sector, prices fall, and a part of the work done goes unrewarded. If some producers have been inefficient, they are in no position to raise their prices arbitrarily in order to cover their unjustified costs. Their product will sell at a price presupposing work of typical efficiency. The inefficient part of labour will go unrewarded. (The efficiently performed part of labour can be described as *socially necessary labour*, a term useful in the development of the labour theory of value in Chapter 3.)

Exchange is, therefore, the institution through which private labour is audited and either becomes accepted as social labour or is rejected. In trying to sell his product the commodity producer is striving to transform his individual labour into social labour. Only if he is successful does he acquire the right to draw a share from the pool of products supplied from all branches in the social division of labour.

It is exchange which makes the individual commodity producer an effective member of the society of all producers. Not, however, in any smooth cooperative manner. The isolated character of private production re-emerges in the market (where implicit social relationships are made explicit and validated) in the form of competitive antagonism. Having worked on his own, at his own risk and cost, every producer tries to get as much for himself as he can out of the market relationship without regard for others. The ensuing competition eliminates inefficient or supernumerary producers, thus promoting a proper allocation of resources. At the same time it creates the temptation and possibility of exploitation in exchange, if some trader – by superior negotiating skill, position of temporary monopoly, force or plain sharp practice – is able to extract for himself more from the market than is required to keep him in his chosen branch of activity at the level of wellbeing customary to society. Antagonistic competition continually opens the way to *unequal exchange*, a concept to be more precisely defined in the following chapter.

(c) The fetishism of commodities

Commodity producers have no conscious control over the production apparatus of society as a whole, because they do not coordinate their activities on the basis of a consciously worked out, mutually agreed plan. Lack of overall conscious control implies also lack of control over each one's individual sphere by every one of them. They have to obey the dictates of the market which follow no-one's intended design. The market puts into effect an average of a vast number of uncoordinated partial decisions. Everyone has to accept this average, which represents no-one's intended project, even if it has gone against his interests. Moreover, the regulatory influence of the market is exercised *ex post*, after production decisions, possibly mistaken ones, have been acted upon and irreversible commitments have been undertaken. Adjustment of errors, when they arise, assumes the form of price revisions, the cost of which falls upon individuals who could not have foreseen them in order to hedge against them.

When confronted with the workings of the invisible hand of the market, individuals are faced with nothing but the consequences of their own decisions and acts. Being unintended consequences, however, they imprint on the economy the feature of uncontrollable objectivity similar, in the eyes of those who experience it, to the objectivity of natural events. The analogy is strengthened by the fact that, parallel to natural reality, a second material reality is created by the producers themselves: the world of commodities. As a result of the anarchy of production this world escapes the control of its own creators, it turns back and through the invisible hand of the market strikes them down and dominates them. Producers, particularly in more advanced market economies, are continually engaged in a struggle to penetrate the opaqueness of market relationships, by market research and to control their market environment by advertising, long-term contracting, speculation etc. They have had some success in this but have on the whole been unable to eliminate the unpredictable, *ex post*, arbitrary character of market adjustments.

Of course, what in fact dominates producers in a market economy is not commodities as material objects but unacknowledged social relationships set up and resolved through commodity exchange. Being unacknowledged in any directly conscious, effective manner (abstract recognition of general interdependence is not relevant), these relationships have become identified with commodities rather than with the individuals who relate through commodity exchange. To take one example, excessive supply in a certain market appears as a relationship between a mass of goods and the subjective needs of consumers, which have been oversupplied. But, at one remove further back, excess supply is discovered to have been caused by the maladjustment of a certain sector with the rest of the economy. Producers in that sector working in isolation have, in the exclusive pursuit of their private advantage, created the excess supply which in its turn destroys them. This maladjustment is the result of an unacknowledged social relationship among producers, not a relationship among objects.

When social relations of production are regulated by relationships among quantities of commodities, and producers reach the point of perceiving their social relations as mere attributes of things (recall the widespread description of inflation as 'too much money chasing too few goods'), the phenomenon is described as the *fetishism of commodities*. In Marxist analysis it is treated as a crucial, widely ramified and inescapable characteristic of commodity production, of which it influences both the perception and the functioning. As a specific concept and as a technical term, commodity fetishism is exclusive to Marxist economics. The phenomenon itself however has, in some form or other, been registered also by non-Marxist economists, particularly students of the economics of unemployment and recession. Keynes is a good case in point. In his discussion of liquidity preference preventing the rate of interest from falling to a level consistent with full employment, he gives a striking description of the paralysing effect of objects on human production relations.[2]

> Unemployment develops, that is to say, because people want the moon; – men cannot be employed when the object of desire (i.e. money) is something which cannot be produced and the demand for which cannot be readily choked off. There is no remedy but to persuade the public that green cheese is practically the same thing and to have a green cheese factory (i.e. a central bank) under public control.

Fetishism of commodities can thus be listed as the fourth characteristic of the coordinating mechanism in simple commodity production, after individual decision making, absence of monopolies and *ex post* coordination by the market. The fifth and final one in the group of economic characteristics is the aim of production.

In general, the aim of all production is the satisfaction of the needs of producers. With commodity production, however, satisfaction cannot be sought from the producer's own product, because, under the regime of the division of labour, he does not produce for himself but for others. (The producer may be a consumer of his own products, but that consumption would cover so insignificant a fraction of his needs as to be negligible.) It follows that the producer is not interested in the usefulness of the product to himself. He is not producing a *use-value* for himself but one for others. What interests him directly in his product is its purchasing power over other goods, the *exchange-value* of his commodity. He can only satisfy his needs if he has to offer to other producers, something which they desire, something exchangeable in sufficient quantity. In one and the same product, commodity producers simultaneously try to produce use-values for others and exchange-values for themselves. In the perpetual antagonism of exchange, producers may, of course, attempt to cultivate desires or even false needs in the minds of the consumers of their products, to pass off shoddy goods for highly useful items, etc.

Use-value and exchange-value, both pertaining to the commodity as two different aspects of it, can be separated conceptually as well as functionally. Use-value (for others) is obviously a condition for the existence of exchange-value, while the latter is a means towards acquiring use-value (for oneself). The direct aim of a producer in this situation can only be exchange-value. But simple commodity production is in some respects patterned on its real-life counterpart of petty commodity production. Small producers are not in business in order to become rich; even if they have an abstract longing for wealth – their type of activity is not what makes large fortunes. They pursue exchange value not as a way of enrichment but simply as a means of satisfying their use-value needs. The direct aim of their economic activity, the acquisition of exchange value, is dominated by their final but none-too-distant aim, which is the possession of goods for the sake of their use-value.

(d) Legal characteristics

It was seen above that social intercourse among commodity producers presents an aspect of separateness (in production) and one of association (in exchange). In the legal sphere their separateness is reflected in the institution of private property, their association in the institution of the contract. These two institutions, together with the guarantee of personal freedom offered to their citizens by modern states that have abolished both slavery and economic tutelage over their citizens, make up the backbone of the legal system in societies based on commodity production. In the following, an attempt to trace the broad correspondence between law and economics in such societies will be made.

(a) Independence in economic decision-making presupposes the capacity of individuals to move freely with respect to society (personified in the state) and with respect to one another. Personal freedom and equal treatment of all in the eyes of the law in the economic (at least, but preferably in every) sphere of social activity are, therefore, instrumental to the proper functioning of commodity production. This freedom (the individual's bill of rights) is not, however, sufficient. To make practical use of their economic freedom, commodity producers must also have absolute and exclusive power of disposal over their material resources and over their products. Private ownership confers on them this power.

(b) Ownership can be acquired originally or by transfer from an existing owner. Original ownership is acquired either by occupation, as in the case of objects without an owner or by construction, with every independent producer being acknowledged as the owner of whatever he himself makes. Occupation, particularly in early times, could also take the form of violent seizure of the territory of a community by a group of invaders. In this case ownership of land would then belong to the invading nation or tribe, which made it available to individual members, while always retaining some residual rights itself.

Historically, such residual rights have functioned as obstacles to the full development of commodity production and exchange. To a regime struggling to become fully commercialised and individualistic, they opposed forms of communal or state ownership expressing the spirit (totally alien to commodity production) of tribalism or primitive communalism. In general, commodity production is basically inconsistent with the existence of political entities claiming rights of ownership jointly with private producers if such entities are not themselves trading agencies but attempt to represent a non-market principle of economic organisation. The reason is that no buyer of commodities could rest secure in the knowledge that he had acquired exclusive ownership over goods that he had paid for, if uncertainty prevailed as to the extent of the ownership rights the seller had the capacity to transfer. It follows that liquidation of communal ownership in sectors taken over by private economic activity is a condition for commodity production.

(c) Self-employment of all producers in simple commodity production presupposes that individuals are not limited to the merely formal capacity of acquiring ownership of productive assets, but that they are *actual, active* owners of their means of production. This assumption is the one which differentiates simple commodity production most sharply from capitalism. It is not a purely legal condition since it goes beyond the abstract formulation of a right, to state that the contents of this right must actually be enjoyed by everybody and that all be in the material position to exercise it. It is included in the legal section of the characteristics of simple commodity production mainly because of its emphasis on the ownership aspect of the position of producers.

(d) Absolute and exclusive power of disposal over one's goods, implicit in the right of private ownership, includes also the capacity of transferring ownership freely to someone else. This aspect of the right of private property is obviously of essence for the functioning of exchange. But as nobody can force the acquisition of ownership on anybody else, exchange presupposes an agreement that property rights are transferred, i.e. reciprocally granted and accepted. This agreement is based on the fact that commodity producers, being free and independent economic agents, can bind themselves by their own free will to certain mutual obligations. Obviously the agreement does not have to take specific form, nor does it have to be executed on the spot. It often is, but separation of the agreement about exchange from the act of exchange itself can become a great advantage. It endows market transactions with a high degree of flexibility which, to some limited extent, counterbalances the anarchic features of commodity production, because it makes possible a certain measure of forward planning.

Contracts are founded on the autonomy of the private will of commodity owners. But with exchange as the only remaining link providing cohesion in an otherwise atomised society, respect for contracts becomes a matter for public concern. Society, through the state, intervenes on behalf of individuals to make private contracts legally enforceable. At a further remove, of course, society intervenes on behalf not of individuals but of its own integrity. In defending individuals against breach of contract by other individuals the state defends the very fabric of commodity production. The dual aspect of the institution of contract – freedom in concluding one, enforceability in executing it – strikingly reflects the dual position of private producers, both isolated (hence autonomous, free of externally-imposed obligations) and mutually dependent (hence forced to undertake, at some stage, self-assumed obligations to one another).

(e) In (b) above, it was seen that the political community, in so far as it is originally based on tribal or communalistic principles, should withdraw from its role of a joint owner of resources to the extent that private production expands. Such withdrawal must be seen in more general terms, as covering all aspects of public life which might exercise an inhibiting influence upon private initiative. The role of the state is restricted to buttressing, by means of its monopoly of armed force, the position of the producer as a private individual. This the state achieves by declaring private property inviolate and also by proclaiming its readiness to enforce properly negotiated contracts. It protects private individuals both in their separateness (private property) and their togetherness (contract). Finally it protects them against the power of the state itself by proclaiming that individuals have rights (human rights) which the state can under no circumstances tamper with, provided that as citizens they remain law-abiding. As a further step in its development the state will also, under democracy, grant to individuals inviolate rights of participation in the running of the state itself (the rights of the citizen).

This is the essence of bourgeois human and political rights. They do represent a great step forward in the progress of mankind. On the other hand it must be seen that they sanctify as universally 'human' a specific, historically limited, type of man: the private commodity producer.

Ideally, therefore, the role of the state is protective and defensive of citizens as private individuals. The political authority assumes no role in initiating or directing economic activity. It has no private interests of its own to pursue. In so far as it safeguards law and order it can arguably be seen as a representative of the general interest. Such interest, however, in conditions of commodity production, is emptied of positive content. It remains as a negative interest, in the sense that the state is expected merely to prevent various things from happening. Private interests on the other hand expand to take up the whole space of positive practical human activity, leaving the general interest as nobody's (positive) interest.

Both in its insistence on the absolute character of private property, the absolute autonomy of private will and the withdrawal of the state from economic life, the above sketch of legal norms in commodity production is highly idealised and, on current experience, obsolete. Private property nowadays is subject to numerous restrictions on behalf of society, private initiative is controlled in all sorts of ways, and the state has become a very active force in the management of the economy. All these developments are very real but they are associated with a mature and complex capitalism, while the legal characteristics outlined above refer to a deliberately simplified model of early commodity production. The picture corresponds better to the idea often attributed to classical economics about the proper relations between the individual and the state, in a society based on commerce. Modifications of this picture under the impact of capitalist development will be examined in due course.

Capitalism: the labour market

The two crucial characteristics – one economic and one legal – of simple commodity production, which must be replaced for the definition of capitalism to emerge, are the assumption that each producer is exclusive owner of his means of production and the assumption about the aim of production.

It might appear contradictory to the principles of historical materialism stated in Chapter 1, that the first change differentiating capitalism from simple commodity production should be located in the legal sphere. But the phenomenon envisaged here is not legal, in the narrow sense of a change in some right or norm. Law remains the same, it is its economic substratum which changes. In the midst of a simple commodity-producing society, a numerous class of people emerges who have no ownership of means of production. Readers may, if they so wish, imagine that competition has worked such ravages among simple commodity producers as to make most of them bankrupt, bringing about the polarisation of a formerly homogenous society into two opposite classes, a small one which monopolises the means of production and a far larger one which finds itself excluded from productive resources. Historically, there is a component of that process in the formation of the modern proletariat, but it is dwarfed by other developments, not considered for the moment.

This propertyless class is technically known as the *proletariat*. Being deprived of means of production, proletarians cannot produce any commodities. They are, therefore, excluded from participating in the social division of labour and from market exchange. They would perish if they found no way of gaining access to the productive resources of society, monopolised now by a minority capitalist class. They gain access by offering for sale the one commodity they are left with, their capacity to work. This they are in a position to sell because propertylessness does not, in the legal context of simple commodity production, disqualify them from formal personal freedom, which, moreover, they cannot renounce by selling themselves into slavery. They remain free to dispose of themselves as they choose and to come to contractual arrangements with other citizens. The content of such arrangements is fixed by private agreement.

Typically the nature of this agreement, the employment contract, is the following: the owners of the capacity to work hire out their services for a period of time to the owners of the means of production. The latter allow the former to make use of such means, under supervision and instructions, with the purpose of making a product. Ownership of the product belongs to the capitalists who undertake the obligation to pay to the direct producers not a proportionate, or any other, *share* of the product but simply a fixed amount of money as wages. (For incentive purposes workers may be paid by the piece. In such cases, piece-rates are set so as to yield, on the average, a total amount per worker equal to the time-wage usual for the trade.)

This transaction is technically described in Marxist theory as the sale of the capacity to work (of *labour power*) for a price (*wages*). The emergence of a labour-market (*the buying-and-selling of labour power*) and of a new form of employment, is the first important set of features distinguishing capitalism from simple commodity production.

For the rest the (theoretically) original mode of production remains unaltered. Products are still produced as commodities, under division of labour, and the regulation of production is achieved *ex post*, through the market. Exchange remains the only social link of an otherwise atomised society. In a sense exchange becomes even more important because producers who under simple commodity production have a direct individual relationship to their productive resources, must now establish this relationship itself through an act of exchange, the buying-and-selling of labour power.

Under the surface, however, important changes begin to take place. The first is the change in the function of private property and of the contract. In simple commodity production the exclusion aspect of private property (the fact that it gives to the owner the right to exclude other persons from using his goods) serves as a guarantee of independence for the private producer, who stands on a par with other private producers. In capitalism, on the other hand, it becomes a means of maintaining the class of working people in a perpetually dependent state of propertylessness.

The changes in the function of the institution of contract go even deeper. In simple commodity production the contract serves the exchange of products among partners who are equal both legally and economically. In capitalism it brings together legally equal but economically very unequal partners who no longer exchange commodities but one of whom buys the other, as if he were a commodity. There is, of course, intentional exaggeration in the description of the capitalist as 'buying' the worker, as indeed there is in Marx's characterising of the employment contract as 'wage slavery'. But the exaggeration serves the purpose of stressing that what the worker alienates is a part of his creative personality, his capacity for producing. This deprives him not merely of the direction of his own work-activity but also of any direct claim on the product of that activity. In simple commodity production the maker and only the maker becomes the original owner of the commodity produced. In capitalism the maker no longer has any ownership rights; by virtue of the buying-and-selling of labour power it is the capitalist (increasingly a non-maker) who has the right of original acquisition.

To bring about this momentous change in social and legal relationships no reform in the legal order is introduced. The contract of hiring of personal services – a contract-type known in pre-capitalist times, but having limited application in the absence of a propertyless class ready to sell its labour power – simply becomes the normal kind of employment contract. The fact that in the new conditions the contract is no longer merely about the rendering of services, but also about the expropriation of the worker from the product of his work, is so deeply ingrained in bourgeois consciousness as to be hardly noticed in everyday life.

Bourgeois political philosophy, on the other hand, sometimes slips into acknowledging the new function of contract. Robert Nozick, one of the most convinced contemporary defenders of capitalist institutions, has rationalised the entitlement of the capitalist on the product in the following remark:[3]

> Whoever makes something, having bought or contracted for all other held resources (transferring some of his holdings for these cooperating factors) is entitled to it.

This rule, setting the 'making' of something as the principle of justice of original acquisition, involve a certain difficulty when among 'other-held' resources which the capitalist buys the capacity itself to make things is included. Who is in this case the 'maker'? The capitalist (assuming he contributes directly to the production process even as a manager – an increasingly unreal assumption) or the worker? If they are both 'makers' why don't they become joint owners of the product? There can be no other explanation except that, having sold his 'other-held' resource (his labour-power) to the capitalist, the worker has alienated his rights as a 'maker'. One is forced to conclude that the contract, from being a mere vehicle for the transfer of ownership in simple commodity production, becomes in addition a (tacit) way of original acquisition in capitalism.

But now it can no longer be claimed as a justification for the contents of the contractual agreement that the contract is the product of the meeting of minds between two free, sovereign individuals. The worker is not free to sell or not sell his labour power. As a result of his propertylessness, he has to sell it, on pain of starvation. The source of capitalist ownership is only formally contractual; in fact it rests on economic compulsion. It is therefore of doubtful legitimacy, even in the context of bourgeois morality.

It is sometimes argued that the compulsion is not unilateral, because capitalists need to employ workers just as much as workers need to be employed by capitalists, since without workers capital is condemned to remain idle and unproductive. In the long run and in an abstract sense this is true, but in any imaginary confrontation in which the two classes would go on strike against each other, the capitalists, as owners of the stocks of goods in society, would be in a position to hold out much longer and probably bring the working class to heel, even without the help of the state, which on such occasions would itself not refrain from intervening. This long-run, structural, imbalance in the relative strength of the two classes finds its day-to-day counterpart in the persistent unemployment of a section of the working class throughout the history of capitalism. Unemployment is the most effective form of implementation of the state of propertylessness of the proletariat.

Another similar argument is that workers could escape their dependent position if they went out to hire capital and set up their own business instead of selling their services to capital owners. In pure logic this argument is unexceptionable. Indeed, there seems to be no reason why capitalists should bother to organise the production process themselves, rather than leaving it to labourers while drawing a comfortable income from the letting out of their productive assets. What, however, appears plausible in abstract logic, collapses, in this case, when put to the test of practical reality. There are very good reasons to be considered further on in the book why the capitalist, particularly in the formative epoch of the bourgeois mode of production, has to combine the roles of owner and manager and why it would be dangerous for his existence to attempt to be the one without the other. Absentee capitalist ownership is indeed possible in advanced capitalism, provided management remains safely in the hands not of workers but of trusted functionaries of capital.

The dependent position of the worker, the perpetuation of his original propertylessness via the expropriation of his product, creates a presumption in favour of the thesis that the worker may be exploited by the capitalist. The theory of exploitation will be discussed extensively in Chapter 3. Here it is merely pointed out that with the capitalist being the exclusive owner of the product, as well as bearing the obligation to pay fixed wages, the less the worker is paid and the more he is made to produce (being a dependent employee), the greater the residual benefit for the capitalist owner. Both motive and opportunity for exploitation would appear obvious in this situation. Moreover, as long as a certain percentage of unemployed labour is always present on the market, capitalists run no risk of having to bid against one another for labour so hard as to cause their advantages to vanish in the face of a universal upsurge of wage levels.

It is useful to conclude this section with one of Marx's passages in *Capital*, where he manages to capture the full contradiction between the freedom and equality enjoyed by the worker versus the capitalist in the formal act of concluding a wage-labour contract and his dependence and inferiority in the process of fulfilling that contract.[4]

The consumption of labour-power . . . is completed . . . outside the limits of the market or of the sphere of circulation . . . This sphere that we are now deserting, within whose boundaries the sale and purchase of labour power goes on, is in fact a very Eden of the innate rights of man. There alone rule Freedom, Equality, Property and Bentham. Freedom, because both buyer and seller of a commodity, say of labour-power, are constrained only by their own free will. They contract as free agents, and the agreement they come to, is but the form in which they give legal expression to their common will. Equality, because each enters into relation with the other, as with a simple owner of commodities and they exchange equivalent for equivalent. Property because each disposes only of what is his own. And Bentham, because each looks only to himself. The only force that brings them together . . . is the selfishness, the gain and the private interests of each. Each looks to himself only, and no one troubles himself about the rest, and just because they do so, do they all, in accordance with the pre-established harmony of things . . . work together to their mutual advantage . . .

On leaving this sphere of simple circulation or of exchange of commodities, which furnishes the 'Free-trader Vulgaris' with his views and ideas, and with the standard by which he judges a society based on capital and wages, we think we can perceive a change in the physiognomy of our dramatis personae. He, who was before the money-owner, now strides in front as capitalist; the possessor of labour-power follows as his labourer. The one with an air of importance, smirking, intent on business; the other timid and holding back, like one who is bringing his own hide to market and has nothing to expect but – a hiding.

Capitalism: the aim of production

The second alteration in the characteristics of simple commodity production that leads to the definitions of capitalism refers to the aim of production. It was noticed above that in simple commodity production the ultimate aim of economic activity is the acquisition of use-value, and that this dominates the immediate aim which is the acquisition of exchange-value. In capitalism, by contrast, the acquisition and accumulation of exchange value, indeed the production of exchange value by means of exchange value, becomes the aim and driving force of business activity.

This second difference from simple commodity production is, in the author's opinion, quite as important as the first, but it is rarely commented on with equal force. A full consideration of its implications must wait until the concept of money is developed in Chapters 3 and 4. What can be said now, by way of anticipation, is that the step from use value to exchange value as an aim of economic activity is equivalent to the step from a stationary or slowly growing to a dynamic, fast and even at times explosively growing economy. With the economy oriented totally towards exchange value (historically only capitalism has shown that trait) the rate of population increase ceases to be the upper limit to the expansion of output. Material production acquires a self-sustaining rhythm of its own which, in the lifetime of a few generations, reaches unprecedented levels of productive achievements. Humanity moves into a totally new era, which brings the abolition of millenial deprivation for the vast majority of people within the realm of the feasible. For as long, however, as this enormous productivity remains subject to the domain of private capitalist interest, it simply provides additional incentives for raising the share of capital even further as against that of labour, the dependent factor of production. This joining together, the mutual reinforcement of labour dependency and economic dynamism (between exploitation of labour and capital accumulation) constitutes the hallmark and distinctive feature of the capitalist mode of production.

CHAPTER 3

The labour theory of value

The aim of this chapter is to present a simple, non-mathematical statement of the labour theory of value, preparing the way for the discussion of exploitation in Chapter 4 and of capital accumulation in Chapter 5. The theory is presented as a quantification of economic relations in simple commodity production described in Chapter 2. Being, however, mainly intended for the analysis of capitalism, the labour theory of value cannot be fully stated until, in Chapter 4, its most crucial application to capitalist production relations is described.

Upon embarking on this exposition notice must be served that, particularly over the last decade, the labour theory of value has lost rather than gained ground. Its critics are no longer limited to the circle of authors generally hostile to Marxism. Even among those who endorse socialism as an aim of a movement of social change, and broadly accept Marxism as the theory of that movement, an increasing number has decided that, for its purposes, the labour theory of value is no longer tenable.

In the present author's opinion this category of critics, who have undoubtedly made interesting and valuable contributions to the development of Marxist or radical economics, risk, by their wholesale rejection of the labour theory of value, throwing out the baby together with the bathwater. For the study and methodical exposition of the specific, basic workings of the capitalist mode of production, the labour theory of value does not yet seem to have found a successor. This, rather than any presumed logical or mathematical perfection (of which, in the author's opinion, no theory of value can boast), is the sense in which it is introduced and defended here.

To avoid obscuring the positive contents of the theory with a fully ramified discussion of the objections to it, no attempt to confront recent criticisms is made in the text. Some of them are taken up in the Appendix to Chapter 4. This compartmentalisation of the argument is made in an attempt to respect objectivity without damaging clarity. On the other hand, the more fundamental and time-honoured critique, based on the claim that the labour theory of value focuses unilaterally on labour, to the exclusion of other equally important factors of production, is discussed in the fourth section of the chapter. The order of the three following sections is: first, basic definitions are stated; second, there follows a discussion of competition as the mechanism by which the predictions of the theory are implemented in practice; third, the relationship between abstract labour and money is briefly commented on.

Basic definitions

(a) Exchange ratios and production costs

In a state of simple commodity production, the exchange ratio between two commodities will conform to their relative labour inputs. If it takes a potter two days to make a clay jar while it only takes one day for a blacksmith to make an axe, the exchange ratio between jars and axes will be one to two. If, by some accident, the rate of exchange, prevailing in a well-stocked market, falls to one to one, nobody will bother any longer to make jars or buy them from the producers. Potters will turn into blacksmiths and produce the market-equivalent of any number of jars they may need, in half the time it would have taken them to produce jars directly. Of course, under such conditions, any existing stock of jars will very quickly run out. The ensuing shortage will push exchange ratios back to two axes per jar and even higher. Potters will resume production with new enthusiasm, probably overstepping the limits and creating excess supply. Exchange ratios will then fall again and continue to fluctuate until equilibrium is established at a rate equal to that of labour inputs. (In the above it is assumed that the materials for making the various commodities are taken free from nature.)

(b) Concrete and abstract labour

The point of this little economic parable is to motivate measurement of the values of commodities by their labour content – the labour expended in their production. This method leads to the following question: it is observed that the act of exchange has the capacity to transform a blacksmith, with regard to the effects of his work, into a potter. An individual has worked making axes, but by the end of the production-exchange cycle he finds himself equipped with a jar, and vice versa. Given this transformability of one kind of work into another, whose labour is it that must become the common standard to measure all labour inputs: the blacksmith's or the potter's? The answer is, neither. For the purpose of ascertaining its quantity the blacksmith can compare his work with that of another blacksmith. He cannot compare it with that of a potter, because their activities differ qualitatively. Only as producers of unspecified commodities, i.e. as suppliers of human labour pure and simple, can producers in different branches of production, establish a common standard by which to measure the relative quantity of their work. This standard is the hour of work, performed in an unspecified manner, in abstraction from the concrete circumstance or the form assumed by labour in the various occupations. Labour in which inter-subjective quantitative measurements of work inputs are made among commodity producers is thus described as *abstract labour*.

This idea may appear to clash with the well-known psychological trait of individuals often trying to attach greater importance to their own activity than to that of their neighbours, particularly if they stand to gain thereby. The blacksmith may not wish to accept three hours of the potter's work as equivalent to three of his own; he may demand four or five. But if he did so his customers would go to some competitor of his, prepared to sell for less, and in the end mutual competitive pressure would force all producers to stand on an equal footing.

The power of the concept of abstract labour becomes more evident if a chain of exchanges rather than one single act of exchange is considered. The potter may not himself make use of the axes he acquired from the blacksmith. He may exchange them further against a quantity of hides which in the end he hands over for a pair of shoes. Exchange makes the potter's work equivalent successively to that of a blacksmith's, a tanner's and a shoemaker's. Given sufficient market links anyone's work can be transformed into anyone else's. The more distant the trades, the more obvious the need for a standard of comparison which, being common to all, is specific to no one.

The chain of transactions demonstrates that private labour – the activity which the producer, in the context of the division of labour, undertakes on his own initiative, without prior agreed coordination with other producers – acquires social validity in the form of abstract labour. For the relevant concept to be defined a chain of barter transactions, or even one single exchange, may be sufficient. But, from the practical point of view, a transaction chain is a rather awkward instrument. The social validity of labour of the commodity producer can acquire its full effect only if he is able to reach the final link of the chain in one leap without having to undergo the trouble and risk of intermediate exchanges. To achieve this, in the context of a market economy, he would need to be able to exchange his product for a general commodity, itself directly exchangeable against any other goods whatsoever. Possession of this one special commodity (which is, of course, money) would immediately translate his private labour into labour of general social validity, i.e. abstract labour. The notional correspondence between money and abstract labour is thus established.

(c) Abstract labour and money

In the absence of money, the producer may assert the social validity of his private work by engaging in a sequence of acts of exchange. His labour needs no endorsement by any public authority to acquire such validity; what the producer needs is possession of exchangeable commodities. However, without money, a certain asymmetry is noticeable between abstract labour and its market manifestation in exchange value. Abstract labour is defined as labour detached from the specific characteristics of any sector of production. Exchange value, on the other hand, appears attached to the physical body of commodities, inseparable from their use value. The emergence of money as the general commodity endows exchange-value with a form detached from any specific good; it makes the expression of exchange value independent of the use value of any commodity, and it thereby restores full symmetry between abstract labour and the material expression of its effectiveness in market exchange. The use value of the money commodity itself (e.g. the ornamental use of gold) fades away in the face of its role as representative of independent exchange value. This triad of concepts – abstract labour, exchange value in independent form, money as the general commodity – provides the most general framework for the quantitative determination of exchange ratios in the theory under discussion.

(d) Socially necessary labour

To the dual nature of the commodity, consisting of a use-value and an exchange-value aspect, the dual character of labour corresponds. Exchange-value is coupled with abstract labour, use-value with concrete labour. Exchange value (and abstract labour) are represented as pure quantities. The value of commodities of any kind is measured by the same unit, the hour of work. In the case of use-value and concrete labour, quality is the predominant characteristic.

If the influence of demand is, for the moment, set aside and the extremely rigid assumption is made of individual producers identical in industriousness and dexterity in all sectors of the economy, concrete and abstract labour (and by extension use-value and exchange-value) can be treated as totally separate categories. The assumption of productively identical individuals is needed to make one hour of work by the same producer objectively worth exactly the same as one hour of work by any other producer (homogeneous labour). It then becomes possible to add together hours of work and estimate values of the various commodities without asking questions about the quality of the labour each one performs. The quantitative aspect (abstract labour) can be totally separated from the qualitative one (concrete labour).

In the author's opinion, it is possible to make the assumption and enforce the strict separation, without jeopardising most of the crucial insights of Marxist economic analysis. Marx himself, however, saw the matter differently. He opted for a less abstract approach of value calculation, in which he tried to make allowance both for the structure of demand and for differences in the skill and industriousness of the various producers. Since such properties, particularly skill, are meaningful only when related to the production of specific objects, Marx's approach leads inevitably to an area of a certain overlap between the concepts of concrete and abstract labour. The result of the overlap is the emergence of the hybrid concept of socially necessary labour and the distinction between skilled and unskilled labour.

The concept of socially necessary labour does not materially affect but it does modify the analysis of abstract labour presented in section (b) above. The transformation of concrete into abstract labour in the process of exchange goes on as before, with two additional conditions: (a) that labour must be of the degree of skill and intensity typical of the branch of industry where it is performed; (b) that it must correspond to the amount of total work just sufficient for satisfying the corresponding social need which is assumed given independently of the unit value of the commodity.

Subject to these two conditions labour, described now as *socially necessary labour*, counts as abstract labour, which corresponds hour for hour to a certain amount of exchange value embodied in the product. Inefficient or supernumerary labour is not acknowledged as valid on the market. Producers who have worked inefficiently receive no value in exchange for the superfluous part of their work; they simply have to bear the burden of their inefficiency themselves. In the example of the parable of blacksmiths and potters, if some blacksmiths need two days to make an axe, while most of their colleagues need one day, they will not be given one jar in exchange for one axe. They will have to work twice as long in order to produce the jar-equivalent. Four days of their work will count only as two days of socially necessary labour. By contrast, if among blacksmiths there happens to be a couple of extremely efficient ones, who produce two axes a day, they will be in a position to buy twice as many jars for the same hours of work as most other fellow-workers. Two days of their work will count as four days of socially necessary labour. Similarly if, as a result of the isolation of producers and of the anarchy of production, more has been produced of a certain item than is needed (effectively demanded), prices will fall below values and the part of the total labour mistakenly allocated to that item will be unrewarded.

(e) Skilled and unskilled labour

In addition to the differences of skill in the same trade discussed in the previous paragraph, there exist certain trades which are considered more skilled than others. A goldsmith or a silversmith is thought to be more skilled than a stonemason, an engineer more skilled than a blacksmith etc. How can it be plausibly argued that the hour of work in any of these professions is worth just one hour of work in any other? Moreover there are certain physical or mental faculties which, without constituting skill in the usual sense, have nevertheless become so scarce and so much sought-after, that their possession is treated as a kind of skill. If the physique of the working class has been generally deteriorating, a man strong enough to work as a navvy counts as a skilled worker, Marx has observed.

In such cases the quantitative equivalence of hours of work irrespective of the kind of product (the idea of abstract labour) no longer holds. Labour of all kinds is still equivalent in the sense that an engineer is in a position to buy the silversmith's product and vice versa. But, from the quantitative point of view, skilled labour must be converted to a larger quantity of unskilled labour before abstract labour and exchange value can be properly measured. It is assumed that coefficients of conversion from skilled into unskilled labour can be ascertained and applied accordingly. One hour of labour of a silversmith will be multiplied, say, by a factor of three to be converted to its equivalent of unskilled labour. A unit of measurement of exchange value common to the products of all kinds of labour – the hour of unskilled work – can thus be established.

Unskilled labour has no special privilege to supply this common unit. The hour of skilled labour would do as well. The hour of work of a navvy would then have to be multiplied by, say, a factor of one third to be reduced into its equivalent in skilled labour time. However, unskilled labour, being relatively more widespread and, for that reason, of a more universal status, appears as a more natural common basis of reduction for all kinds of work.

The idea of conversion of all kinds of labour into an unskilled labour equivalent is plain enough. Much less plain are the exact principles for fixing the relevant conversion coefficients. A similar problem arises in the case of the fixing of norms which determine how much of the labour actually performed in each branch is to count as socially necessary labour for purposes of value calculation.

On these questions Marx appears to have reasoned as follows. For as long as human labour rather than mechanical automata remains the central element of production, the labour process has required both a degree of discipline concerning the skill, intensity and efficiency of work, and a gradation of tasks into more or less skilled. All societies need such disciplinarian or hierarchical institutions. In addition, for the sake of proper coordination, production in all societies has to respect certain proportions among its various activities. For this reason, the concept of socially necessary labour (in *both* its aspects) as well as the distinction between skilled and unskilled labour are applicable to societies of all kinds.

Societies belonging to different modes of production each develop different institutions for defining or imposing standards of discipline and hierarchy in their labour processes. In the Middle Ages, for example, it was up to the guilds to set the standards of artisanal production and up to the masters in the various trades to enforce them on their apprentices and journeymen. Societies also develop different techniques for maintaining their productive activities in the right proportions among themselves. Village communities have, for long ages, depended for this on the reproduction of a traditional pattern. A planned economy tries to achieve the same result through its central plan. But all economies have to resolve these tasks somehow. The methods vary, the tasks themselves remain the same. They are not conditional on historically changing relations of production. They constitute part of a substratum of 'laws of production' common to all types of socioeconomic organisation. This is the reason why the concept of socially necessary labour (in *both* its aspects) and the distinction between skilled and unskilled labour are applicable to economies of all kinds.

The market economy (the economy of commodity production) also has to satisfy the 'laws of production' common to all. In that sense, the norms that determine the socially necessary character of labour, or the relations between skilled and unskilled labour, are independent of the market. They are implicit in the production process. But they can only be known, they can be ascertained by producers, only *via* the market. By transforming concrete into abstract labour, exchange makes explicit the norms implicit in production relations and, through competition, it enforces them on all individuals. By establishing differential rates of reward the market informs producers about the hierarchical importance of the various tasks. But the problem remains that, in the context of commodity production, no other source of information on all such norms and/or conversion coefficients outside the market exists.

How serious is this problem? For a number of economists of the very first order, both opposed and sympathetic to Marx (Böhm-Bawerk, Morishima) it is very serious indeed. In their view it constitutes the Achilles heel of the labour theory of value, embroiling Marx's argument, as soon as it is extended to cover heterogeneous labour, in an incurable circularity. Conversion coefficients of skilled into unskilled labour are first sought in the market. On their basis the total number of hours of work to be imputed to labour is estimated. Finally the claim is made that a measurement of total exchange-value in the economy (as well as of the value of particular commodities) can be arrived at exclusively on the basis of the expenditure of labour in production. The claim is spurious and the argument circular because what must be taken as the number of hours of work spent in production has been shown to depend on the conversion coefficients of skilled into unskilled labour, ascertained exclusively in the market.

A brief arithmetical example may clarify this point. Assume there are two types of labour, A and B, of different skill, and that fifty hours of actual labour of each type are performed in the economy. The total number of hours of work actually performed is therefore 100 hours. If the market rewards labour of type B twice as highly as that of type A, and this is taken as the rate at which hours of B labour must be converted into hours of A labour for purposes of value calculation, total labour in that economy amounts to a value of 150 hours of A-equivalent labour. If, now, the reward differential changes, under the impact of supply and demand, into A = 3B, total value in the economy rises to 200 hours of A-equivalent labour. It follows that the measurement of value, apparently derived from the labour process, is sensitive to the fluctuations of supply and demand in exchange.

Although Marx did not hesitate to point to the market as the source of conversion coefficients of skilled into unskilled labour, the question of circularity never seems to have preoccupied him. He perceived no fundamental difference between the case where exchange converts the labour of a carpenter (embodied e.g. in a chair) into that of a presumed equally skilled blacksmith (embodied in an iron kettle), and the other case where it converts the embodied labour of a blacksmith to that of a more highly skilled silversmith or watchmaker. For grasping the substance of the functions of exchange in the economy, for unravelling the secrets of the historical specificity of commodity production, the former case seemed to Marx, rightly, the basic one. It is in these areas that he made his most important contributions and from that point of view no circularity is present in his thinking, since the production and exchange processes operate at different levels. Production is the more basic activity, exchange simply enforces (albeit in a 'blind' manner) the requirements, priorities and norms implicit in production.

On the other hand, Marx paid insufficient attention to the strictly quantitative difficulties of his approach in the presence of heterogeneous labour, as illustrated in the arithmetical example given above. Various attempts have been made since to iron out these difficulties, the most promising one having been conducted along the lines of treating education as a production process which turns unskilled into skilled labour (Hilferding, Morishima, Rowthorn). No complete theoretical resolution of the problem has, however, been achieved so far. In its absence two alternatives to the abandonment of the labour theory of value remain. The first is to persist with the counterfactual assumption of labour homogeneity, an assumption which, in the author's already stated opinion, does not materially diminish any of the crucial insights derivable from Marx's theory. The second alternative is to estimate long-run averages of reward-differentials among variously skilled jobs, long-run averages of the total demand of various commodities as well as long-run averages of efficiency norms in the execution of the various tasks, and treat these three categories of estimates as constants in the calculation of values. The assumption here would be that such averages represent the basic structure of the economy, revealed through the market but not dependent on the fluctuations of supply and demand. Values calculated on this basis could then be set against and compared with ordinary market prices.

(f) Present and past labour

Production of commodities absorbs not only current labour but also materials, which are products of past labour. Their cost, as well as the cost of any part of durable equipment (also a product of past labour) which has been currently used up, must be repaid from the value of current output and is charged accordingly. With such charges in mind the value of the commodity can now be defined as the sum of past and present socially necessary labour, with all types of skilled work having been converted into one type of homogeneous, simple (i.e. unskilled) labour. In making charges for past labour, however, one additional condition must be imposed. Of the hours of labour embodied in commodities produced in the past, only so many count as current costs as are necessary to produce the same commodities in the present, not as many as actually, historically spent. Value accounting is based on the principle of reproduction rather than of historical cost. For example, if 10 per cent of the value of an item of equipment, acquired originally for £1000, must be charged to current depreciation costs, but the same item can be purchased today for £500, a charge of only £50 rather than £100 will be made.

Durable equipment has not been described above as capital, because this concept has not been introduced yet. Marxist theory insists that durability of the means of production, a purely technical characteristic, is neither necessary nor sufficient for defining capital, a social relationship which may be embodied in either durable or in non-durable commodities. Since the labour theory of value is still discussed in the institutional context of simple commodity production, where every producer is his own boss, none being a capitalist employer, durable equipment cannot be treated as capital, the latter presupposing capitalistic ownership of such equipment.

Strictly speaking, the theoretical model of simple commodity production does not allow for the existence of any class of owners, capitalist or other, of means of production separate from the immediate producers; in particular it rules out a separate landlord class. Rent, therefore, does not appear as a cost in the calculation of the value of a commodity, seen exclusively as a crystallisation of past and present labour. This exclusion leaves open the problem of what happens to non-produced factors of production like virgin land, the 'original and indestructible' powers of the soil, or mineral deposits still in the ground. Are these to be used free of charge by every producer? Should they not be rationed among users by a system of pure scarcity prices?

Actual market economies do, of course, include both a landlord class and a practice of setting prices according to the relative scarcity of non-labour factors. The presence of landlords introduces an element of monopolistic exploitation which may distort the pure scarcity character of non-produced factor prices. To the extent, however, that a pure scarcity element enters into price formulation, it obviously cannot be explained on the basis of any labour theory of value. What is not a product of labour, or even what has been a product of labour but cannot be reproduced currently by labour (art masterpieces, antiques, vintage cars), cannot have its value determined by the hours of work necessary for its production. Such items, as well as the non-producible aspect of land (i.e. virgin land as distinct from the tilled field), have a price but have no value.

It follows that, as an explanation of exchange ratios among commodities or of production costs, the labour theory of value can give complete coverage only in a purely industrial economy, where all inputs are objects manufactured by labour out of non-scarce resources and nothing else.

No such economy exists in reality. If in practice charges for rent, royalties etc. constitute a significant part of the costs of production, then the gap left uncovered by the labour theory of value is an important one. If, on the contrary, they constitute a very small proportion of total costs, a purely manufacturing economy may be a tolerable approximation to reality. Whether this is in fact so, is an empirical matter. It is remarkable in this connection that in advanced capitalism the share of rent in GDP has been steadily declining. In Britain it fell from about 14 per cent in 1855 to about 5 per cent in recent years, with a considerable part of it consisting of urban rents which are, in part, charged for buildings, i.e. for products of labour. Therefore, payments to genuinely unproducible factors of production are even less than 5 per cent and may, perhaps, be treated as negligible.

A theory of value based on the principle of scarcity would not suffer from the particular deficiency of being unable to account for the cost of non-producible factors of production. In addition, it would be capable of explaining the price of no-longer-producible commodities, like vintage cars, works of art by past masters, etc. It would be a more general theory, very successful in the analysis of some aspects of the allocation of resources but not as suitable for those particular tasks which are discharged, with a fair degree of success, by the labour theory of value. It will be argued in Chapter 4 and in its Appendix that these tasks are associated with the analysis of the problem of exploitation. Therefore, choice between the two theories of value (scarcity or labour), boils down to a choice of which problem, allocation or exploitation, is selected for study. This choice is prior to the selection of a theory of value; in that context it is pre-theoretical and, like any choice, it involves the cost of a foregone alternative. A certain loss of generality in the explanation of market-prices is the opportunity cost of the labour theory of value.

Competition and unequal exchange

(a) The law of value

In Chapter 2 an analysis of competition stated in qualitative terms was outlined. It is now possible to construct its quantitative counterpart, which will also serve as a means of relating the labour theory of value with Marshallian supply and demand theory.

Competition has both functional and exploitative aspects (with exploitation not being restricted to capitalism here). In practice, it is impossible to separate the one from the other, but they can be separated conceptually. Functional effects are studied through the idea of socially necessary labour, exploitative ones through the idea of unequal exchange. The quantitative measurements which have to be brought into play consist of (i) the difference between individual and market value and (ii) the difference between value and price.

Socially necessary labour operates as a control on the expenditure of effort by individual producers. Quantitatively, as far as socially necessary labour in the first sense is concerned (i.e. as a norm of skill and efficiency typical in an industry), the control works through the difference between individual value and market value. It is only the latter which corresponds to socially necessary labour, but there is nothing to stop the producer from individually achieving results better than the industry achieves on average. Producers whose costs are lower than those typically incurred in their branch produce their commodities at an individual value lower than the market value, but they do not have to sell at a lower value. They may use their competitive advantage to broaden their market by undercutting the price of their competitors, while at the same time earning normal profits themselves. Or, they may continue trading the same volume as before but use their lower costs to reap supernormal profits from the difference, with given selling prices. By contrast those producers for whom individual value is higher than market value are forced to make losses and have either to improve their performance or suffer elimination from the industry.

There are two ways whereby a difference between individual and market value may arise. Demand may increase under conditions of rising long-run costs, so that less and less efficient producers have to be mobilised to supply the market with a certain commodity. In such cases market value is not determined by labour of highest or even average, but by labour of lowest productivity. Given the extent of the need, it is this kind of labour which dictates the efficiency norm required for entry into the industry. Intra-marginal producers find, in this case, their individual value falling below market value without any additional effort of their own. They become able to reap efficiency rents analogous to the differential rent accruing to intra-marginal plots of land in Ricardian analysis.

Alternatively producers may themselves take the initiative to increase the productivity of their labour, thereby reducing their individual value below market value, by introducing improved technical methods which their competitors have not yet had time to imitate. For as long as their technological advantage lasts, producers are placed in a position to make extra profits, or to expand their market, or some combination of the two. Their profits are best described as entrepreneurial, since they constitute a reward of initiative in improving production methods. They are eliminated to the extent that other producers arrive to copy the pioneers. A new market value becomes, then, gradually established at the lower level of costs, previously covered by the individual value of some untypical producers only. The process in question presents striking analogies with Schumpeter's description of the innovating activity of entrepreneurs; this part of Marxist analysis has probably constituted one of the sources of inspiration for the theories of the Austrian economist.

Socially necessary labour in the second sense represents the share of total labour available in the economy which, if allocated to a certain sector, is just sufficient to supply a need at the existing level of long-run demand. When mistakes happen, as they inevitably do in a market economy, prices rise above or fall below the corresponding values. If the allocation actually prevailing in practice is the ideal one, the sector is in a state of long-run equilibrium. With all sectors in this kind of balance, the economy as a whole is in a state of general equilibrium with price and value coinciding everywhere. Conversely, the assumption of their coincidence (an assumption which underlies the statement in value terms of the main propositions of Marxist economics), can be interpreted as tacitly pre-supposing general equilibrium. This does not mean that Marxist economics is general equilibrium economics in the sense of arguing that the market achieves a harmonious state of proper universal interdependence among all parts of the economy. It does, however, imply that Marx and later Marxists have frequently used general equilibrium concepts, even if only to demonstrate the inevitability of disequilibrium in capitalism.

Under this second aspect of socially necessary labour, competition no longer functions as the enforcer of a social norm of efficiency. Its role is to promote a proper allocation of resources in circumstances of unplanned, spontaneous division of labour. Under the impact of random deviations of either supply or demand from their equilibrium positions, short-run prices are formed, and it is the difference between such prices and commodity values that eliminates supernumerary producers (or attracts new suppliers). If a sector has been oversupplied, competitors start undercutting one another's prices in an effort to get rid of their stock first. The fall in price may stimulate increased demand and persuade consumers to absorb all existing stocks (Marx fully accepts this point, so that an ordinary demand curve is not at all inconsistent with his basic value theory). Producers, however, will in such cases be able to sell only at a loss, so that some of their labour expenditure will go unrewarded and some of the weaker ones among them may suffer bankruptcy as a result and be eliminated.

Figure 3.1 summarises and illustrates the discussion on the interplay between value and price. In the diagram cost, price and value are measured vertically, in units of socially necessary labour, and quantity of output is measured horizontally. D and D' are ordinary demand curves, S and S' are short run supply curves, and the shift from S to S' (or from S' to S) is a

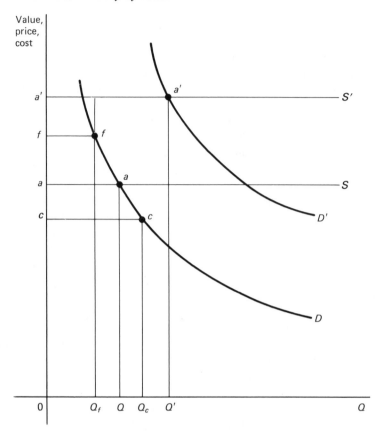

FIGURE 3.1

long-run shift, reflecting either changes in technology or rising long-run costs. Value is either *a* or *a'* and, in the short run it is independent of demand (because of the horizontal slope of the supply curves). *Q* and *Q'* are the equilibrium quantities in the two cases. At *c* and *f* less or more labour than is socially necessary has been mistakenly allocated to the industry; price therefore either falls below or rises above value. Ideally the demand curves should be of unit elasticity, so that the total amount of socially necessary labour *paid* (*ex post* as distinct from allocated *ex ante*) does not vary (rectangles $0_{aa}Q_f$, $0_{ff}Q_f$ and $0_{cc}Q_c$ are then all equal). If demand increases permanently to *D'* less efficient producers set the norm for the sector so that value rises to *a'*. The long-run change in value is shown as discontinuous, to stress its independence from short-run fluctuations of demand and cost.

The mechanism of competitive adjustment, operating through the discrepancy between individual and market value and between market value and market price, is described as *the law of value*. In the word 'law' it is emphasised that value and competition, as regulators of the economy, operate like natural forces, in a blind manner, disregarding hardships or benefits distributed to individuals who did nothing to deserve either. The law of value does express the needs of society but it does this in an uncoordinated, asocial, hit-and-miss manner. An association of producers, conscious of its aims and its potentialities, could, in principle, plan its production activities in such a way as to make them dovetail *ex ante*, without the need of large corrections *ex post*. Planning of this kind would replace the law of value and avoid its blind destructiveness. But in the context of commodity production, conscious *ex ante* coordination is made impossible by the antagonistic nature of relations of production and ownership.

(b) Exploitation in exchange

The blind character of the law of value is not the only damaging effect associated with the competitive regulation of commodity production. Competition generates a spirit of antagonism as well as the opportunities for producers to take advantage of one another in the market. Individualism, inherent in commodity production, conditions people psychologically to treat the other person as an alien, whom it is permissible and even honourable to exploit, in the expectation that he or she is going to reciprocate fully, given a chance. Society, mindful of its own preservation, imposes through its conscious organ of the state, certain limits to prevent mutual aggressiveness by individuals against one another from getting out of hand. In private transactions, naked violence, outright fraud and the more blatant forms of monopolistic market power are officially repressed. Even so, a wide margin for the legitimate exercise of force and deception in trade does remain, nourished by the attitude of foreignness among individuals, which inevitably accompanies the isolating, private charter of the production process.

Exploitation in exchange takes the form of a difference between value, determined by socially necessary labour content, and the price which the consumer is able to negotiate for his commodity on the market. Any price which, being superior to value, is not the result of purely random, unforseeable shifts in demand or supply but derives from the exercise of some kind of market power, is clearly exploitative. The phenomenon is described as *unequal exchange*, to account for the fact that the seller acquires a greater counterpart, measured in terms of abstract labour, than what he has handed over. To the extent that unequal exchange is an occasional occurrence in day-to-day transactions, it can, perhaps, be treated as negligible. It becomes, on the other hand, a serious matter, if a certain group in society or a certain nation, or group of nations internationally find themselves in a perpetually disadvantaged negotiating position, so that exchange against them is permanently and systematically unequal. Discrimination against ethnic minorities or against women on the labour market as well as unequal trade between advanced capitalist and dependent former colonies in the Third World are the two main areas where unequal exchange is believed to be practised most in the modern capitalist world. The monopolistic oil-pricing policies of the OPEC countries are supposed to be the first and so far the only case where the tables of unequal exchange have been turned against industrial capitalism by its underdeveloped trading partners.

Discrimination on the basis of race or sex and unequal international trade are two areas which, over the last fifteen years, have attracted considerable attention from Marxist and other radical economists. Of these two areas only international trade has been subjected to any systematic study of value and unequal exchange. If labour power is a commodity (a topic extensively discussed in the following chapter) there is no reason, in principle, why discrimination on the labour market cannot be treated similarly with discrimination on the world commodity market.

Coming back to international trade, it would appear that measurement in terms of abstract labour does offer a way of cutting through the tangle of comparative costs, negotiating positions, transport costs, political events etc. By looking not at quantities and prices but at total amounts of abstract labour exchanged via commodity exchange, one might hope to discover whether one nation exploited another. But the comparison is plagued by an internal problem jeopardising its robustness. It has been seen above that, for purposes of being treated as abstract, skilled labour is converted to an equivalent larger amount of unskilled labour. It may be argued, however, that labour in advanced industrial nations is more skilled than in underdeveloped countries, or, at least, that it is more productive and should count as more skilled. Even, therefore, if on a straight count underdeveloped countries hand over more hours of their own labour (embodied in their products) than they receive back, one may still not be able to speak of unequal exchange. The coefficients of conversion of skilled into unskilled labour between countries will have to be established first. Given such coefficients it may turn out that fewer hours of work embodied in the exports of an industrially advanced country are equivalent to substantially more hours of work embodied in the exports of an underdeveloped country, so that despite the difference in the total number of hours during which the labour force in one country works for supplying the other, no unequal exchange can be said to exist. Only under the heroic assumption that one hour of work in an industrialised capitalist economy is exactly equivalent to one hour in a developing economy, does unequal exchange in international trade acquire unambiguous meaning.

Abstract labour and money

The idea of abstract labour is motivated by the equivalence of all types of labour which exchange establishes among producers. In its capacity of abstract labour the producer's work acquires purchasing power over the labour (i.e. the products) of others. This of course is, in some ways, a theoretical metaphor. In practice nobody buys anything directly with labour; purchases are made with money. The correspondence of abstract labour and money (exchange-value which has become independent of use-value) has already been noted above. It has been suggested that money is the dual of abstract labour in the process of exchange, while abstract labour is the dual of money in the process of production, and that both are aspects of exchange value, which has become independent of any specific use value. The argument of the labour theory of value is usually presented as maintaining that value is determined by the labour content of commodities. If labour is the only factor of production and under the assumptions already explained above, the validity of this argument can be established. In equilibrium, exchange ratios of commodities cannot differ from their relative labour costs. In that sense the arrow of causality may be said to run from labour input to exchange value.

Outside equilibrium, matters differ. The law of value is implemented by flows of money among industries. If an industry has overexpanded it makes losses; money flows out of it. If it has contracted too much it makes supernormal profits; money flows into it. To flow from industry to industry, money must be in a form which does not bind it physically to any specific use; in this sense the independence of exchange value from use value is essential to the regulation of the economy.

Flows of labour must correspond to inter-industry flows of money. This is possible only if labour can detach itself from one specific industry to migrate to another as easily as money does. Ideally, abstract labour, being labour of no specific character, labour in general, represents in production an instrument as flexible as money in exchange. But while in the case of money its concept corresponds to an empirically given object (to a money-commodity that has no other main use, like gold or to a money-artefact, like paper money), it is not as clear that something empirically tangible corresponds to the idea of abstract labour. Whether some such empirical property exists is a matter for further investigation.

Commodity production, which begins with a division of labour based originally on individual aptitudes, tends increasingly towards severing the subjective link between the producer and the product. In simple commodity production this separation takes the relatively mild form of the producer's becoming indifferent to the use-value of his product, as far as his own consumption is concerned, because he is not producing use-value for himself but for others. In capitalism the separation takes the much more drastic form of the worker having no ownership over his product and no control over his own labour activity, since he works under instructions. In such conditions, it becomes a matter of indifference to the worker what he produces or what industry he moves into, if conditions of employment are comparable. Subjectively his labour is, in his eyes, already abstract at that stage.

Objectively, the difficulty still remains that workers do not receive the kind of training which would enable them to move more or less freely from one job to another. Simplification of tasks with the aid of mechanisation and scientific management may lead to the point where workers are so fully substitutable that the sector of their activity becomes a matter of indifference to them and to society. This would establish perfect correspondence between money and abstract labour. In practice such a state of affairs is hardly likely ever to materialise completely. But, for some authors, there is evidence of movement in this direction in modern industry. They would claim that this is the main insight to be gained from the labour theory of value.

The remark that when the economy is out of equilibrium allocation of labour is steered by money flows, raises the question of the relative primacy of production and exchange. In equilibrium, exchange ratios are determined by relative labour costs; outside equilibrium, exchange value in its independent form leads the process of re-allocation of resources. Should one perceive in this the operation of two symmetrically opposite forces, which ultimately turns out to be nothing more than an ordinary balance of supply and demand?

Marxist theory does not contradict supply-and-demand analysis; it proposes a different analysis. It emphasises that a developed economy is controlled by flows of money, to which flows of productive activity and ultimately of labour correspond. But productive activity is not the willed outcome of the conscious initiative of the producers. Rather it dominates producers in the form of a labour discipline that derives its norms not from any conscious human agency (either the producer himself or a social agency with which the producer could identify), but from the material reality of exchangeable objects. It is not so much that exchange dominates production, as that the unacknowledged needs of production (in terms of intersectoral balance, degree of effort etc.) acquire an objective form and dominate the producers through exchange, by virtue of the law of value. The following quotation from Marx is very pertinent here:[1]

> The social character of activity, as well as the social form of the product, and the share of individuals in production here appear as something alien and objective, confronting the individuals, not as their relation to one another, but as their subordination to relations which subsist independently of them and which arise out of collisions between mutually indifferent individuals. The general exchange of activities and products, which has become a vital condition for each individual – their mutual interconnection – here appears as something alien to them, autonomous, as a thing. In exchange value, the social connection between persons is transformed into a social relation between things; personal capacity into objective wealth. The less social power the medium of exchange possesses . . . the greater must be the power of the community which binds the individuals together, the patriarchal relation, the community of antiquity, feudalism and the guild system . . . Each individual possesses social power in the form of a thing. Rob the thing of this social power and you must give it to persons to exercise over persons.

The determination of exchange value by abstract labour consists of this whole network of relationships by which production of commodities is regulated. The penetration of production by exchange which this system makes necessary is expressed in the idea of abstract labour. Value in its independent form, i.e. as money, corresponds to it not because labour, in some mystical manner, 'creates' a metaphysical entity called 'value', but because abstract labour *is* value. It is the flow of labour which corresponds to the flow of money. (This correspondence is, however, only qualitative. It does not amount to money prices being identical with the abstract labour content of goods, except under special conditions. The question of quantitative correspondence is considered in the discussion of the transformation problem, in the Appendix to Chapter 4.)

Labour and waiting

What seems to offend commonsense most in the labour theory of value is the selection of labour as the factor of production on the expenditure of which, to the exclusion of all others, exchange value is dependent. Mainstream economics, in distinguishing three basic factors of production, land, labour and capital (and sometimes a fourth one, entrepreneurship), appears to be more reasonable. It also appears to be practically more relevant in the determination of exchange value (or price). It begins with establishing scarcity prices for the basic factors of production via the interplay of supply and demand for each. In then derives the cost, which under equilibrium coincides with the price of the commodity, by summing together all direct and indirect payments to factors of production. This method has the undeniable advantage of directing attention to the problem of the best possible allocation of resources. Under the ideal scheme described, the scarcest factors would be given the highest price tags, being consequently allocated to the most important uses (those which consumers were willing to pay the highest costs for); the second scarcest would follow; and so on down the scale, until all scarce factors had been used up.

It has already been admitted that in the face of basic scarcity the labour theory of value is powerless. It provides no explanation for the pricing of non-reproducible commodities and has to give way to an alternative theory. What, in each case, constitutes fundamental scarcity is another question; one particularly difficult to answer in the case of productive capital, which consists of reproducible objects (durable equipment, machinery, stocks of materials or even stocks of means of subsistence).

The most plausible candidate for the role of an element of basic scarcity in the case of capital is 'waiting'. This represents one aspect of production that has gone unnoticed so far: the fact that a certain period of time must elapse between the first substantial expenditure of labour in production (say, the digging up of the foundations for a building) and the moment when something saleable emerges as a final product. During this whole period (which obviously becomes longer if durable means of production – capital as most commonly understood – have to be supplied before final production starts), the producer must not only work but also wait for the result of his efforts to take final shape. There are even cases where he can do nothing *but* wait – like the farmer who waits for the harvest, the tree-planter who waits for timber or the viniculturist who waits for wine to mature in his cellars. In these cases 'waiting' appears as one aspect of production, even physically distinct from 'performing'. This suggests the possibility of a notional distinction between the two, even when no physical distinction is possible (when the working period coincides with the time of production).

Given this distinction, the question arises: (a) whether it implies a cost not reducible to past and present labour; (b) in case of an affirmative answer to (a), whether a separate charge for 'waiting' will necessarily invalidate the labour theory of value.

One straightforward way of dealing with (a) would be to define hours of 'waiting' as hours of work and calculate the value of commodities not only according to the hours of active labour absorbed by their production, but as a sum of active labour time and 'waiting' time. In such case commodities having average working but longer production times would only be produced if buyers were willing to give in exchange for them enough of their own time (embodied in their products) to cover the additional cost. The labour theory of value, modified in the manner of the present paragraph, would lead to sensible exchange ratios, from the allocation point of view. (It has to be stressed, however, that Marx himself, in discussing the difference between working time and the time of production, implicitly rejected this interpretation. This aspect of his work is not pursued further here. Interested readers are referred to *Capital*, Vol II, chapters XII to XVI.)

Whether an identification between labour time and 'waiting' is possible in practice (so as to be reasonable to assume in theory), depends on the social relations of production prevailing in a particular economy. If it is producers who themselves supply their own 'waiting', as just another aspect of their work, the identification makes sense. If, on the other hand, 'waiting' is supplied by a special class of non-producers, the problem of its allocation as a separate factor of production does arise and a separate charge to costs must be introduced to this effect.

How is it possible to specialise in the supply of 'waiting'? Simply, by storing up means of consumption for the use – at a price higher than their current market price – of those producers who, occupied in making commodities of long production times, are unwilling or unable to wait for the sale of their product before they start consuming. Obviously, such producers are in no position to make their own purchases directly. Not having produced anything saleable yet, they lack means of buying. They can only acquire consumer goods from the suppliers of 'waiting' by purchasing on credit. Or alternatively, and much more practically, they can borrow money, so that ultimately, suppliers of 'waiting' need play no other role except that of money lender. By enabling some producers who would otherwise not have undertaken it, to engage in the production of commodities requiring long production times, the supply of 'waiting' in this form does become a factor of production and interest a legitimate production cost.

The labour theory of value cannot properly cover this case. 'Waiting', from being just one aspect of productive labour, inseparable from other aspects, has itself acquired autonomous existence, and must be counted as a second, independent principle of value determination. Commodities have to be valued as a sum of direct labour costs and of 'waiting' costs. To conflate the two under a homogeneous accounting in terms of hours of work could only generate confusion, given the difference in the source of supply.

This sounds like a vindication of capitalist incomes, typically represented by interest, but it it nothing of the sort. No such apologetic use of the legitimacy of a certain kind of interest is allowed, before the question of the existence of a class, who supply 'waiting' by shouldering the burden of abstaining from immediate consumption themselves, is resolved.

Marxists obviously deny that the capitalist class engages in any such activity. They are quick to point to the rarity of any capitalist actually postponing his gratifications, while working men typically have to wait – sometimes for ever – to see even quite elementary needs of theirs satisfied. Marxists conclude that, under institutions of capitalist ownership, both labour and 'waiting' are burdens carried by just one class, the working class.

That Marxists should argue thus is something to be expected. Less well known is the fact that they are by no means alone in pressing this point of view. Economists as far removed in other respects both from Marxism and from each other as J. B. Say and J. M. Keynes have said essentially the same thing. Attacking Adam Smith's panegyric of frugality as a source of capital accumulation, J. B. Say asked:[2]

> But this frugality which Smith praises in individuals, is it not feasible exactly because of some faults in the political system, which weigh upon the most numerous class? . . . It is not the poor who do the saving . . . it is at their expense that saving is done.

A hundred years later, in one of his first works to attract wide attention Keynes described pre-First-World-War capitalism in the following terms:[3]

> This remarkable system depended for its growth on a double bluff or deception. On the one hand the labouring classes accepted from ignorance or powerlessness, or were compelled, persuaded, or cajoled by custom, convention, authority . . .

into accepting a situation in which they could call their own very little of the cake, that they and Nature and the capitalists were cooperating to produce. And on the other hand the capitalist classes were allowed to call the best part of the cake theirs and were theoretically free to consume it, on the tacit underlying condition that they consumed very little of it in practice.

Keynes should, perhaps, be forgiven for not belabouring the obvious – that in terms of 'waiting' capitalists did rather better out of their theoretical freedom to consume the best part of the cake, than workers out of the ignorance and powerlessness, which constituted their lot.

Orthodox economic theory insists that in free enterprise (i.e. capitalistic) economies, there develops a separate market for 'waiting', the capital market, on which interest rates simply represent the price of 'waiting'. If so, the price is not paid to the actual supplier of this particular good – the worker – but to the person who stands to him in an exploitative relation (to be explained in the following chapters). Capitalists do generate 'waiting', but only by enforcing involuntary frugality on working men and women.

In treating the rate of interest as the ordinary price of just another factor of production, economic theory directs attention to two functions of any such price: (a) its incentive function, in calling forth sufficient 'effort' to supply 'waiting', and (b) its optimising function in allocating the factor to those activities where it is most in demand.

If the assumption of a separate class specialising in the art of waiting were true, a separate price for waiting would indeed have these functions. It would, then, be a very useful accounting and allocative device. The same would hold if not a specialist class but workers were themselves the voluntary suppliers of 'waiting', separately however from other aspects of their productive labour.

As matters stand in capitalism, interest performs neither of these two functions. With respect to its incentive effect, Keynesian analysis has shown that it operates rather as a disincentive to an adequate capital supply. If capital were allowed to accumulate without hitches, it would under modern conditions soon, at least in Keynes's perception, cease to be a scarce factor of production. Capitalists, who implement their exploitative relations *vis-à-vis* labour by virtue of their ownership of this particular scarcity, would find themselves deprived of the material basis of their privileges. They guard against this danger by stopping the accumulation of capital (by withholding investment) at crucial moments, pinpointed for them by the fall in interest rates.

With respect to its allocative function, interest does not perform well either. Given its exploitative origins, coupled with the anarchy of the market, acquisition of a share of this privileged income is gained far more by aggressiveness or speculation, than by careful, considered weighting of the relative urgency of social needs. Keynes's comment on the Stock Exchange is worth repeating:[4]

When the capital development of a country becomes a by-product of the activities of a casino, the job is likely to be ill-done.

Keynes's analysis, supported by the experience of the practical workings of the capitalist economy, demonstrates the failure of interest rate in both its incentive and in its allocative functions. Of this malfunction, Marxist analysis can contribute an explanation. Interest cannot perform well as a price, because it is not mainly a price; in capitalist conditions it is an economic expression of the plundering of one social class by another. Any price functions it may also fulfil are always subject to its main role as an exploitation-generated income. Orthodox economic theory chooses to ignore this reality and treat interest as if it were a pure scarcity price and nothing else. On the basis of this distorting assumption it manages to build quite elegant but totally unrealistic allocative models of capital formation, which end up in mere apologetics.

The labour theory of value recognises the futility of elaborate models of ideal resource allocation in the presence of exploitative relations of production, which, in the phase of their decline, make a mockery of every genuine principle of economic rationality. The labour theory might be developed as an alternative accounting method, intended to disclose the deformation to the allocation of resources caused by the phenomenon of exploitation. It would then give rise to a kind of Marxist welfare economics. Some Marxist economists have attempted openings in the direction of a critique of the allocation of resources in modern capitalism, but they have found the labour theory of value unhelpful for that purpose.

This is not surprising. This theory has been adopted as the result of a deliberate choice of disregarding the problem of allocation of resources ('waiting' being interpretable as just one resource), in favour of concentrating on an analysis of the problem of exploitation, considered by them as by far the more urgent one. (The decision is analogous to that of the Keynesians in disregarding allocation in preference for the question of unemployment.) The labour theory of value, as developed by Marx, is ideally suited for an analysis of exploitation in the context of a free market economy. By contrast, in conflating the various characteristics of the production process into just one – the expenditure of abstract labour – it becomes inherently weak on the question of allocation. This is also the reason why – having enabled social scientists to acquire a number of crucial insights into the workings of capitalism – it has fared rather poorly in post-capitalist regimes, where its weakness as a planning instrument was exposed. Its abiding strength, as will be argued in the next chapter, is in the analysis of the combination of exploitation and a free market. This is the source of its vitality.

CHAPTER 4

Value, labour power and exploitation

Exploitation in economic theory: two views

Following on from the general presentation of the labour theory of value in Chapter 3, the present chapter goes on to apply that theory to the question of exploitation. It begins with a description of the attitude of economic theorists to this problem, continues with a detailed analysis of the Marxist view and concludes with some comments on two non-Marxist explanations of the phenomenon of profit.

The one most striking difference between Marxist and non-Marxist economics is in the insistence of the former on the importance of exploitation of labour by capital as a cornerstone of the capitalist mode of production. Two main consequences flow from this basic premise. First, that theoretical analysis must be focused on this crucial feature of capitalism. Second, that there is no other way for the working-class to rescue itself from exploitation except by getting rid of the capitalist system altogether. These two tasks, the theoretical and the practical, are interdependent – a point which the last section of this chapter, as indeed many other sections in the rest of the book, restate and expand on. In attaching so much importance to exploitation Marxist economics is unique among schools of economic thought.

A study of exploitation is either totally absent from mainstream economics, or it is treated as merely peripheral. As long as the market settles down at a point reasonably close to the general competitive equilibrium position, economic theory can show that every rational consumer (and/or producer) finds himself in a state as prosperous as possible, consistent with his initial asset endowment (the Pareto optimality of general competitive equilibrium). No individual can fall victim to exploitation in a perfectly competitive market, as long as he behaves rationally. Irrational people may, of their own fault, suffer losses, but these cannot be ascribed to any intrinsically exploitative characteristics of the economic system. Therefore individuals, expected in social science (that is to say *bourgeois* social science, because Marxism allows no hard-and-fast, unhistorical generalisations about human nature) to be purely self-seeking, can proceed with the game of antagonistic competition confident in the knowledge that, in principle, their hard-headed, egoistic behaviour is also, by the fortunate order of things, the only one consistent with maximisation of general welfare. The whole ethos of bourgeois society is focused on this ideological exaltation of self-centred individualism. Economic science contributes its part by offering an analytical justification for such ethos. In the eyes of Marxist critique, this gives to economics its ideological function, consisting, as Marx put it, in the writing of prescriptions for the tranquillisation of the bourgeois mind.

Non-Marxist economic theory will not deny that the distribution of assets with which the market-game begins may be unfair. The market itself will tend neither to redress this unfairness nor to make it much worse. This makes a dual response to the problem of inequality of wealth possible. Some economists, critical of capitalist institutions, will argue that the market is an instrument for perpetuating an unfair situation, and will stress the propertylessness of the working class as a particularly damning instance.[1] Most others will emphasise that through market-exchange, gains from trade are possible for every participant and that changing the distribution of wealth and income is not a matter for economics but for politics. The market will serve any distributional ideal preferred by the public, with equal even-handedness.

Against the widespread complacency of the second group two serious objections have been raised: (a) that the market in our epoch is essentially monopolistic rather than competitive and (b) that *laissez-faire* capitalism is unable to maintain the economy at a full employment level (the Keynesian criticism). For those insisting on (a) exploitation may become a matter of some interest. There may be cases where wages fall below the marginal product of labour; this is how exploitation of labour is defined in standard welfare economics. But labour is not unique in that respect. Other factors of production may find themselves similarly exploited. Even if it turns out that labour is the exploited factor on a specific occasion, it does not follow that capital will necessarily benefit. It is even possible that the imperfection of the market will benefit labour at the expense of capital.[2] What turns out to be the definitive and ultimate loser from exploitative situations, defined as deviations of factor prices from their marginal value products, is the welfare of consumers. Exploitation implies not that capitalists exploit workers; rather that monopolists exploit consumers. The cure for this kind of exploitation is the restoration of conditions as close as possible to those of the competitive market, not the abolition of the capitalist ownership of the means of production (although state intervention to control monopolies may require inroads into capitalist ownership).

It may appear that the Keynesian critique of *laissez-faire* capitalism has found in unemployment a failing of the system as deep-seated as exploitation but more relevant, or, at least, more urgent for the great majority. However, in its Keynesian conception, unemployment is different from exploitation, in the sense that while it causes suffering among the workers, it directly benefits no other social class, and it is less basic in the sense that it can be eliminated by corrective reforms rather than by a revolution to overthrow the system.

Marxist emphasis on exploitation does not imply a rejection of the case made by mainstream economics for the existence of gains from trade. In a brief, but significant, comment Marx pointed to such gains even in the presence of unequal exchange. In *Theories of Surplus Value*, III, he wrote:[3]

> Profit can also be made by cheating, one person gaining what the other loses. Loss and gain within a single country cancel each other out. But not so with trade between different countries . . . Here the law of value undergoes essential modification. The relationship between labour days of different countries may be similar to that existing between skilled, complex labour and unskilled, simple labour within a country. In this case, *the richer country exploits the poorer one, even where the latter gains by this exchange* as John Stuart Mill explains in his 'Some Unsettled Questions' [italics added].

If benefits from trade are consistent with exploitation under unequal exchange they are more strongly consistent with it under equal exchange (the strong case of exploitation which Marx sought to establish). On the basis of the passage in the *Theories of Surplus Value* the generalisation can be attempted that the proof of the Pareto optimality of general competitive equilibrium is quite compatible with Marx's own proof of the possibility of exploitation, implemented through the very same optimising market mechanism, in conditions of universal freedom and formal equality for all participants. Between neoclassical and Marxist economics there exists not so much a clash on the character of the market (or commodity production), as a decision to look at the market from different points of view, to concentrate on different problems. This pre-theoretical choice is by no means arbitrary. In the eyes of Marxists neoclassical economics, no matter how admirably refined in its formal analysis, constitutes one gigantic ideological evasion of the negative aspects of a bourgeois economy.

Exploitation in general and capitalistic exploitation

In the Marxist context, exploitation is defined as the appropriation by a certain class of the productive labour of another class, without the appropriators themselves supplying to the other class an equivalent counterpart in terms of productive labour. The appropriation of the product by the exploiters is a consequence of the prior (in some form) appropriation of productive labour by them. Under this broad definition exploitation is not peculiar to capitalism. It runs through all class-divided societies of the past, all 'antagonistic forms of society' mentioned in the 1859 *Preface* (see Chapter 1). In all of them exploitation is premissed on a productivity condition: the labour of the exploited must have become productive enough to enable them both to support themselves and cater for the exploiters. Their labour is accordingly split into two parts: one by which they maintain themselves (*necessary labour*, a concept different from that of *socially necessary labour* of the previous chapter) and *surplus labour*, performed without counterpart for their exploiters. Output also is split in a similar manner into *necessary* and *surplus product*. Historically cases of exploiters who have, on occasion, seized from the labourers not only surplus but also a part of the necessary product are not unheard of but they cannot become the norm, or labourers would be forced to perish. In their turn, exploiters would, then, also perish or they would be reduced to supporting themselves by their own work, a fate worse than death for most of them. In either case exploitation would cease to exist. Therefore, in the interests of the exploiters themselves, there can be no such thing as absolute, total exploitation that would turn virtually all labour into surplus labour (unless the decision has been made to exterminate by overwork one section of the workers, as in the Nazi labour camps).

At the end of the previous section it was suggested that the choice of exploitation as the central theme of analysis in Marxist economics is pre-theoretical. Is there any *prima facie* evidence to justify this choice? In slave-owning or self-based economies, the socio-political institutions themselves constitute an open admission that a large part of the section of the population working productively is exploited. By contrast in capitalism no such presumption can be founded on its political or even its economic institutions. The very opposite seems to be the case. The system rests on the freedom of trade and the free pursuit of private interest. Hence anyone who insists on the systematic rather than incidental nature of exploitation in capitalism is faced with a double task. First, he has to seek *prima facie* evidence in the material, rather than the institutional condition of the workers. Assuming this condition justifies further concern, theoretical analysis is needed to make transparent what the everyday appearance of things masks or renders opaque. There is no obviousness about the exploitive appropriation of labour in capitalist markets.

The commodity character of capitalist production has the effect that labour in its concrete, useful form is an activity that presents no interest to exploiters. It is not labour in this form that they seek to appropriate; it neither possesses universal social validity to be used as a means of exchange, nor does it produce use-values for those who happen to employ workers. The owner of a factory which makes ball-bearings, or shirts, has no need for the use-value of the product (i.e. his own need is infinitesimally small, compared to the volume of total output). To place themselves in a position of command in a commodity economy exploiters must aim at appropriating not concrete but abstract labour, materialised in money. Production of use value through the direct labour process intervenes only as a means of acquiring, without counterpart, a certain amount of exchange value. Free appropriation by capitalists of a certain proportion of the total of exchange value circulating in the economy is, under commodity production conditions, the only meaningful kind of exploitation. This proportion corresponds to the surplus labour and to surplus product of precapitalist exploitative regimes. In a term which Marx made famous, it is described as *surplus value.* The definition of exploitation, in its specifically capitalistic form, as appropriation of surplus-value, constitutes the first step in the analysis necessary for going beyond the appearance of equitable relations in the capitalist market. The next step is to demonstrate the possibility of a mechanism which makes such appropriation possible, not in violation of but in accordance with the principles of commodity production and exchange.

The paradox of trade

In the first part of this chapter it was suggested that Marx deliberately chose to demonstrate the possibility of exploitation under the most unfavourable assumptions to such proof; to establish a strong case for the existence of exploitation. He set out to show that exploitation through the market could and did take place in the capitalist economy even in the absence of unequal exchange. This decision is implicit in his assumption that, for the purposes of his discussion, all commodities exchange at their values, neither above nor below. The economy is in a state of general equilibrium. Capitalists on the other hand, are first and foremost traders. They buy to sell for profit, not only as merchants but also as industrialists. In the latter capacity their trading consists in buying materials and labour power, in order to resell for profit the output produced by these means. But, as traders, capitalists have to pay a counterpart for the values they acquire. In a state of general equilibrium, where no unequal exchange occurs, it is impossible for any of them to obtain surplus value free of charge through exchange. They all pay full value for whatever they buy. Exploitation appears to be inconsistent with the assumptions made about exchange in a commodity-producing economy. It seems a logical impossibility.

The paradox of the labour theory of value

But is it not possible that this logical dead end has been reached because of the concentration of the argument on capitalists as traders? Could there not be a special kind of unequal exchange on the labour market, in their relations with their employees, which owners of capital take advantage of? The answer should be that the theorist has no right to acquit himself of his task by special, *ad hoc*, assumptions of this kind. If payment according to full value is assumed, it must hold in all markets, not all markets minus one. The labour market cannot constitute the sole convenient exception. Moreover the fact that capitalists as employers appear to buy labour-hours on this market increases the difficulties of a solution on the basis of the labour theory of value. Excluding costs for materials etc. capitalists pay wages at full value for a certain number of hours of work. They expect to recover their costs from the sales of the product. The value of the product is determined by the hours of work directly and indirectly absorbed in its production. In purchasing materials and hours of work, capitalists have already paid the proper value equivalent for the hours constituting the value of the product. It should follow that the proceeds from the sales are just sufficient to cover the wage costs, without leaving any margin for surplus. Far from unearthing exploitation from the bowels of the capitalist system, theoretical analysis seems to have buried it even deeper. The acquisition of surplus value from the transactions between labour and capital seems as logically impossible as its extraction from equal exchange of goods. This second logical impossibility constitutes the paradox of the labour theory of value.

The commodity 'labour power'

To resolve the paradox Marx introduced into the analytical apparatus of Classical Political Economy a new concept which, by its simplicity, originality and power was destined to burst the old discipline asunder and extract from it a new synthesis, or a new paradigm, that of Marxist economics. He went back to the transaction between labour and capital to ask the following question: was it really hours of work that the capitalist was purchasing from the worker or was it some other commodity? Not surprisingly, he came up with the answer that hours of work were not, as such, the object of the transaction. Capitalists would buy not a certain number of work-hours, but the capacity of a person to work an unspecified number of hours.

It is conceivable that Marx might have produced this answer purely by means of theoretical speculation. In actual fact, he was prompted in this direction also by the experiences still fresh in memories at his time of an epoch in Britain (his prototype of a capitalist economy), when no legal limit of any kind on anyone's hours of work existed. (Some legislation imposing maximum limits on the working day dates from 1833.) One sample of evidence on this matter, quoted by Marx in *Capital*, after he had sifted through massive volumes of official documents, is particularly striking. It consists of a sentence from an 1860 Report of the Inspector of Factories:[4]

P[rior] to the Act of 1833, young persons and children were worked all night, all day, or both, ad libitum.

From such conditions of a rude and early capitalism, unadulterated by humanitarian considerations or legislative intervention, Marx could distil the idea that the natural behavioural tendency of the buyers of labour power (the capitalists) was to squeeze out of the hired men not a number of hours stipulated in law or in an agreement, but as many hours of work as labourers could possibly physically stand. Marx devoted to this aspect of capitalist behaviour some of the finest polemical pages in *Capital*. It is worth it, at the cost of a small deviation, to taste a sample.[5]

> But, what is a working day? At all events, less than a natural day. By how much? The capitalist has his own views of this *ultima thule*, the necessary limit of the working day. As capitalist, he is only capital personified. His soul is the soul of capital. But capital has one single life impulse, the tendency to create value and surplus-value, to make . . . the means of production absorb the greatest possible amount of surplus-labour.
>
> Capital is dead labour, that, vampire like, only lives by sucking living labour, and lives the more, the more labour it sucks. The time during which the labourer works is the time during which the capitalist consumes the labour-power he has purchased of him.
>
> If the labourer consumes his disposable time for himself, he robs the capitalist.

In the original labour contract of pristine, unregulated capitalism the exact number of hours for which the wage-labourer works is, therefore, left undetermined. Its determination is achieved through as much slave driver's pressure as the capitalist is able to exert and the worker to stand. It follows that the worker does not contract to sell a specified number of hours of labour, but rather he sells his capacity to perform work together with his acceptance to subject himself to alien supervision and discipline. This capacity, the only commodity that, being otherwise propertyless, he has to offer for sale, is described as his *labour-power*. Legislative regulation of the length of the working day in developed capitalism makes the relationship less transparent, but does not change its substance. The worker still sells his capacity to work. The capitalist still tries to extract as much effort out of him as possible, although now he has to act within legal limits and apply more refined methods of psychological motivation rather than crude pressure. As an individual, the worker has virtually no control over his working hours, these are fixed by works regulations similarly for all employees. Legislation defines an open and a closed season for exploitation within every twenty-four hours; legal protection, in the context of a capitalist economy, can amount to no more.

The formulation of the concept of labour power makes it possible to analyse this factual situation with the help of the labour theory of value. The capitalist buys labour-power and, in the absence of unequal exchange, he must pay for it at full value. What is this value? The first obstacle on the way to determining it is that labour power is obviously not an industrial product. No costs of production, at least none in the usual sense, are incurred in its case, so that its value cannot be determined by the amount of abstract labour absorbed in its manufacture. It becomes a commodity not because it is a product, but because the worker is forced to make a part of his human personality available for use by somebody else, in exchange for a wage.

Indirectly, however, labour power may be treated as a product, exactly because it is one aspect of the worker's person. To be sustained, the human being requires to consume goods. In capitalism, the consumption goods, or *means of subsistence*, take the form of commodities which themselves represent a certain total of value. They embody the proportion of abstract labour which the market mechanism has allocated for the support of individuals belonging to the working class. Neglecting for the moment household labour, the value of the means of subsistence determines the value of (unskilled) labour power in its entirety. In addition, it is not the subsistence of the worker as an individual but as a family which is envisaged. The capitalist system, in order to perpetuate itself over time, requires a renewable supply of labour, a race of workers rather than one single generation of them. (Whether the working man's family becomes, in his own eyes and for his own pecuniary benefit a 'workshop' producing exploitable human material is a special question, discussed briefly towards the end of this chapter.)

Having to pay for labour power, hence for the value of the means of subsistence, the capitalist does not advance an amount of money equivalent to the hours of work performed by whomever he hires, but to the hours of work performed by the producers of the means of subsistence which the worker consumes. The two do not come to the same because, in view of the level of productivity already achieved at the beginning of the capitalist era, one producer of means of subsistence can supply more than one consumer. If he supplies, say, himself and four others with the net product of a ten-hour working day, to each of the five only two hours of *necessary labour* correspond. All five, on the other hand, work a ten-hour day each. It follows that *surplus labour* is equal to eight hours per worker. Correspondingly, their product also can be divided into *necessary product* and *surplus product*.

The resolution of the paradox of the labour theory of value is illustrated by this numerical example. All commodities, including labour power, have been paid at their full value. No unequal exchange has occurred anywhere (the assumption of a general competitive equilibrium has been maintained throughout). Yet the capitalist has been able to appropriate a certain amount of surplus value, equal to the difference between the value of the means of subsistence consumed by the worker (2 hours of labour) and the value of the worker's product (10 hours of labour), which integrally belongs to the capitalist. The absence of unequal exchange has not prevented the emergence of surplus value, as the latter was not generated in the sphere of exchange but in that of production. The presumption formulated at the end of Chapter 2 about production being the fulcrum of exploitation is now rigorously confirmed by the combined application of the labour theory of value and the concept of labour-power. The capitalist production process can, therefore, be analysed as a process of production of surplus value.

Constant and variable capital

The capitalist organises production by a sequence of acts of buying and selling. He appears on the market as the owner of a certain amount of money (of value in the form of money) which he invests in non-human and in human factors of production by purchasing means of production and labour power. He has these combined together in the production process, at the end of which he emerges as the owner of a new commodity. Given the difference between the value of labour power, measured in hours of labour, and the duration of the working day, the commodity produced represents a value greater than the sum of values invested at the start of the process. The last stage consists of the capitalist's selling the new commodity and recovering an amount of money larger than he originally spent. Surplus value acquires thus a palpable money form, as the difference between the two sums of money involved in this operation. Money has been exchanged for more money, or money has been made to give birth to money.

The process of acquiring surplus-value through production is described as *the circuit of capital* and can be schematically represented as follows:

$$M - C \prec \begin{array}{c} MP \\ LP \end{array} \ldots P \ldots C' - M'$$

where M stands for money, C for commodity, MP for means of production, LP for labour power, P for the production process, with primed quantities defined as greater than non-primed ones ($M' > M$, $C' > C$). It must be stressed that, although the appropriation of surplus-value is impossible without the process of production, it is equally impossible without the last step $C' - M'$, or the *realisation* of surplus-value. The circuit of capital represents thus, in a specific, concrete manner, the merging of production and circulation into one unified process of extraction and appropriation of surplus-value on behalf of the capitalists. (On the merging of production and circulation see also Chapter 3.) No matter how closely merged, however, and how indispensable both of them to surplus-value appropriation, production and circulation maintain their distinct functions. In the absence of unequal exchange $M = C$ and $M' = C'$. No surplus value is generated in circulation; no surplus-value is realised in production.

The discovery of the way in which, despite general competitive equilibrium, absence of unequal exchange, freedom and equality for all participants, a market economy is still consistent with systematic class exploitation gives to the labour theory of value its typically Marxist form and flavour. This theory can now be stated completely and with its help a theoretical image of the exploitation process, backed up by empirical illustrations, can be drawn.

So far the value of the commodity has been defined as a sum of past and present labour. This definition remains valid but, for commodities produced in a capitalist regime, it is modified to take into account the fact that labour acts only under the command of capital; that it only becomes productive of value and surplus value after it has been purchased by capital and absorbed into capitalist ownership. Past labour now appears in the shape of means of production bought by the capitalist at the beginning of the process. As for present labour, it falls into two parts: necessary labour which corresponds to the value of means of subsistence, the necessary product consumed by labour, and surplus-labour which corresponds to surplus value appropriated by capital. The capitalist has paid wages for the value of the means of subsistence, hence for necessary labour only. Only that part of labour constitutes *paid labour*, surplus labour is *unpaid labour*.

This is clearly not the way in which matters appear in everyday life. From the capitalist's point of view, his capital, which coincides with his original expenditure, consists of the value of the means of production and of the wages. To these, surplus value is added as if by a miracle. He has no reason to make any distinction between the two parts of his capital because to him they appear as equally productive of profit. In the eyes of the theorist, on the other hand, the difference is very striking. Only that part of money capital which has been paid for the purchase of labour power is capable of expanding into a sum larger than itself. The generation of value is associated with the performance of work, which only labour, not the means of production, is capable of. This difference has motivated the coining of two terms that have taken their place among the hallmarks of Marxist economics: *constant capital* for the value of the means of production, and *variable capital* ('variable' because of its expansionary capacity) for the value of labour power. Constant and variable capital each constitute, from the point of view of the capitalist, costs of production that must be recovered from the sales of the product. They are, therefore, additive parts of the value of the commodity to which a third part, surplus value, is also accrued. The well-known definition of a commodity's value as

$$W = c + v + s$$

is thus derived. (*W* stands for value, *c* and *v* for constant and variable capital and *s* for surplus value).

The new concepts of constant capital, variable capital and surplus value can now be used for formulating a number of other quantitative relationships, crucial for the further development of the theory.

The definition $c + v + s$ with its distinction between constant and variable capital is comprehensible and of great interest to the theorist, but, on the basis of his everyday experience, it is scarcely accessible or interesting to the practising capitalist. The latter's concern lies with the relationship between surplus value and his total advances (his costs) measured by the ratio:

$$r = \frac{s}{c + v}$$

With the help of this ratio (the *rate of profit*), the expression for value, W, can be rewritten as follows:

$$W = c + v + s = c + v + \frac{s}{c + v}(c + v)$$

$$= (c + v) + r(c + v) = (1 + r)(c + v) = p.$$

The expression

$$p = (1 + r)(c + v) = (c + v) + r(c + v)$$

is known as the *price of production*. It is a form of value represented as a sum of cost per unit of output $(c + v)$ and of profit, $\pi(c + v)$, calculated as a proportion (a percentage) of unit cost. It thus corresponds to the widespread business practice of determining price as a sum of unit costs (in ordinary money, not in Marxist value terms) and of a markup which is a percentage on unit cost, intended to cover overheads and profits. Through the mediation of the price of production $[(1 + r)(c + v)]$, the Marxist theoretical formula of value $(c + v + s)$ is brought into some correspondence with practical economic notions.

At the present level of analysis the difference between value and price of production remains purely formal. Algebraically and quantitatively, the two expressions are equivalent. They do not, however, remain so as the analysis becomes more concretised, a fact which leads to the emergence of the *transformation problem*, discussion of which has been postponed to the Appendix of Chapter 4.

Absolute and relative surplus-value

The practising capitalist is, for obvious reasons, crucially interested in the rate of profit on his capital advances. By contrast the theorist and, to some extent, even the theoretically untutored worker, are concerned with the reality covered by a different concept – the *rate of surplus-value*. This is expressed as the ratio s/v and quantifies, in value terms, the degree of exploitation suffered by the worker. It has been seen above that exploitation boils down to a division of the labour performed during a working day into necessary and surplus labour. The quantitative relationship between the two parts, in hours of work, or the relationship between paid and unpaid labour, in units of value, measures the intensity of exploitation, the *degree of exploitation* of the worker. Algebraically the correspondence can be shown as:

$$\frac{s}{v} = \frac{\text{surplus labour}}{\text{necessary labour}} = \frac{\text{unpaid labour}}{\text{paid labour}}$$

(in   (in hours of   (in money units)
value   work)
units)

Capitalists have an obvious interest in raising as much as possible the degree of exploitation, because of its beneficial repercussions on their rate of profit. The relationship between the two ratios can be demonstrated by the following manipulation of the rate of profit formula:

$$r = \frac{s}{c + v} = \frac{\dfrac{s}{v}}{\dfrac{c}{v} + 1}$$

Assuming c/v constant, r increases with s/v. Again this relationship is far from obvious. To grasp it in its full generality would require concepts far removed from the everyday experience of business practice. However, its empirical counterpart, the fact that profitability benefits from longer and harder working hours of the employees, for a given wage, is something that requires no great analytical insight. To keep labourers doing their best and working their hardest is one of the principal maxims of every capitalist manager. It is his function as a boss.

There are two ways whereby the balance of exploitation can be tipped in favour of capital. One is to lengthen the working day (or to increase the intensity of work, during a day of constant length). The working day must be long enough for the worker to be able at least to cover the value of his means of subsistence. With the productivity of labour in industries producing wage-goods given, this part of the working day is a fixed magnitude because the unit value of the means of subsistence remains constant. Work must be prolonged beyond that minimum limit, for surplus value to start flowing. From then on, the longer the working day, the larger the amount of value falling to the share of the capitalist. This method of exploitation is described as the production of *absolute surplus value*.

With modern hours-of-work legislation, capitalists no longer have it in their power to push the hours of work to the limit of the physical endurance or the moral resistance of the workers. Absolute surplus-value may still be increased through intensification of the rhythm of production while total working hours remain constant. Workers, on the other hand, tend to take advantage of the legal limits imposed on hours of work to boost their earnings by offering to work overtime. Whether they gain or lose in the process depends on the additional strain that overtime imposes on them, wearing down their lifetime faculties (their labour power) faster, and on whether such faster wear and tear is adequately compensated for by their increased overtime earnings. If not, modern legislation notwithstanding, capitalists may still attempt to increase absolute surplus-value.

The second method of raising the rate of exploitation consists of reducing the part of necessary labour within the limits of a working day of a given constant length. This is described as increasing *relative surplus value*. To bring about such an increase, two conditions are required:

(a) The productivity of labour in industries producing wage goods must be increased, probably as a result of mechanisation, or by some other means of technical progress. The increase in productivity does not have to be limited to wage-goods industries but, if spread throughout the economy, it must not leave them out. Given this, a larger volume of commodities will be produced with a constant number of hours of work and, by the accounting rules of the labour theory of value, the individual unit of the product will become cheaper, in value terms. The empirical counterpart of this theoretical prediction is the fall in prices which accompanies gains in productivity from important technological breakthroughs.

(b) The monetary remuneration of labour must be reduced, in proportion with the fall in value of the wage-goods (real wages must remain constant). This assumes, of course, that the value of money remains constant (or rises). By contrast, if the value of money is falling together with the value of wage-goods, no reduction of money wages is necessary.

The two methods of raising the rate of exploitation differ drastically in the manner of their operation. The importance of absolute surplus value is easy to grasp. Methods for raising it are consciously, although not confessedly, pursued by every capitalist manager at the microeconomic level. With relative surplus-value matters are different. Technical progress is not a variable under the control of individuals, to be mobilised whenever they need it. It follows its own course of development, charted both by the increase in scientific knowledge and the emergence, if it occurs at the right moment, of organisational talent among industrialists. In the sense that it responds to the efforts of no one individual in particular (the industrial innovator needs the gifted engineer, they both need the research scientist conducting research in state-funded laboratories or in those of big corporations and supported by a whole scientific discipline sometimes stretching back for centuries), it has the character of a general social force. Only the capitalist system as a whole, not any individual capitalist, may generate it without, even then, being in a position to have it totally regulated. Moreover, pressure on money wages, necessary if capital is on balance to gain as against labour from increases in productivity, cannot be exercised by individual capitalists acting in isolation or competing for labour. This is much more a matter for action by the class as a whole and may involve the financial and monetary policies of the state. It is concluded that, while efforts to increase absolute surplus-value usually operate at the microeconomic level, the increase in relative surplus-value is much more dependent on macroeconomic developments which it shapes as much as being shaped by them. It will be argued in subsequent chapters that the whole course of development of the capitalist mode of production can, from one point of view, be seen as determined by the struggle to increase relative surplus-value.

Unpaid labour and the wage-form

The morphology of exploitation presented in previous sections is derived from the joint application on the analysis of capitalism of the labour theory of value and of the concept of labour power. These theoretical concepts are by no means obvious and in some respects clash with spontaneous ideas generated by everyday experience. One such clash, not to be taken up again because it has already been discussed in Chapter 3, is the assumption that labour is the only factor of production associated with the generation of exchange value. The others are the assumption of general equilibrium and the claim that only one part of the worker's hours of work are paid, while a certain other part remains unpaid. The implications of the general equilibrium assumption will be discussed again later in this chapter. Here it remains to examine the problem of unpaid labour.

Exploitative mechanisms (slavery, serfdom) operative in modes of production anterior to capitalism, are transparent with respect to the performance of unrewarded labour on the part of the producers. When the serfs perform compulsory work in the fields of their lord, they, and everybody, can see immediately that they are working for someone other than themselves. Their self-interest is not directly involved in this work, which may be one of the reasons why they have to be compelled to do it. Historically, pre-capitalist exploitation is always associated with compulsory work and with the direct intervention of the organised forces of repression of society in the labour process. Productive workers spent their lives under some kind of military captivity (slaves are literally prisoners, working under overseers, serfs cannot deplace themselves from their areas without permission) which gave to exploitation an immediately recognisable, political character.

Capitalism is, by contrast, based in principle on the maximum possible separation of the state from the economy. The forces of repression available to the state do not intervene directly to act as recruiters, foremen and supervisors in the capitalist factory. Their role in pre-capitalist exploitative regimes has to be taken over by the economic self-interest of the worker himself. That is why essential for the system is to instil into workers' minds the belief that no such thing as unpaid labour exists. It is not indeed claimed that a conscious organised conspiracy of deception on the part of some capitalist general staff has been set afoot and maintained over the centuries. Ordinary capitalists are, perhaps, as much deceived as everybody else by appearances in capitalist society. With the exception of certain bourgeois ideologists who, particularly nowadays, may be more or less cognisant of the real function of their activity, it is the institutions themselves, without anyone's conscious design, that encourage certain opinions, a certain view of the world, without which they could not function. The wage-form of the price of labour-power is a good case in point. If every time a worker sought work he was told clearly at the gate that he would be allowed into the factory only on condition that he explicitly abdicated from the reward of a part of his labour time in favour of the owners, every employment contract would constitute for the workers a call to insurrection against capitalist ownership. It is very doubtful whether, in such conditions, any work would get done without direct compulsion, which would deprive capitalism of one of its great advantages, the presence of a dynamic and flexible free labour market.

Such insurrectionary tendencies do not arise, because the employment contract is stated in terms that conceal the exploitative character of the relationship. A rate of payment is fixed per hour of work done, so that all hours appear to be paid for. By creating the impression of fully paid labour, the wage-form, without any explicit propaganda, cultivates a view of the economy favourable to the perpetuation of a system of wage-labour. It is not difficult to make the analysis of exploitation presented above consistent with the appearances of the case, and hence revealing the reality behind them. The worker is in fact paid the value of his labour power, which is divided by the number of hours in an average working day to find a rate per hour worked. This constitutes the wage rate. The worker reproduces the value of the daily wage in less than a day. But as for every hour he works he receives only a fraction of the hourly value he produces, he has in the end to work a full day in order to be paid the value corresponding to half-a-day's production. If, for example, the value of labour power is £20, the value added per worker per day £40 and the working day consists of eight hours, the wage rate will be £2.50 per hour. To make a living wage a worker must work eight hours. He probably has no choice in the matter as he is subject to factory rules, but he would have to work that long by sheer necessity, even if he was free to fix his own hours. Payment at that rate allows for a comfortable 100 per cent ratio of surplus value, or for a 100 per cent ratio of unpaid to paid labour, and yet every single hour worked seems to have been accounted for in the wage. Similar concealment takes place in the case of piece wages, where the work contained in every item of the product seems to be paid.

Of course, no capitalist accountants sit down to make estimates of that kind. These are implicit in the fact that employment is offered only as long as a certain commodity can be profitably produced and sold. The mechanism of supply and demand on the labour market, working impersonally like a force of nature, sees to it that wages are kept to a level consistent with the rate of profitability usual in the economy. On the assumptions stated above (general equilibrium, labour the only factor associated with the generation of exchange value), the residual turned into profit can only arise as the result of the exploitation of labour.

Some peculiarities of labour-power

Exploitation being at the heart of Marxist economics and the concept of labour-power at the heart of the theory of exploitation, it is not surprising that a vast amount of attention has been focused on it. This questioning has brought to the surface a number of problems: (a) problems relating to the definition of the concept; (b) following on from (a), problems associated with the applicability of the labour theory of value to the determination of the value of labour power; (c) more fundamentally than (a) or (b) questions which challenge the very idea that labour power can be conceived as a commodity. To outline the problems and discuss some of their implications is the task of the present section.

(a) The definition of labour-power

It has been noticed in the literature[6] that Marx has given not one but three alternative definitions of labour power, each with different implications for the determination of the value of that particular commodity. The first definition, in *Capital*, Vol I, Chapter 6, associates labour power with the means of subsistence and determines its value by the value of these means. If the remuneration of labour were to fall below that level, demographic consequences would follow. The strength of workers would start declining, they would become unfit for industrial labour, even their numbers might begin to fall. Consumption by workers under this definition is strictly functional. They consume the minimum necessary for their daily reproduction as workers and nothing beyond that.

The second definition tempers the starkness of the first by introducing an element of tradition and fairness, 'a historical and moral element' as Marx put it.[7] Purely functional consumption is only one element of the worker's consumption. A second element is determined by historical and social conditions, reflecting presumably the general level of civilisation which a society has reached and the working class has won a share of. The value of labour power is in this case determined by the value of the means of subsistence plus of those other commodities that raise the worker's consumption from the purely functional to the traditional level. If the remuneration of labour falls below traditional living standards, no demographic consequences follow. Social unrest, on the other hand, may well be sparked off, as workers resist encroachments on what they have come to consider their acquired rightful share. As a result of such unrest, industry might find itself deprived of working hands for some time, an outcome not dissimilar to that following upon a reduction of wages below their functional level under (a).

The third definition associates labour-power with the coexistence in the same economy of capitalist and pre-capitalist forms of commodity production in which the capitalist class monopoly of the means of production is not complete. In a socio-economic formation[8] of this kind producers accept exploitation only if by working on their own in the non-capitalist sector they earn less than in the capitalist one. In fact, given the non-pecuniary advantage of being one's own boss, they might have to earn considerably less before they decide to make a move. This is the least familiar version of Marx's definition; it will, therefore, be supported by a quotation:[9]

> As to the limits of the value of labour, its actual settlement always depends upon supply and demand. I mean the demand of labour on the part of capital, and the supply of labour by the working man. Hence the relatively high standard of wages in the United States. Capital may there try its utmost. It cannot prevent the labour market from being continuously emptied by the continuous conversion of wage labourers into independent self-sustaining peasants.

In this case the value of labour power is obviously determined as the opportunity cost of working in the capitalist sector of the economy. If wages fall below that, workers abandon capitalist industry for the self-employed sector.

Marx's three definitions have one point in common: that they fix a lower bound to the value of labour power, below which the worker ceases to be available for exploitation by capital. The worker's reward and his consumption may, and in the case of the third definition must, rise above the lower bound, however determined. By how much? Is there also an upper bound to correspond to the lower one? An explicit answer to this question does not exist in Marx but one can easily be inferred from the overall tenor of his analysis. The same principle which determines the lower bound will also determine the upper one. The value of labour power can never rise above the point where the typical worker is placed in a position of being able to accumulate capital from his earnings, because in that case he would soon cease to be a worker. He would no longer supply dependent labour to capitalist industry and would be lost to it as exploitable material.

This idea of an upper bound can be elaborated by some comments on the circuit of capital, described on p. 64 above. Considering the schema

$$M - C \prec \begin{matrix} LP \\ MP \end{matrix} \ldots P \ldots C' - M'$$

it is noticed that, at the end of one production cycle, the capitalist reappears as the owner of the original sum of money he invested, increased by the amount of surplus-value ($M + \triangle M$). He is, therefore, equipped to begin the cycle all over again, as a capitalist, i.e. as a buyer of labour power, indeed, on a scale expanded by the addition of surplus-value to the original capital. The worker, on the other hand, has received wages, spent them on consumer goods and performed the labour required of him. At the end of the cycle he remains as propertyless as he was at the beginning, ready to reappear on the market as a worker. It may be concluded that capitalist production is not simply a process which turns out commodities; it also reproduces the worker as a worker and the capitalist as a capitalist. With every cycle of production it reproduces the capitalistic relationship, it recreates the conditions for the perpetuation of the system.

The upper and lower bounds to the value of labour power fix a rather wide range of numerical values for it. Within this range, is it possible to select one point to represent *the* value of labour power? In the present author's opinion, the answer must be in the affirmative. The two bounds are determined by the structural characteristics of the system. If the workers' reward were to move outside these bounds, the normal functioning and even the very survival of the system would be called into question. In the context of such structural characteristics, the actual distributional share of the working class is determined by class struggle between labour and capital at various levels, of which market bargaining is the most common, mildest but, in the long run, not the most decisive.

Like any protracted campaign, distributional class war is not one continuous battle. It is characterised by its big strategic confrontations, its day-to-day skirmishing and its periods of truce. Conflict at the structural bounds of the value of labour power (particularly the lower bound where most of the struggle takes place) mobilises large, basic class forces and energies, because it has drastic implications. At most, it may lead to a proto-revolutionary crisis (as in the French May 1968 Paris events); at the very least it will require painful upward or downward revisions of their accustomed economic position by one of the two main combatants, the working or the capitalist class.

Strategic battles may not resolve everything. Given the broad balance of class-power established by them, the struggle can be continued and some additional ground gained or lost, by non-revolutionary, trade-union methods. Eventually a truce is arrived at, characterised by acceptance on all sides, partly formally, partly in practice, of a certain average level of wages as constituting the customary norm. This average norm, for the time it remains valid *is* the value of labour power.

(b) The labour theory of value of labour power

The norm discussed in (a) is an average in two senses (i) among industries and/or types of skill and (ii) over time, with regard to fluctuations caused by short-run changes in the supply and demand of labour power. It therefore displays the general characteristic of the concept of value as it relates to all commodities, and may be contrasted to price in the same way. In general, value, either in its basic form or modified into price of production, is a long-run equilibrium point at which exchange ratios between commodities settle for a relatively extended period of time. Ordinary price, on the other hand, is the day-to-day exchange ratio, determined by brief aberrations of supply and/or demand from the level consistent with long-run equilibrium. It has been argued that through market bargaining, collective or even uncoordinated but massive, workers may exercise pressure to increase and maintain higher wages and that such improvements may become traditional, establishing a new level of value for labour power (on its second definition). If so, the value of labour power cannot remain conceptually distinct from its price; in fact the market, supply and demand, is the sole determinant of this value, which risks becoming a tautologous concept, merely stating that the workers receive what they receive.

The flaw in this argument lies in its making no distinction between a price determined under the influence of competitive demand and supply, and one forced into shape by the exercise of market power. When the workers engage in one of their periodic battles to improve their standard of living they use their concerted economic, social and political power to alter significantly in their favour the distribution of income. If they are successful, they have exercised extraneous power over the market, leading to the establishment of the norm of value for labour power. This does not exclude random, short-run shifts of demand or supply causing deviations of current wages from the norm, so that a meaningful difference between value and price of labour power can still be established. Workers adapt more or less passively to short-run fluctuations of this kind, but they join battle to defend their basic norm. The difference between value and price is preserved and, on these grounds, the tautology criticism fails. One may point out various moments in the experience of the modern working class movement at which the working class has achieved historical victories, or suffered historic defeats, affecting the value of labour power for long periods of time. The introduction of compulsory paid holidays in France under the Popular Front government of 1936, the introduction of the National Health Service in Britain after the war or, more recently, the Pompidou compromise with the unions which ended the Paris 1968 upheavals are all cases in point. Conversely, the wage discipline imposed by the Nazi regime in Germany was an example of a downward revision of the norm.

A point of additional interest here is that such discontinuous shifts in the worker's standard of living nowadays implicate the State in either introducing legislation (paid holidays) or making a basic new public good available (the NHS). The conclusion must follow, and be registered as one of the peculiarities of surplus-value in *modern* capitalism, that the workers' consumption, and hence the value of labour power, consists partly of private and partly of public goods. It is, therefore, no longer in all respects determined through the market place but via a more complex process which is becoming increasingly political. From the point of view of the tautology criticism this development makes any confusion between value and price of labour power less rather than more likely, since an increasingly important determinant of such value, the political process, lies outside the scope of influence of market negotiations about the wage.

(c) The commodity character of labour power

The most radical questioning of the validity and usefulness of the concept of labour power takes the form of a challenge of its commodity character. The criticism has two prongs: that labour power is not produced as a commodity, is not a product of labour, and that it is not treated as such in economic life. These two lines of attack touch upon both the economic and the legal characteristics of the definition of a commodity.

In order to appreciate this challenge fully, it is helpful to place it in perspective, starting with Marx's own understanding of the matter. In proposing that a certain part of the human personality of the worker, his capacity to perform productive labour, becomes an object of trade, Marx certainly did not feel that he was proposing anything very original (in substance, as distinct from emphasis). He believed that this was the implication of the standard approach of his bourgeois predecessors in Political Economy and although he found the thing morally reprehensible, he also considered their views on it as a realistic, hard-headed reflection of bourgeois conditions. Commenting on Ricardo's analogy between the costs of production of hats and that of men, he wrote in the *Poverty of Philosophy*:[10]

Doubtless, Ricardo's language is as cynical as can be. To put the cost of manufacture of hats and the cost of maintenance of men on the same plane is to turn men into hats. But do not make an outcry at the cynicism of it. The cynicism is in the facts and not in the words which express the facts.

And in the *Theories of Surplus Value* he added:[11]

It is not a base action when Ricardo puts the proletariat on the same level as machinery or beasts of burden *or commodities*, because (from his point of view) their being purely machinery or beasts of burden is conducive to 'production' or because they *really are commodities* in bourgeois production.

[Italics have been added]

Thus, when Marx proceeded to define labour-power as a commodity, what he believed himself to be clarifying was not that some aspect of the human personality was being commercialised in capitalism, but which aspect that was. Moreover, he knew full well that workers were commodities from the point of view of the bourgeoisie, 'in bourgeois production'. If the bourgeoisie could have it all their own way, workers would be reduced to passive, submissive quiescent performers, not much differing from beasts of burden. It did not follow that the workers themselves accepted this kind of status, that they did not actively oppose it. On the contrary, he expected them to fight their ground and, in so doing, place continuous obstacles on the way to consummation of the natural tendencies of 'bourgeois production', which thus remained an unattainable normative ideal for the bourgeoisie.

In criticisms of the idea of a commodity character of labour power it is stressed that, if it were a commodity, it ought to possess both a use- and an exchange-value aspect. Labour power is, indeed, theoretically defined in such a manner as to include both. In the opinion of the critics, however, these two theoretical aspects bear little correspondence with the facts. The use-value of labour-power is its capacity to perform surplus-labour. That is why the capitalist buys it. Having bought it, however, he is not in a position to use it in the same way that any ordinary consumer uses commodities he has bought. The fact acquires significance here that the employment contract is not legally a sale, a contract about transferring ownership and possession, or about *dare* ('handing over', to use the term of Roman Law) but is about *facere* (about doing something). Were it a sale, the transfer of ownership would fix a precise moment when control of the commodity would cease to belong to the seller and pass totally to the buyer, who could make any use of it or destroy it at will.

No clear-cut separation is possible in the case of the employment contract. The worker always retains a certain residual control over his labour power, despite never-ceasing efforts to subjugate him, which fill many a volume in the history of industrial relations in capitalism. In Chapter 2, the point has been made that strict, absolute private ownership, leaving no room for ambiguities about the rights of persons over things, is one of the conditions of commodity production. It now emerges that in the case of that one commodity which, more than any other, lies at the heart of the capitalist mode of production, such clarity of the legal position is impossible to achieve. Even after the sale, capitalist and worker remain, in some way, joint owners of labour power, so that the manner and duration of its utilisation generate endless friction at the workplace.

In Marx's perception no legal arrangement could ever clarify the balance of rights on the use of labour power, both because of the inherently contradictory character of the relationship between buyer and seller of this particular commodity and because of its nature – its inseparability from the human being. He thus formulated a Marxist impossibility theorem concerning conflict at the workplace, the resolution of which could only be of a political, dictatorial nature. Having dramatised the conflict in an imaginary dialogue between the Worker and the Capitalist concerning the proper length of the working day, he concluded:[12]

Apart from extremely elastic bounds, the nature of the exchange of commodities itself imposes no limit to the working-day, no limit to surplus-labour. The capitalist maintains his rights as a purchaser when he tries to make the working day as long as possible, and to make, whenever possible, two working days out of one. On the other hand, the peculiar nature of the commodity sold implies a limit to its consumption by the purchaser, and the labourer maintains his right as seller when he wishes to reduce the working-day to one of definite normal duration. There is here, therefore, an antinomy, right against right, both equally bearing the seal of the law of exchanges. Between equal rights force decides. Hence it is that in the history of capitalist production, the determination of what is a working-day presents itself as the result of a struggle, a struggle between collective and capital, i.e. the class of capitalists, and collective labour, i.e. the working class.

As with use value, ambiguities and peculiarities beset the commodity concept of labour-power in its exchange value aspect also. With commodities in general, their exchange value is determined by their costs of production in terms of abstract labour. Labour-power has no costs of production in that sense, because it is not an industrial product. Its production is a natural process, supported by inputs which are themselves commodities and some inputs which are *not* commodities. Marx has defined the production of the commodity inputs as equivalent to the production of labour power. His definition does create a link between the value of labour power and the production process but, as noticed already at the beginning of the paragraph, production is, in this case, only one of the determinants of value. The others are tradition and the class-struggle, which jointly determine the category of commodities that normally constitute the worker's consumption bundle.

Furthermore, by focusing entirely on the industrial plus social origins of the value of labour power, Marx makes no mention of the domestic labour required for supporting the working man to keep him fit and ready for work. This makes the concept of labour power inappropriate for the analysis of the household exploitation practised against women, not by capitalists but by members of the opposite sex. Marx was only peripherally interested in this crucial human confrontation, mainly because he perceived the class struggle as gradually absorbing all other social and even human contradictions. On the question of household exploitation of women, or indeed of children by their parents, his intuition, only partly verified by developments and for the rest so far over-optimistic, was centred on the effects of industrialisation. He expected that industrial development, by drafting women and children into productive labour, would eliminate the monopoly position of the single male breadwinner in the household, thus creating a basis for a free, equal and presumably mutually caring family relationship. His analytical apparatus of the labour market is clearly not suited to problems originating in differences of age and sex, apart from the case where the working man's family has degenerated to the point of becoming a commercial enterprise for the benefit of the head of the family, who hires off his offspring to factories and pockets their wages (instances of such behaviour were recorded during the Industrial Revolution).

Even when looking solely at the commodity element determining its value, the difference between labour-power and ordinary commodities remains striking. Like all other commodities, labour power may respond to technical progress and become potentially cheaper as a result of increases in productivity. Unlike other commodities, however, it may turn back and claim a share of the productivity gains to be added to and increase its value. In the discussion of relative surplus-value, earlier, it was stated that, for the value of labour-power to be reduced, technical progress in the production of wage goods must be accompanied by reductions in the money-wage, assuming the value of money has remained fixed. The reaction of the working-class to any encroachment on the money value of their wages will be very negative. To increases in productivity they are likely to respond by regular productivity bargaining, capable of making such increases quite consistent with the maintenance of the value of labour-power.

In *Capital* Marx has come very close to formulating a thesis similar to the one proposed here. In discussing the adaptation of the price (as distinct from the value) of labour-power to increases in productivity, he wrote:[13]

> If in consequence of the increased productiveness of labour, the value of labour-power falls from 4 shillings to 3, or the necessary labour-time from 8 hours to six, the price of labour-power may possibly not fall below 3s. 8d., 3s. 6d., or 3s. 2d., or 3s. 10d. The amount of this fall, the lowest limit of which is 3 shillings (the new value of labour power), *depends on the relative weight, which the pressure of capital on the one side, and the resistance of the labourer on the other, throws into the scale.*
> [Italics added]

Marx's thesis envisages a lag of the price of labour power, achieved by working-class militancy, behind the decline in value of labour power, caused by technical progress. There is no reason why such militancy will stop at 'lagging' price behind value and not establish a new typical wage-norm – hence a new value of labour-power centred on the price rather than the technologically reduced old value. Working-class struggle may 'promote' the price of labour power into the value of labour power. In the perception of Marx, evidenced by the quotation above, this value would, even so, keep on declining with technical progress but not as rapidly as the bundle that constituted labour's original means of subsistence. The outcome would be a rising real wage combined with a falling value of labour power and a rising rate of exploitation. It seems more consistent with the evidence about the constancy of relative shares in advanced capitalist economies that the value of labour power (the typical wage-norm measured in hours of labour) has remained broadly constant during the last century.

This claim rests on the assumption that the working class remains a fairly stable percentage of the population in advanced industrial capitalism. If, under this assumption, the value of the whole of output is imputed to labour (as it should be on the basis of the labour theory of value) and if technical progress increases productivity uniformly in all sectors, then the constancy of the relative distributive share of labour implies constancy of the proportion of hours of work allocated to the production of wage goods. It follows that the aggregate value of labour power remains constant, as a proportion of the value of output. This, combined with the constancy of the labour force, as a proportion of the population, yields the result of a constant average value of labour power.

With the value of labour power constant, increases in productivity will give a rise in real wages considerably higher than under Marx's assumption of a value of labour power declining (although not as fast as productivity increased).

It must, therefore, be considered as established that the factor which makes labour power behave differently from all other commodities is its sensitivity to the effects of class struggle. It might appear justified to jettison the commodity definition completely and proceed to a study of wages and conditions of work exclusively in terms of unmediated class-struggle analysis.

However, no important analytical insight seems to be gained while some may be lost in any such research strategy. An interpretation of capital–labour economic relations as an unmediated class relationship would impoverish the concept of the class struggle itself. The labour market, with the commodity character it imparts on the capacity to work, is one of the most formidable class weapons in the hands of the bourgeoisie for maintaining long-term social and economic compromises. Labour market institutions give to the workers a place in the scheme of economic life, consistent with bourgeois interests but also apparently dictated by an ubiquitous alleged economic rationality which no good, or service, or factor of production can escape. It instils into their minds day-to-day subconscious compliance with the capitalist way of organising the social relations of production.

Maintaining the definition of labour power as a commodity, while exploring its peculiarities, is defended here as the most promising theoretical avenue. There are sound reasons, referring to the theory of commodity production, why labour power could not possibly have behaved like other commodities in the course of capitalist development. The conditions of its emergence, captured in its definition, are not the same as with other commodities; they are totally peculiar to it. In general the preconditions under which commodities appear and develop into the standard form of economic intercourse fall into two classes, technical and legal (see Chapter 2). With other commodities the technical condition is small-scale division of labour, the legal one is universal private property spread among all products. Unplanned coordination of production through exchange is the steering mechanism of the economy that corresponds to these conditions. With labour power, the technical condition (as will be argued in some detail in the following chapter) is large-scale production, while the legal one consists of the propertylessness of the producer. Buying and selling of labour power is the crucial institutional arrangement in this case.

The technical presupposition of the commodity labour power is thus the very opposite of that for other commodities. In the case of the latter, atomisation of effort reigns in the production sphere; in the former large-scale cooperation prevails. To the extent that the buying-and-selling of labour power spreads, the sphere of atomised commodity production recedes. It may be inferred that the kind of production which forms the basis of market economies is restricted to the extent that one of the commodity markets (the market for labour power) expands. The coordinating mechanisms of the economy are also realigned accordingly. The competitive market of non-Marxist economics, or the blind operation of the law of value in Marxism, become obsolescent, increasingly replaced by the various kinds of organised markets that pave the way to a planned economy. These insights into the course of development of the capitalist mode of production are not obvious consequences of the class struggle between capital and labour; they also become accessible through a study of commodity production which includes labour-power treated simply as a commodity.

Surplus-value and general equilibrium: the analysis of Schumpeter and Hicks

The definition of labour power apart, the other point in Marx's proof of the compatibility of exploitation and free trade, which may appear contentious, is his assumption of general equilibrium. Marx made this assumption (or, rather, its equivalent, of all commodities exchanging at their values) because he wished to establish his fundamental theorem under the strictest possible conditions, without any support from assumptions about unequal exchange.

From the point of view of individual capitalists, the absence of unequal exchange is both necessary and sufficient for ruling out the extraction of surplus-value from the sphere of circulation of commodities. On the other hand, from the more interesting point of view of the capitalist class as a whole (from a macro- rather than a micro-economic perspective) absence of unequal exchange, while still sufficient for that purpose, is no longer necessary. In a closed economy what one of the capitalists gains from unequal exchange, another loses, so that on balance aggregate surplus value should remain nil, if exchange were the sole source of surplus-value. In an open economy, on the other hand, capitalists in one country may well increase their surplus-value collectively by unequal exchange with capitalist, or non-capitalist, traders in another country. From a Marxist point of view this was the rational kernel in the theories of Mercantilism. Gains in surplus value by unequal exchange in the interior of a country are also possible in case the capitalist sector 'colonises', so to speak, some non-capitalist sector; usually if industry is able to impose monopolistic terms of trade on a presumed non-capitalist agriculture. Capitalists would then exploit simple commodity producers by unequal exchange, while at the same time exploiting workers through the buying and selling of labour power.

To the extent that a capitalist economy approximates the Marxist ideal image of a two-class society, where only capitalists trade in goods and services, while worker-producers trade exclusively only in labour-power, such sources of surplus-value dry up. Consequently trade, without labour exploitation, does not leave to capitalists any residual of aggregate surplus-value, whether the economy is in a state of general equilibrium or not.

Non-Marxist economists, who have not disdained from venturing into Marxian-style large-scale historical analysis of the development of capitalism, tell a somewhat different story. Rejecting tacitly the concept of surplus value, they concentrate on its empirical market counterpart, capitalistic profit. This they find possible to explain under conditions of disequilibrium while, faithful to the conclusions of perfectly competitive analysis, they perceive profit as vanishing in conditions of general equilibrium. Capitalism implies and is implied by profit; hence, given the origins of profit in that kind of analysis, capitalism cannot exist without a long-lasting, persistent disequilibrium in some or all markets. It is sometimes argued that capitalism itself creates the disequilibrium it sucks life from. But as every disequilibrium is, on the grounds of competitive analysis, self-corrective, in the sense of setting in motion forces that lead to a new equilibrium, without profits anywhere, capitalism economically is a self-abolishing system. What it leaves behind it, after its demise, becomes a matter for speculation.

Two very interesting examples of this type of analysis are represented by some work of Professor Sir John Hicks and by Joseph A. Schumpeter. Sir John Hicks[14] published his version in 1969 under the title *A Theory of Economic History*, while Schumpeter[15] had essentially published his own already in German in 1911 and in English in 1934 in his book *The Theory of Economic Development.*

Sir John Hicks can be said to take a consistently 'mercantilistic' view to the phenomenon of profit. He begins with a model of Mercantile Economy where there are two 'outside' areas, in one of which corn is scarce but vegetable oil is plentiful, while in the other the opposite is the case. Merchants perceive the opportunity and start making a profit by buying corn at a low price in one market and selling it at a high price in the other. By this arbitrage operation, however, they narrow their margins of profit, which vanish altogether when relative scarcities, and hence relative prices, become equalised in the two markets. For profit-making to continue, new opportunities have to be discovered (hence the enormous expansionary dynamism of market economics).

Artisans and manufacturers are in the same position with merchants, and so by extension are industrial capitalists.[16]

> The distinction between the pure trader, who buys to re-sell, to re-sell what is physically the same as what he had bought, and the artisan or 'producer' who works on the things he has bought, so as to re-sell them in a different form, is often regarded as fundamental; but economically and socially, it is not as fundamental as it looks. It is a technological, not an economic difference.

Industrial capitalists of our modern epoch, the progeny of the Industrial Revolution, are mercantile capitalists who discovered two new opportunities of profit-making: to buy cheap labour and to reduce costs by the application of science to production. Sir John Hicks offers an explanation (unfortunately too long to be summarised here but, it must be said, very ingenious) as to how labour came to be cheap. He then goes on to suggest that, as with everything else, this source of profit is also destined to dry up, as increasing industrialisation puts pressure on the labour market, ending up with a secular wage explosion. The restoration of equilibrium in all markets, including the labour market, switches off the taps of what Marxists would consider surplus value in the economy.

Is this the end of capitalism? According to Sir John Hicks it is one possible end of the expansionary phase of the Mercantile Economy, but not the only possibility. Trading centres (in the case of commercial capitalism) may perceive where competition is leading them and agree to some sort of monopolistic arrangement. This will arrest expansion (the relations of production will act as fetters on the forces of production) but it will have other saving graces:[17]

Yet this moment, when expansion is arrested, may from other points of view be a wonderful moment. Profits are still high, but it is a condition for their maintenance that they should not be invested in further expansion. Once that condition is accepted, there is wealth, and there is security. What can be better? The hurly-burly of the market-place has been brought into order. People have their places in society, places to which they must keep, but which are preserved for them, by protection against the intrusion of others. Through their guilds and suchlike associations, which are the means to protection, they can explore new forms of human fellowship. It is almost a socialist Utopia; and it is the fact that many socialist Utopias have had elements of it.

However, when he turns to modern industrial capitalism Hicks becomes more sceptical about the virtues of the arrested phase. He perceives that nationalism leads modern states to support monopolistic industrial empires, which block the world-wide spread of industrialisation, perpetuating the presence of a cheap-priced proletariat on a world scale in the underdeveloped nations. In some parts he paints a genuinely sombre picture:[18]

Tariffs [became] established as the principal form of protection, because they were the principal instrument which at that stage was usable . . . Quantitative controls, import and export monopolies, controls over capital movements (outgoing and incoming), manipulations of the tax system (even such as appear on the surface to be internal taxes); new devices, that go the same way, are continually invented.

Thus, at the end of the day, capitalism can save itself from its self-evaporation over the sands of the Stationary State only by transforming itself into a state-managed monopolistic system. In the very long run, only state monopoly capitalism has a chance of saving a regime based on the extraction of surplus value. Lenin could have said it no better.

Schumpeter's historical field of vision is narrower than that of Sir John Hicks. Not concerned with a pre-capitalist mercantile economy, he plunges directly into an explanation of profit as the result of a self-created capitalist imbalance. Agents of the disturbance are the entrepreneurs whose mission, talent, and peculiar contribution to the economy is to lead on the process of economic change. They are the innovators, the gifted visionaries with an eye for new ideas and new ways of doing things, and with the energy, the character and the ability to put them into practice, carrying the passive or recalcitrant common crowd along with them, against its own inertia and opposition. Entrepreneurs intervene in an established state of general competitive equilibrium, where the market value of each product just covers its factor cost. Their activity (say, the introduction of a new product) brings about a situation in which the cost-value equality is upset, and a positive difference, in favour of the product, emerges. This positive difference is profit, which splits further into entrepreneurial profit and interest on productive loans. It is of the nature of profit (consequently also of interest) not to last. Innovators are followed by imitators, who increase the output of the once scarce new product, reduce its price and raise the demand for the factors appropriate to its production, thus squeezing profit margins for all, the original entrepreneur included. Profits are competed away, so that aggregate surplus value can persist only as long as the stream of innovation continues to flow on; hence only if the disequilibrium state is maintained on a prolonged basis or if competition is replaced by monopoly. In full competitive equilibrium no surplus value is possible.

For Schumpeter, who assumes a competitive market as the starting point of capitalist development, this creates one problem: how is investment in innovating projects to be started, if no prior accumulation of an investible fund can take place? (Savings from wages or rents the Austrian economist considers so unimportant as to treat almost with contempt!)[19] He resolves the problem by the introduction of one of the most ingenious devices of his analysis – the capacity of the banking system to create new money, new purchasing power, and make it available to entrepreneurs. Sir John Hicks does not face the same problem. Unlike Schumpeter, he does not begin his analysis from a state of any airtight general competitive equilibrium but allows his original mercantile traders, the forerunners of industrial capitalists, to discover and take advantage of existing opportunities of unequal exchange.

In their treatment of profits Sir John Hicks and Schumpeter can be considered representative of all non-Marxist economics, in which surplus value or, rather, the phenomenon Marxists would describe as surplus value, is explained either as a result of disequilibrium or of the exercise of a degree of market power (or monopoly), both cases being varieties of unequal exchange. As far as one can see, a theoretical explanation of the persistence of surplus-value in full competitive equilibrium is to be found only in Marxist economics, where it depends on the labour theory of value. Whether in real economic life surplus-value persists in equilibrium is a matter of observation and essentially of judgement. With capitalism always caught up in the turmoil of change, no one can hope to observe equilibrium in its pure state in the world. Judgement must, therefore, be exercised, to decide how close or how distant from a state of equilibrium the economy is at any given moment. Observation can then sort out all ascertainable sources of unequal exchange from all *prima facie* equal exchange transactions, and consider whether the sum total of surplus-value payments can be plausibly explained by unequal exchange only. If (as this author would expect), it were found that unequal exchange explains only one part of the aggregate surplus-value, the fact should be registered in favour of the labour theory of value. This theory would, in such a case, explain all phenomena explained by its rivals plus one left unexplained by them. In this area, therefore, it would be the more general theory (while, as noted in Chapter 3, it remains less general in respect of its inability to explain the price of non-reproducible commodities).

For the rest it is remarkable how close to some of Marx's main conclusions both Sir John Hicks and Schumpeter have come, despite their radically different approach to the theory of value. The fact that, like Marx, they perceive the foundation of the capitalist economy to be undermined by the very progress of capitalism is particularly striking. It must also be noticed that Sir John Hicks hints at the possibility of a successor regime with some socialist features, while Schumpeter in his *Capitalism, Socialism and Democracy* has made an explicit forecast of a socialist future (which he believed as inevitable as much as he deplored it). Should it be concluded that differences in the theories of value, adopted by various economists, are not all that important, when the really large questions of social and economic development are brought forward?

Instead of a direct answer, it might be preferable to consider certain implications of value theory for Marxist and non-Marxist thinking. For the latter, clearly, the implication is that, in the absence of monopoly, capitalism is not an exploitative system. Surplus value is not the product of the workers, but of the traders who discover or, even more emphatically, create opportunities. Schumpeter is the one who makes this point most aggressively. The leaders create profit; if you distribute it to the totality of producers, you exploit the leaders. And, in self-justification, he adds:[20]

> If development required no direction and no force then profit would indeed exist; it would be a part of wages and rents, but it would not be a phenomenon *sui generis*. As long as this is not the case, that is *as long as the bulk of the people have the slightest resemblance to the masses of all nations of whom we have any knowledge*, so long the whole return cannot be imputed to the services of labor and land, even in the ideally perfect case of frictionless and timeless economic process. [Italics added]

It is perhaps true that, in the context of capitalist institutions, initiative cannot be exercised by 'people [who] have the slightest resemblance to the masses of all nations' but by the chosen few. Does it follow that these few have in fact created the surplus product alone? To argue this would be to show defective logic. The few were but one of the conditions. There also had to be a system of production relations which usurped the opportunity of creative work from 'the masses of all nations' to make it available to an elite minority.

Schumpeter is far too subtle a thinker to miss the point. In a footnote to the passage quoted above he tried to defend his position:[21]

> A word about the argument which is so often heard today: that the entrepreneur produces nothing, organisation everything; that no one's product is his own but the product of the social whole. At the bottom of this is the truth that everyone is the product of his inherited and personal milieu and that no one can produce anything

for which the conditions do not exist. But we can do nothing with this in the realm of theory, *which is not concerned with the moulding of men but with men already formed.*

In other words theory has to accept the *status quo* which turns out man as 'the product of his inherited and personal milieu'. What produces the milieu? By what mechanism is it maintained? These questions are not to pre-occupy theory, in Schumpeter's view. His explanation of surplus value, hence also his theory of value, implies and is implied by the acceptance of the capitalist *status quo.*

By contrast, the labour theory of value is sometimes mistakenly reduced to the claim that total output belongs exclusively to the workers who make it. In fact, in contemporary capitalist reality, workers 'make' only a rather small part of the product. Science and entrepreneurship, both belonging to capital, make a much larger part. The only way to do justice to the labour theory of value, in such a context, is to recognise in it an accounting system associated with a methodical rejection not merely of capitalist ownership but of the sum total of economic, legal, social and technical relations that in practice alienate the workers from the creative part of work to which they devote most of their lives.

Marxism rejects capitalism not because it is exploitative but because capitalist exploitation has served its historical purpose. The time has come for it to clear the way to new forms of human social intercourse. It is, on the other hand, acknowledged that capitalism, being a class-antagonistic mode of production, will not just lie quietly down and wither away, when its historical usefulness is spent. The ruling class will try to prolong the existence of the system, it will defend it even against its own progress. Ending capitalism is, therefore, a matter of conscious rejection, of conscious political action aimed at the replacement of the existing system with a differently conceived one. The Marxist labour theory of value is also premised on a, sometimes tacit, rejection of the basic assumption of the capitalist system. Thus (and not by any naïve claim that the whole of output 'belongs' by some sort of natural right to the workers) it associates the interest of the most numerous class of modern society, the working class, with the abolition of capitalist institutions. It lays the foundation of a political economy opposed to the existing organisation of economic life. It is this which ultimately differentiates Marxist economics from other large-scale studies of capitalist development, like those surveyed in this section. (For further discussion of the points mentioned at the beginning of this paragraph see Chapter 1, and, in particular, Chapter 10.)

Appendix to Chapter 4: The transformation problem, and the Fundamental Marxian Theorem

Presentation of the subject in this book has so far proceeded on the assumption that basic Marxist theory is best stated in terms of the labour theory of value. Given this choice (announced in Chapter 3) it appeared sensible to the author to treat the theory as if it were an unproblematic tool of analysis, postponing examination of some of the most important controversies until the main exposition had been completed.

A second reason for this postponement was the intention to offer a non-mathematical introduction to the main ideas of Marxist economics. This would have been rendered impossible by any attempt at simultaneous presentation of the labour-theory-of-value controversy, which depends heavily on the mathematical restatement of certain of Marx's propositions and arithmetical illustrations. This restatement has led to the emergence of a *corpus* of mathematised Marxist economics of considerable complexity which, even in the absence of fully rigorous proofs, makes the use of extensive mathematical symbolism necessary.

Value and price of production

The controversy on the meaning and relevance of the labour theory of value begins in the late nineteenth century as a by-product of a quarrel between Engels and some early critics (or detractors) who had accused Marx of almost plagiarising certain of his key ideas on surplus value from the work of the little known German economist Rodbertus. To confound the critics Engels asked them to anticipate (on the basis of Rodbertus's work) Marx's solution, before it was published, of what came to be famously known as the transformation problem. This early phase of the controversy will not be followed up here.[1] The survey will begin with Marx's solution.

The transformation problem regards the transformation of values into prices of production. (The price of production has already been defined on page 66.)

(1) $p \equiv (1 + r)(c + v)$

with

(2) $r \equiv \dfrac{s}{c + v}$

Definitions (1) and (2) obviously imply that, in any one sector model of the capitalist economy, price is identically equal to value defined as:

(3) $W \equiv c + v + s$

It does not, however, follow that value and price can be used interchangeably for all analytical purposes. Only prices of production can represent the behaviour of the practising capitalist with an adequate degree of realism. The capitalist can be described as an entrepreneur supplied with funds who, having advanced the amount $(c + v)$ in the production of some commodity, finds his selling price by adding to his total cost the customary profit markup, estimated as a percentage of his total cost. Profit per unit would, on this basis, be defined as

$$(4) \quad \pi \equiv r(c + v)$$

The capitalist certainly does not determine price by adding together hours of past and present labour absorbed by the commodity. He is not interested in value definitions. The theorist, on the other hand, when he examines not conscious capitalist behaviour but the unintended effects of their intentional action by individual capitalists or the aggregate characteristics of the capitalist economy, can use value accounting, confident that price accounting will yield identical results, as long as the assumption of a one-commodity economy (a one-sector model) is maintained.

Problems arise from the moment that a multi-commodity economy (a multi-sector model) is introduced. Taking as an example a three-commodity economy, prices will have to be calculated as follows:

$$(5) \quad \begin{aligned} P_1 &= (1 + r_1)(c_1 + v_1) \\ P_2 &= (1 + r_2)(c_2 + v_2) \\ P_3 &= (1 + r_3)(c_3 + v_3) \end{aligned}$$

If

$$(6) \qquad r_1 = \frac{s_1}{c_1 + v_1} = r_2 = \frac{s_2}{c_2 + v_2} = r_3 = \frac{s_3}{c_3 + v_3}$$

prices will continue to be identically equal to values. No sector will have any influence on the profitability of any other sector. The economy could, in this case, be decomposed into its constituent parts without loss of information regarding profitability.

If, for the sake of comparison, capitals invested in the three sectors of the economy are assumed to be equal, or that

$$(7) \quad c_1 + v_1 = c_2 + v_2 = c_3 + v_3$$

then (6) shows that $r_1 = r_2 = r_3$ only if $s_1 = s_2 = s_3$ which, with the rate of exploitation (s/v) equalised throughout the economy, can only be true if the organic composition of capital is also equalised among sectors, i.e.

$$\text{if} \quad \frac{c_1}{v_1} = \frac{c_2}{v_2} = \frac{c_3}{v_3} \, .$$

Given workers who, by moving from more exploitative to less exploitative employers, see to it that the balance of advantages and disadvantages in each job is roughly equalised, the assumption of an equal rate of exploitation can be accepted as a fair approximation. No such approximation can, on the other hand, justify any assumption of equal organic composition, since that would do violence to the elementary empirical datum of the different degree of capital intensity observed among industries.

As soon as it becomes accepted that

$$\frac{c_1}{v_1} \neq \frac{c_2}{v_2} \neq \frac{c_3}{v_3}$$

it follows that $s_1 \neq s_2 \neq s_3$. An arithmetical example will make this clear. Let $c_1 + v_1 = c_2 + v_2 = c_3 + v_3 = 100$, measured either in hours of work or in some monetary equivalent – on the assumption that the money commodity costs just one hour of work per unit to produce under conditions of average organic composition of capital. Let the rate of exploitation (the rate of surplus value) be 100%, v_1 be 20, v_2 be 10 and v_3 be 30 (with $c_1 = 80$, $c_2 = 90$, $c_3 = 70$). Then

$$\frac{s_1}{v_1} = \frac{20}{20} = \frac{s_2}{v_2} = \frac{10}{10} = \frac{s_3}{v_3} = \frac{30}{30}, \text{ and } s_1 = 20 \neq s_2 = 10 \neq s_3 = 30.$$

It follows that $r_1 \neq r_2 \neq r_3$.

But this is not an equilibrium position. Capital will migrate from less profitable into more profitable sectors, until the rate of profit is equalised. Marx, assuming that an equilibrium rate of profit has been achieved, proceeded to impose the condition

$$(8) \quad r \equiv \frac{s}{c + v} \equiv \frac{s_1 + s_2 + s_3}{c_1 + c_2 + c_3 + v_1 + v_2 + v_3}$$

This definition appears as a natural, unproblematic, extension of (2). Yet, when (8) is introduced in a three-sector model with unequal organic composition, it no longer yields the result of identical equality of price and value. The following illustrates this effect:

$$\begin{aligned}
W_1 &= c_1 + v_1 + s_1 = 80_c + 20_v + 20_s = 120 \\
(9) \quad W_2 &= c_2 + v_2 + s_2 = 90_c + 10_v + 10_s = 110 \\
W_3 &= c_3 + v_3 + s_3 = 70_c + 30_v + 30_s = 130
\end{aligned}$$

By (8) $r = 60/300 = 1/5$ or 20%. Price of production calculation then yields the following results:

$$\begin{aligned}
p_1 &= (1 + r)(c_1 + v_1) = 1.20 \times 100 = 120 \ (l_1 = 120) \\
(10) \quad p_2 &= (1 + r)(c_2 + v_2) = 1.20 \times 100 = 120 \ (l_2 = 110) \\
p_3 &= (1 + r)(c_3 + v_3) = 1.20 \times 100 = 120 \ (l_3 = 130)
\end{aligned}$$

In general, therefore, $p_i \neq W_i$. Equalisation of the rate of profit with equal rate of exploitation but unequal organic composition across industries leads to systematic deviation of prices from values.

The exception in industry 1 is explained by the coincidence of its organic composition with that of the aggregate social capital; (it can be seen from the arithmetical example that

$$\frac{c_1 + c_2 + c_3}{v_1 + v_2 + v_3} = \frac{c_1}{v_1} \ ).$$

But if

$$\frac{c_1}{v_1} = \frac{\sum\limits_{i=1}^{n} c_i}{\sum\limits_{i=1}^{n} v_i}$$

price is again identically equal to value, as order definitions (1) and (2). This can be demonstrated as follows:

Definition (5) of the price of production in industry 1

(5.1) $p_1 \equiv (1 + r)(c_1 + v_1)$

can be rewritten as

(5.2) $p_1 \equiv (1 + r)(\frac{c_1}{v} + 1)v_1$

and again, using (8) (the definition of the rate of profit) is

(5.3) $p_1 \equiv \left(1 + \dfrac{s_1 + s_2 + s_3}{c_1 + c_2 + c_3 + v_1 + v_2 + v_3}\right)\left(\dfrac{c_1}{v_1} + 1\right)v_1$

By the assumption that organic composition in industry 1 coincides with the aggregate organic composition in the economy, i.e. that

$$\frac{c_1}{v_1} \equiv \frac{c_1 + c_2 + c_3}{v_1 + v_2 + v_3} \quad,$$

(5.3) can be restated as

(5.4) $p_1 \equiv \left(1 + \dfrac{s_1 + s_2 + s_3}{(c_1 + c_2 + c_3) + (v_1 + v_2 + v_3)}\right)$

$\left(\dfrac{c_1 + c_2 + c_3}{v_1 + v_2 + v_3} + 1\right)v_1 = \left(\dfrac{(c_1 + c_2 + c_3) + (v_1 + v_2 + v_3) + (s_1 + s_2 + s_3)}{(c_1 + c_2 + c_3) + (v_1 + v_2 + v_3)}\right)$

$\left(\dfrac{(c_1 + c_2 + c_3) + (v_1 + v_2 + v_3)}{v_1 + v_2 + v_3}\right)v_1$

Cancelling the numerator in the right-hand side bracket with the denominator in the left-hand side one in (5.4), the expression is changed into

(5.5) $p_1 \equiv \dfrac{(c_1 + c_2 + c_3) + (v_1 + v_2 + v_3) + (s_1 + s_2 + s_3)}{(v_1 + v_2 + v_3)} \cdot v_1$

$$= \left(\frac{c_1 + c_2 + c_3}{v_1 + v_2 + v_3} + 1 + \frac{s_1 + s_2 + s_3}{v_1 + v_2 + v_3} \right) \cdot v_1$$

But

$$\frac{c_1 + c_2 + c_3}{v_1 + v_2 + v_3} = \frac{c_1}{v_1}$$

by assumption. Also, the other assumption of an equal rate of exploitation in all three industries ($s_1/v_1 = s_2/v_2 = s_3/v_3$) implies that

$$\frac{s_1 + s_2 + s_3}{v_1 + v_2 + v_3} = \frac{s_1}{v_1} .$$

This is easy to show. Write

$$\frac{s_1}{v_1} = \frac{s_2}{v_2} = \frac{s_3}{v_3} = \alpha.$$

Then $s_1 = \alpha v_1$, $s_2 = \alpha v_2$ and $s_3 = \alpha v_3$. Substituting for s_i ($i = 1, 2, 3$) in the fraction above it follows that

$$\frac{s_1 + s_2 + s_3}{v_1 + v_2 + v_3} = \frac{\alpha v_1 + \alpha v_2 + \alpha v_3}{v_1 + v_2 + v_3} = \frac{\alpha(v_1 + v_2 + v_3)}{(v_1 + v_2 + v_3)} = \alpha = \frac{s_1}{v_1}$$

Therefore (5.5) can be finally rewritten as

$$(5.6) \quad p_1 = \left(\frac{c_1}{v_1} + 1 + \frac{s_1}{v_1} \right) v_1 = c_1 + v_1 + s_1 = W$$

and price of production, in this special case, is identically equal to value.

With the exception of the case just considered, price will always deviate from value when the organic composition of capital differs across industries. This is *the transformation problem* – the transformation in question being that of values into prices of production. At first sight it appears as if the admission that prices will differ from values in any, even minimally, realistic representation of the capitalistic market economy, is quite fatal for Marxist economic theorising. Commodity exchange seems no longer capable of being analysed with the help of value definitions. More seriously, since the rate of profit, and hence total profit for capitals of equal size, is equal across industries, while total surplus-value, corresponding to total surplus-labour for capitals again of equal size, is different from industry to industry as a result of the unequal organic composition, it would seem as if profit and surplus-value were totally unrelated. Either of these results, but particularly the second, is sufficient to destroy the validity of the Marxist theory of exploitation.

Marx's own defence against the possibility of such conclusions rested on three main arguments: (a) that, although prices inevitably deviated from values under the stated conditions, price relations could in fact be explained on the basis of the labour theory of value, (b) that in the aggregate the same totals (price, value, profit and surplus value) of the various economic magnitudes would result, whether one started with values or with prices and (c) that value actually coincided with price in any industry of average organic composition (i.e. of an organic composition equal to the aggregate one in the whole economy), if there happened to be one. All three points are illustrated in the arithmetical example given above. (In particular, total value = 120 + 110 + 130 = total price = 120 + 120 + 120, and total profit = 0.20 × 300 = 60 = total surplus value = 20 + 10 + 30.)

For Marx, point (b) was of special importance. If magnitudes estimated on the basis of prices coincided in the aggregate with those estimated on the basis of values not only total price (the sum of all prices or the total amount of transactions in price terms) would be equal to total value, but also total profit would coincide with total surplus value (again as illustrated in the arithmetical example given). By contrast, in individual industries, profit would differ from surplus value. Comparing equations (9) and (10) makes it obvious that in the second industry profit is equal to 20 units but surplus-value only to 10, while in the third industry profit is equal again to 20 units but surplus-value is equal to 30.

From this discrepancy Marx derived the conclusion that the process of capitalist enrichment proceeded in two stages. Each individual capitalist extracted surplus-value from the wage-labourers directly under his command. The number of labourers depended on the technical composition of capital in the relevant industry. But each individual capitalist had no immediate claim on the surplus-value produced by his own workers. In general, he could claim either more, if he operated in sectors of higher than average organic composition, or less, in the opposite case. Capitalists participated in the extraction of surplus-value in proportion with the number of their workers (the size of their variable capital) but they participated in the appropriation of surplus-value in proportion with the size of their total capital advanced ($c + v$).

In this redistribution of surplus-value, *pro rata* to the total amount of exchange value in the form of capital controlled by individual capitalists, the superiority of capital as a social versus capital as a technical relation of production, is made manifest. The superiority of the social relation, however, acquires operational character only in the fetishised form of exchange-value (of capital advanced). As a fetishised social relationship, capital dominates the direct relationship of exploitation in any specific production process. And rightly so. In the fetishised form, it is the class structure of society (which fades away into the background when the capitalist deals with his workers on a personal basis) that reasserts itself. Without expressing it quite like that, Marx had perceived and underlined the crucial importance of the fetishism of commodities in the present connection:[2]

The relationships of capital are obscured by the fact that all parts of capital appear equally as the source of excess value (profit). The way in which surplus-value is transformed into the form of profit by way of the rate of profit is, however, a further development of the inversion of subject and object that takes place already in the process of production. The latter, has been seen to make the subjective productive forces of labour appear as productive forces of capital. On the one hand, the value, or the past labour, which dominates living labour, is incarnated in the capitalist. On the other hand, the labourer appears as bare material labour-power, as a commodity. Even in the simple relations of production this inverted relationship necessarily produces certain correspondingly inverted conceptions, a transposed consciousness which is further developed by the metamorphoses and modifications of the actual circulation process.

Capital, a social relation that has become separated and independent of its subjects, dominates workers impersonally, by assigning to them places of subordination; it benefits capitalists equally impersonally by assigning to them places of command. Just as the division of labour, in the analysis of simple commodity production, is regulated by relations among objects, the commodities produced, so the class relation between capitalists and workers is set up and implemented via objectified exchange value, capital. Class reality, with its manner of operation revealed in this part of *Capital*, is strikingly illustrated in the following oft-quoted, clearly more than metaphorical passage.[3]

[Capitalists] do not secure the surplus-value, and consequently the profit, created in their own sphere by the production of commodities . . . So far as profits are concerned, the various capitalists are just so many stockholders in a stock company in which the shares of profit are uniformly divided per 100, so that profits differ in the case of the individual capitalists only in accordance with the amount of capital invested by each in the aggregate enterprise, i.e. according to his investment in social production as a whole, according to the number of his shares.

The collective, class, character of exploitation in the capitalist mode of production is an important non-obvious prediction of the labour theory of value.

From value definitions to price equations

The first thoroughgoing criticism of Marx's solution of the transformation problem came from a near-contemporary of his and Engels's, the Austrian neoclassical (by today's descriptions) economist, Böhm-Bawerk.[4] In 'Karl Marx and the Close of his System' (1896) Böhm-Bawerk claimed that *Capital*, Volume III did not at all contain the solution of the transformation problem, which Engels had kept promising, but rather confirmed the presence of an unresolved contradiction between the value accounting system in *Capital*, Volumes I and II and the price-of-production system in Volume III. Böhm-Bawerk's criticism, a total and unsympathetic rejection of Marx's procedure, was probably intended by its author to say the final word on the matter and more generally, to silence Marxist economic theorising once and for all. He did not prove successful, either in his specific or in his general aim. Marxist economic theory continued to develop (admittedly with gaps and in a very unequal manner) the transformation problem remaining as fertile of ideas for its solution over its hundred year career, as when Engels first launched his challenge back in 1885.

Of Böhm-Bawerk's early criticisms the one point that still receives attention and even approbation today occurs in his claim that heterogeneous labour cannot be converted into homogeneous, for purposes of value accounting, without reference to market valuations, hence to prices. The argument, therefore, becomes circular. The validity and significance of this criticism will be considered later. His other claims of contradiction in Marx's argument, have been successfully confronted by the German statistician and economist Ladislaus von Bortkiewicz, in two papers of 1907.[5]

Bortkiewicz was himself critical of Marx's solution, but sympathetically so. He objected to the specific method of production price calculation, not to the general idea of beginning the calculation with values. As to that he found, like many another sympathetic critic of Marx subsequently, that the author of *Capital* had been on the right track.[6]

> [I]n trying to make clear the origin of profit, Marx had the lucky inspiration to construct a model in which profit exists, without any norm other than the (original) law of value being decisive for the relationship in which products are exchanged for each other. Such a model made it obvious that profit could neither have its first cause in the mark-ups which were a phenomenon of an exchange-economy, or needed to be regarded as a counterpart of the 'productive services of capital'. In other words, by making value calculation precede price-calculation, Marx succeeded – much more sharply and emphatically than Ricardo had done – in delimiting the theory of withholding against other theories of profit and in shaking off any common feature.

Granting that, Bortkiewicz went on to object to a specific inconsistency in Marx's method. His objection can best be understood if Marx's definition of the price of production (or, indeed his definition of value), are interpreted as input–output relationships, which they undoubtedly are. In the value equation

$$(11) \quad c + v + s = W$$

physical means of production, multiplied by their relevant values (the term c) are combined with hours of work $(v + s)$ to produce one unit of a certain commodity, evaluated as the sum of past and present hours of labour used up in the production of a commodity. This sum of labour hours obviously does not hang in the void, it is attached to the unit of some produced commodity, some output. With the symbols W_1 and W_2 representing unit values of input and output, q_1 and q_2 representing quantities of input and output and l representing total current labour, $(s + v)$, the basic value equation can be rewritten as

$$(12) \quad W_1 q_1 + l = W_2 q_2$$

Assuming $q_2 = 1$, the correspondence between (11) and (12) becomes complete. Furthermore, with l' representing hours of current *necessary* labour only, the price of production equation can be rewritten in the same manner as

$$(13) \quad (1 + r)(W_1 q_1 + l') = p_1 q_2 \text{ or } (1 + r)W_1 q_1 + l') = p_1(q_w = 1)$$

Equation (12) suffers from no accounting-system inconsistency. The same is not true of equation (13), where quantities are multiplied by values (W_i) on the left-hand (the input) side while they are multiplied by prices on the right-hand (the output) side. However, in any system of economic reproduction, where produced commodities are used to produce commodities, certain outputs, evaluated in production prices, become inputs and should continue to be evaluated in a similar manner. This makes equation (13) with values on the left and prices on the right hand side, incorrect, as a representation of the production of commodities by means of commodities, and formally inconsistent.

This inconsistency had been noticed and commented upon by Marx, but he dismissed it as immaterial to the development of his argument. In view of the quite extraordinary implications attributed to the correction of this point, it is worth starting with Marx's own comment:[7]

> The foregoing statements have at any rate modified the original assumption concerning the determination of the cost-price of commodities consumed in its production. But for the buyer the price of production of a specific commodity is its cost-price, and may thus pass as cost-price into the prices of other commodities. Since the price of production may differ from the value of a commodity, it follows that the cost-price of a commodity containing this price of production may also stand above or below that portion of its total value derived from the value of the means of production consumed by it. It is necessary to remember this modified significance of the cost-price, and to bear in mind that there is always the possibility of an error if the cost-price of a commodity in any particular sphere is identified with the value of the means of production consumed by it. Our present analysis does not necessitate a closer examination of this point.

(Cost-price in the above is defined as $(c + v)$ which obviously differs from production-price $(1 + r)(c + v)$.)

Bortkiewicz made the difficulty, noticed by Marx, the central point of his analysis. He proposed to solve the transformation problem fully consistently by stating and solving a system of simultaneous equations, where values would be the known parameters and prices of production the unknown variables. His solution proceeded along the following lines: The economy is divided in three sectors. Sector one produces means of production; all constant capital spending in the economy $(c_1 + c_2 + c_3)$ constitutes demand directed to sector one. Sector two produces wage goods; all wage payments in the economy $(v_1 + v_2 + v_3)$ are spent on the products of this sector. The third sector produces luxuries; capitalists are assumed to accumulate no capital, therefore all surplus-value earned by them $(s_1 + s_2 + s_3)$ is spent on the purchase of the products of sector three. In all three sectors demand (for means of production, for wage-goods and for luxury-goods) is assumed equal to supply. The Bortkiewicz system is thus a general equilibrium model of a stationary economy; a development from Marx's schemes of simple reproduction (see Chapter 6). It is represented by the following equations:

$$(14) \quad \begin{aligned} (1 + \varrho)(c_1x + v_1y) &= x(c_1 + c_2 + c_3) \\ (1 + \varrho)(c_2x + v_2y) &= y(v_1 + v_2 + v_3) \\ (1 + \varrho)(c_3x + v_3y) &= z(s_1 + s_2 + s_3) \end{aligned}$$

In (14) c_i, v_i, s_i $(i = 1, 2, 3)$ are assumed to be known value magnitudes; x, y and z are undetermined multipliers (conversion coefficients) by which values are converted into prices. The multipliers are *not* prices of production; the prices are cx, vy and sz. As they now appear both on the input and on the output sides of the equations, the inconsistency of Marx's method is overcome.

Bortkiewicz's system must be solved for x, y, z and ϱ, the rate of profit, treated here not as a given quantity (as $r = s/(c + v)$) but as an unknown, to be solved for simultaneously with the prices of production. This constitutes a major departure from Marx's method based, as it was, on a prior determination of the rate of profit in the value accounting system. After Bortkiewicz a distinction has to be made between r, the value and ϱ, the price rate of profit.

The simultaneous solution for prices and the rate of profit is, as will be shown, a mathematical necessity for the solution proposed by Bortkiewicz. At the same time it strengthens the general equilibrium character of his procedure which had already asserted itself in the imposition of the conditions of simple reproduction on the system of equations.

In the event, these conditions can be dropped without damaging the solution. On the basis of Bortkiewicz,[8] a more general system of equations can be set up, which leaves the question of balance of demand and supply among the three sectors of the economy open. This system is stated as follows:

$$(15) \quad \begin{aligned} (1 + \varrho)(c_1x + v_1y) &= xa_1 \\ (1 + \varrho)(c_2x + v_2y) &= ya_2 \\ (1 + \varrho)(c_3x + v_3y) &= za_3 \end{aligned}$$

where a_i is total output in value terms in each sector. Writing $\gamma_i \equiv c_i$, $(i = 1, 2, 3)$

$$\beta_i \equiv \frac{v_i}{a_i} \ (i = 1, 2, 3), \text{ and } m \equiv (l + \varrho)$$

(15) can be rewritten as

$$(16) \quad \begin{aligned} (m)(\gamma_1x + \beta_1y) - x &= 0 \\ (m)(\gamma_2x + \beta_2y) - y &= 0 \\ (m)(\gamma_3x + \beta_3y) - z &= 0 \end{aligned}$$

The system is homogeneous (there are in its equations no independent additive constants, which could be collected on the right hand side). Neglecting for a moment the fact that m is also an unknown, the system can be seen as containing a subsystem, consisting of the first two equations in the two unknowns x and y. This subsystem is linear in x and y and homogeneous, so that for it to have a non-zero solution, the determinant of its coefficients matrix must be zero. Rewriting the first two equations of (16) as:

$$(17) \quad \begin{aligned} (m\gamma_1 - 1)x + m\beta_1y &= 0 \\ m\gamma_2x + (m\beta_2 - 1)y &= 0 \end{aligned}$$

yields the following condition for a solution:

$$\begin{vmatrix} m\gamma_1 - 1 & m\beta_1 \\ m\gamma_2 & m\beta_2 - 1 \end{vmatrix} = 0$$

$$(m\gamma_1 - 1)(m\beta_2 - 1) - m^2\beta_1\gamma_2 = m^2(\gamma_1\beta_2 - \beta_1\gamma_2) - m(\beta_2 + \gamma_1) + 1 = 0$$

Solving this quadratic in m immediately yields the price rate of profit, since $m = 1 + \varrho$. The solution demonstrates also the mathematical necessity of refusing to introduce a predetermined, value rate of profit in (17). If ϱ, and therefore m, were treated as predetermined constants, the determinant of the coefficients matrix of (17) could be zero only by accident; therefore only in special cases could (17) be solved for prices of production. On the other hand, if the rate of profit is treated as an unknown, the value of m can be chosen so as to make the determinant of (17) always equal to zero, which guarantees that a successful transformation from values to prices is always possible.

With m determined, (17) can be solved for the ratio of x/y (since systems of homogeneous linear equations with zero determinants of their coefficient matrices can be solved for ratios of their variables only). The solution for x/y together with (16) will finally yield the solution for z/y. Since x, y and z are intended to be conversion coefficients from values to prices of production, x/y and z/y can be used for the transformation from relative values (c/v say) to relative prices (cx/vy). To make the solution fully determinate, one additional relationship, that will make it possible to solve for absolute prices, is the next requirement.

Invariance conditions between value and price accounting

One way in which this problem has been tackled is by assuming that the organic composition of capital in the sector represented by the third equation of (16) (the luxury goods sector) coincides with the average organic composition of aggregate social capital, so that no difference between value and price exists in that sector; therefore $z = 1$. With z/y given from the solution of (16) and z set at 1, y and then x can be found. The step from relative to absolute prices is complete.

However, there is no particular reason why the luxury goods sector should be one of average organic composition. If it is not, but its product (say, for the sake of the analysis, gold) is treated as the money commodity in both the value and the price systems, the following anomaly occurs: the sum of prices is greater than the sum of values, if organic composition in the production of gold is lower than average and the opposite if it is higher than average. The reason for this is that with the price (or value) of gold, in terms of itself, being by definition equal to 1, (the exchange-rate of gold in terms of itself is one in both the value and the price system) the fact that the price of production of gold is lower (or higher) than its value, as a result of the transformation from values to prices, can find expression only in the sum of the prices of all other commodities rising above (or falling below) their values; (the purchasing power of gold falls or rises, while nominally both its value and its price are fixed at unity).

It has been seen, however, that for Marx equality of aggregate price with aggregate value was one of the links that connected the detail behaviour of individual capitalists, realistically describable in terms of production prices, with value analysis, theoretically applicable both in detail and in the economy as a whole, but observable only in the aggregate. If as a result of the solution of the transformation problem, the aggregate value-price invariance was found not to hold in general, the significance of the labour theory of value would again be shaken.

To avoid this anomaly, it has been suggested that Marx's invariances (total price equals total value and total profit equals total surplus-value) might be used as postulates for supplying the additional relation required for going from relative to absolute prices. This is indeed possible. Defining $q = x/y$, and using the first equation of system (15) to express ϱ in terms of the parameters

$$(\varrho = \frac{xa_1}{c_1x + v_1y} - 1),$$

the third equation of (15) can be solved for z as follows:

$$c_3x + v_3x + (c_3x + v_3x)(\frac{a_1q}{q}\frac{}{c_1q + v_1} - 1) = za_3$$

$$\frac{a_1c_3qx + a_1v_3x}{c_1q + v_1} = a_3z$$

$$z = \frac{a_1(c_3q + v_3)x}{a_3(c_1q + v_1)}$$

The additional condition (total price equals total value) can now be used:

$$a_1x + a_2y + a_3z = a_1 + a_2 + a_3 = a$$

Substituting for y and z,

$$a_1x + a_2\frac{x}{q} + \frac{a_1(c_3q + v_3)x}{c_1q + v_1} = a$$

or

$$x\left(a_1 + \frac{a_2}{q} + \frac{a_1(c_3q + v_3)}{c_1q + v_1}\right) = a$$

and finally,

$$x = \frac{aq(c_1q + v_1)}{(a_1q + a_2)(c_1q + v_1) + a_1q(c_3q + v_3)}$$

Since $q = x/y$ has already been found in terms of the parameters of the system in the previous section, the last expression gives a solution for x that does not involve y or z. This solution, together with the already known ratios x/y and z/y gives the values of x, y and z separately in terms of the parameters of the system, and thus completes the solution, making the calculation of absolute price levels possible.

The trouble is that for the solution for production prices to become fully determinate (i.e. for absolute production prices to be found) only *one* additional relation is needed. If more than one such relation is imposed as a condition, the system of equations becomes overdetermined, unless the value coefficients (c_i, v_i, s_i) take on numerical values capable of satisfying two or more invariances simultaneously. Such systems do exist, but they represent special cases. (For example, the double assumption of simple reproduction and identical-with-the-rest-of-the economy value structure in the luxury goods department yields systems with the specified characteristics.) In general there is room for only one independent additional condition in the solution of the transformation problem. This leads, sometimes, to the rather pointless search of one condition (either total price equals total value or total profit equals total surplus value, or some other still) as representing more crucially the spirit of Marx's analysis and as better deserving to be maintained in any value-price transformation. The fact of the matter, however, is that any such choice between invariance postulates inevitably reduces the scope of the labour theory of value, as envisaged by Marx, and can only partially reflect his original purpose.[9]

From values to technical input coefficients

Recent research has shown the possibility of solving the transformation problem fully consistently (i.e. without confusing value with price accounting) while maintaining both invariances, considered crucial by Marx, under conditions much less restrictive than those mentioned in the previous paragraph. These solutions will not be presented here[10] in order to maintain the historical continuity of the narrative.

The impact of Bortkiewicz's solution on the further development of Marxist theory has been ambivalent. His demonstration of the possibility of a consistent transformation removed one formal problem from the labour theory of value, but also took the first step towards splitting the price and value models apart in a manner that appeared to make their reconciliation problematic. Critics of the labour theory of value – on the whole inimical to everything that Marxist analysis stood for – seized upon this point to argue increasingly that Marx's value model was nothing but an awkward, politically motivated, incubus on general equilibrium price analysis; that it could add nothing to what could be learnt from price general equilibrium models; that, even if it had some sociological merits, for economics it was totally irrelevant.

Such was not Bortkiewicz's attitude (for his opinion see p. 94 above). In the setting up of the problem, he tried to make as much use of value data as his mathematics would allow him. He started from the same value definitions of the constituent parts (constant, variable, surplus) of capital as Marx, and would probably not object to defining the rate of profit as $r = s/(c + v)$, if it did not stand in the way of the solution of his system of equations. But the further development of Bortkiewicz's solution introduced a far more radical departure from the original value starting point.

Bortkiewicz's solution, as developed by Winternitz was generalised by Francis Seton,[11] who gave to the discussion its modern form. Seton's new idea was essentially to proceed from the three-sector economy, studied by Bortkiewicz and his successors, to an n-sector economy, similar to the one studied by Leontief in input–output analysis. Marx's elementary disaggregation of production costs into constant and variable capital is extended by Seton to cover a complete breakdown of the cost structure of every industry, so that the original Bortkiewicz system appears in the following form:

$$k_{11}p_1 + k_{12}p_2 + \ldots + k_{1n}p_n = \phi a_1 p_1$$

$$k_{21}p_1 + k_{22}p_2 + \ldots + k_{2n}p_n = \phi a_2 p_2$$

$$(18) \quad k_{n1}p_1 + k_{n2}p_2 + \ldots + k_{nn}p_n = \phi a_n p_n$$

where k_{ij} represent the cost input (c_{ij} and v_{ij}, in the constant/variable capital terminology of Marx) of industry j's product into industry i, reckoned in terms of labour value: p_{ij} are value/price conversion coefficients; a_i is output in value terms ($a_i = c_i + v_i + s_i$), and $\phi = 1 - \varrho$ (so that the left-hand side of equations (18) represents cost as a summation of value inputs duly transformed into prices of production, while the right hand side represents cost as a difference between total price ($a_i p_i$) and total profit ($\varrho a_i p_i$) per sector. Obviously ϱ is the price rate of profit).

Dividing both sides of (18) by a_i and transfering ϱp_i to the left-hand side, the system is put in the form:

$$(k_{11} - \phi)p_1 + k_{12}p_2 + \ldots k_{1n}p_n = 0$$
$$k_{21}p_1 + (k_{22} - \phi)p_2 + \ldots k_{2n}p_n = 0$$

(18a)

$$k_{n1}p_1 + k_{n2}p_2 + \ldots (k_{nn} - \varepsilon)p_n = 0$$

$$\text{where } \varkappa_{ij} = \frac{k_{ij}}{a_i}$$

(18a) can obviously be written

(19) $\quad | K - \phi I | \, \bar{p} = \bar{o}$

$$\text{where } K = \begin{vmatrix} k_{11} & k_{12} \ldots k_{1n} \\ k_{21} & k_{22} \ldots k_{2n} \\ & \cdot \quad \cdot \\ & \cdot \cdot \cdot \cdot \cdot \\ & \cdot \quad \cdot \\ k_{n1} & k_{n2} \ldots k_{nn} \end{vmatrix}$$

I is an identity matrix, $\bar{p}$ and $\bar{o}$ are vectors of conversion coefficients and of zeroes respectively. System (19) is a homogeneous system of n equations in $n + 1$ unknowns (the p_i ($i = 1, \ldots, \eta$) and ϕ). Treating ϕ not as an unknown but as an undetermined coefficient, a solution for (19) can always be obtained by selecting an appropriate value for ϕ, such that:

(20) $\quad | K - \phi I | = \varrho$

Such ϕ are described as the eigenvalues or characteristic values of matrix K, while the vectors $\bar{p}_i$ associated with them in the system $K\bar{p} = \phi\bar{p}$ are known as the eigenvectors or characteristic vectors of K. By certain well known theorems on non-negative square matrices,[12] K, which is such a matrix, has one maximum, non-complex positive eigenvalue, which implies a positive fractional rate of profit (since $\phi = 1 - \varrho$).

Bortkiewicz's favourable opinion on Marx's adoption of value accounting as the starting point of his analysis of exploitation has already been mentioned. It has also been explained that Bortkiewicz could not accept to have the rate of profit predetermined as $r = s/(c + v)$ in the fashion of Marx, because that would make it impossible for him to solve the system of equations which he set up. Even so, in the

Bortkiewicz solution the price rate of profit remains a transformed value magnitude, because it is solved for the value coefficients that constitute the elements of the system (17) or of the matrix in (18a). The only significant dissociation of the value and price systems, which emerges as a result of the Bortkiewicz solution is the impossibility of maintaining both invariances of aggregate magnitudes considered crucial by Marx.

With Seton's formulation, however, the way for a far more drastic dissociation of the two accounting systems is opened. As Seton has himself pointed out, the coefficients k_{ij} in (18a) can be seen as the product of physical input coefficients and the unit values of the respective commodities. Writing k^*_{ij} and a^*_i for the inputs into and the output of a certain commodity and recalling that $\varkappa_{ij} = k_{ij}$, the coefficients of (18a) can be represented as $k^*_{ij}\omega_i$, where ω_i, ω_j are the appropriate unit values. Physical input coefficients can then be defined as

$$K^*_{ij} = \frac{\varkappa^*_{ij}\omega_j}{a^*\omega_i} \cdot \frac{\omega_i}{\omega_j}$$

or

$$(21) \quad K^*_{ij} = K_{ij}\,\frac{\omega_i}{\omega_j}$$

Referring back to the matrix of value coefficients of (19), these can all, on one block, be transformed into input–output coefficients as in (21) by the following operation:

$$
\begin{vmatrix} W_1 & 0 & \dots & 0 \\ 0 & W_2 & \dots & 0 \\ 0 & 0 & & W_n \end{vmatrix}
\begin{vmatrix} k_{11}k_{12} & \dots & k_{1n} \\ k_{21}k_{22} & \dots & k_{2n} \\ k_{n1}k_{n2} & \dots & k_{nn} \end{vmatrix}
\begin{vmatrix} \frac{1}{W_1} & 0 & \dots & 0 \\ 0 & \frac{1}{W_2} & \dots & 0 \\ 0 & 0 & & \frac{1}{W_n} \end{vmatrix}
$$

$$
= \begin{vmatrix} k_{11}\dfrac{W_1}{W_1} & k_{12}\dfrac{W_1}{W_2} & \dots & k_{1n}\dfrac{W_1}{W_n} \\ k_{21}\dfrac{W_2}{W_1} & k_{22}\dfrac{W_2}{W_2} & \dots & k_{2n}\dfrac{W_2}{W_n} \\ k_{n1}\dfrac{W_n}{W_1} & k_{n2}\dfrac{W_n}{W_2} & \dots & k_{nn}\dfrac{W_n}{W_n} \end{vmatrix}
= \begin{vmatrix} k^*_{11}k^*_{12} & \dots & k^*_{1n} \\ k^*_{21}k^*_{22} & \dots & k^*_{2n} \\ k_{n1}k^*_{n2} & \dots & k^*_{nn} \end{vmatrix}
$$

or, in brief:

$$(22) \quad K^* = WkW^{-1}$$

where W is a diagonal, unit value matrix (the elements of the diagonal of $\wedge$ are the unit values of commodities).

Transformation (22) is known as a similarity transformation, and has the property of preserving eigenvalues, so that the same eigenvalue, ϕ, and the same price rate of profit $\varrho(\phi = 1 - \varrho)$ will be found whether a matrix of value coefficients, K, or of physical input–output coefficients K^* is used as the starting point. It follows that for finding the price-rate of profit, a value model is no longer necessary. Exactly the same average rate of profit for the economy can be computed, on the basis of a physical input-output coefficients matrix.

As for the conversion coefficients vector $\bar{p}$ (the vector consisting of elements which convert the value expressions into prices of production), this, in general, does not remain invariant under the similarity transformation, but neither should it. The elements of a new vector $\bar{p}^*$ which will now emerge as the solution of the system

(23) $k^* a p^* = \phi p^*$

are no longer conversion coefficients from values into prices of production; they are interpreted as these prices of production themselves. The computation of the price set of the capitalist economy acquires, therefore, the following form. Starting with a technologically determined matrix of input–output coefficients, a unique price-rate of profit and a set of production prices, using this rate of profit as a mark-up, can be computed, without any reference to a prior value model. This is a rather strange and unexpected culmination of the efforts to find a proper solution of the transformation problem, which solves it by conjuring out of existence the entity (value) originally meant to be transformed into a set of production prices.

This particular turn of the argument (the possibility of computing general equilibrium prices of production and a rate of profit, without needing to make any reference to value magnitudes) has been exploited heavily by unfriendly critics of the labour theory of value and of Marxian economics generally. They have argued that Marx's value model, far from contributing a simplified essential picture of capitalism amounts, in fact, to a 'complicating detour'. (The expression in quotation marks belongs to P. A. Samuelson[13] the main proponent of the anti-value view.) Samuelson's challenge is relative to the possibility of reintroducing value in the discussion, from which it had apparently evaporated.

This reintroduction was successfully effected by Morishima, in his *Marx's Economics* (1973). Morishima took his point of departure from his joint research, with F. Seton, on the transformation problem (M. Morishima and F. Seton: 'Aggregation in Leontief Matrices and the Labour Theory of Value', *Econometrica*, 1961). Subsequently Morishima extended the scope of the methods pioneered in that article to some of the main topics of Marxist economic theory. His mathematical presentation is both lucid and dense, so that any attempt to summarise it here would only do it an injustice. Instead of repeating his proofs, a sketch of his basic ideas on exploitation will be offered.

The centrepiece of Morishima's construction consists of an advanced restatement of Marx's well-known relationship

$$\frac{s}{v} > \frac{s}{c + v}$$

(the rate of surplus value – the rate of exploitation – is always higher than the rate of profit). Let it be noted that $s/(c + v)$ is simply a good approximation to ϱ. Though

Morishima has shown that they are equal to each other, under certain stringent conditions, the Fundamental Marxian Theorem is a proposition which rigorously holds between s/v and ϱ rather than s/v) and $s/(c + v)$. For the sake of explanatory convenience, however, I shall, in the following neglect the errors produced by replacing ϱ by $s/(c=v)$.) While in Marx, however, the relationship is proven in a one-sector economy and for a single rate of profit and surplus value, Morishima achieves a fully general proof, in a u-sector economy and for any rate of profit or surplus value.

Morishima has named this proposition (which was proven independently from Seton–Morishima also by N. Okishio: 'A Mathematical Note on Marxian Theorems', *Weltwirtschaftliches Archiv*, 1963) the Fundamental Marxian Theorem. The gist of the theorem is conveyed in Figure 4.1 (see M. Morishima: *Marx's Economics*,

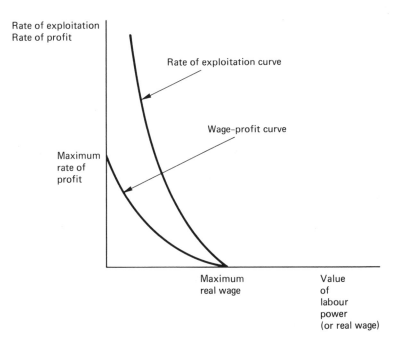

FIGURE 4.1

Cambridge, 1973, p. 64. The rate-of-profit curve is dominated by the rate of exploitation curve for all values of the real wage. The rate of profit, in Marx's approximation $s/(c = v)$ reaches a finite value when $v = 0$; the rate of exploitation, s/v, tends to infinity for a zero value of v).

Significance of the Fundamental Marxian Theorem

Casual reading of the Fundamental Marxian Theorem might suggest that it contributes nothing very significant to knowledge already acquired, since the result that the rate of surplus-value is always higher than the rate of profit can be seen directly from the Marxist formulation

$$\frac{s}{v} > \frac{s}{c + v}$$

The difference, of course, is that while Marx uses the same accounting system, in terms of labour-values, both for the rate of exploitation and for the rate of profit, in the case of the Fundamental Marxian Theorem the rate of profit has been estimated quite independently of labour-values, on the basis of prices of production derived not from values but directly from a matrix of technical coefficients. The value and price systems have been developed in parallel on a common technical base, as illustrated in Figure 4.2.

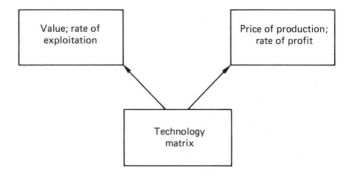

FIGURE 4.2

To relate these two independent accounting systems, in a way that preserves Marx's result (rate of exploitation necessarily higher than rate of profit) is certainly nothing trivial. It demonstrates that surplus-value is both necessary and sufficient for the existence of profits, or that exploitation is necessary for capitalism. Given that, at least in the opinion of a respectable section of Marxist theorists (to which the present author also adheres) (a) the best, and probably the only convincing, explanation of exploitation under conditions of free and equal exchange is via the construct of the buying-and-selling of labour-power and (b) that a definition of the latter rests on the labour theory of value, the Fundamental Marxian Theorem provides a solid basis for the continuing relevance, indeed indispensability, of that theory in the analysis of capitalism. This is the reply to Samuelson's claim that the labour theory of value, far from being a simplifying assumption, constitutes, in fact, a 'complicating detour' and is, therefore, totally irrelevant, even harmful to the understanding of exploitation through the market. (It should not be inferred from the above that Morishima subscribes unconditionally to the labour theory of value. On the contrary, in the final chapter of *Marx's Economics*, he expressed serious reservations about it and proposed the recasting of Marxist economics in terms of von Neumann prices.)

Some further problems

So far the labour theory of value has been formulated under two assumptions, relaxation of each of which creates certain further theoretical problems.

The first assumption is that each industry in the economy in question produces just one product. If this assumption is relaxed and joint production allowed, it can be shown that, in certain cases, positive profits are consistent with negative surplus-value. This is supposed to provide one further demonstration of the irrelevance, indeed the invalidity, of the labour theory of value.

The second assumption is that of homogeneous labour. If heterogeneous labour is allowed, any labour theory of value becomes impossible, because no unambiguously defined unit of measurement exists. The way to overcome this problem is to fix conversion coefficients for each type of labour that will transform all various kinds into one basic type (in Marx's case unskilled manual labour) one hour of which will then serve as a unit of measurement. The objection to this is that such coefficients can only be arbitrary and may lead to values which are negative or indefinite. The rate of surplus-value may also emerge as unequal among industries.

In the possible negativity of value the consequences of admitting joint production or heterogeneous labour in the analysis, coincide. With regard to joint production the criticism concerning negative surplus value has now been met on the theoretical level on the basis of a linear programming definition of value.[14] Heterogeneous labour on the other hand has proved far more intractable. Despite many worthwhile attempts the problem still defies theoretical solution of a mathematical type.[15]

The undesirable results flowing from the assumption of heterogeneity of labour and the associated arbitrariness of conversion coefficients may, on the other hand, be avoided if wage-relativities are adopted for the conversion of one type of labour to another. (If, for example, skilled is paid four times more than unskilled labour, one hour of the former will count as four hours of the latter.)

This way out (the one that Marx himself favoured) can be criticised on the grounds that it makes value magnitudes dependent on price relativities and price fluctuations, since the hours of converted labour time necessary to produce a certain commodity will change with every shift of relative wages. Differences in relative wages may also reflect natural scarcities of certain talents or capacities peculiar to certain individuals. In either case, expenditure of labour in production ceases to be the sole determinant of value; exchange appears to stake a claim as an equal partner.

For some, the difficulties associated with heterogeneous labour are so serious as to impose considering the abandonment of the labour theory of value as a basis for Marxist economics. If the matter were to be decided exclusively on the grounds of the impossibility, so far, of constructing a satisfactory mathematical model of heterogeneous labour with fully general conversion coefficients, rejection of the labour theory of value would indeed be inevitable.

If on the other hand one were prepared to accept relative wages as conversion coefficients, as the present author feels more inclined to do, then the two objections against their use ought to be confronted.

With regard to the inherent instability of values that would reflect short-term wage fluctuations, the reply can be proposed that the labour theory of value presupposes the establishment of a long-run equilibrium situation. Wage fluctuations are, therefore, not relevant. On the contrary, in the long run wage differentials can be explained on the basis of the difference in the costs of producing (i.e. of training) various types of labour power. If it is assumed that such costs are relatively stable over long periods of time, wage differentials (appearing now as differences in the value of various types of labour-power) can give a stable basis for the conversion of one type of labour into another.

Alternatively, stability of relative wage rates may be assumed without being explained; a procedure which is not very satisfactory but is not unprecedented either.[16]

Obviously, none of the above can eliminate the element of natural scarcity in the determination of wage relativities. Supply and demand will inevitably play a role then, even in the long run. This is a general difficulty that affects all aspects of the labour theory of value. It has already been discussed and its significance circumscribed, in Chapter 3. Apart from that, the incursion of exchange in the determination of the value unit is not so unmarxist as might appear at first sight. Marx has stressed that the very basis of quantitative measurement in the labour theory of value, the concept of abstract labour (see Chapter 3, page 35) is dependent on the functioning of an exchange economy. On the same principle that the various types of concrete labour, embodied in commodities, are equalised through exchange, the various types of heterogeneous labour can be homogenised through the market.

Provided a reasonable degree of stability prevails in markets a labour value accounting system can be developed, to demonstrate the consistency of free market exchange and with labour exploitation.

CHAPTER 5

Money and growth

The psychology of money-making

It is sometimes argued that Marxist economics disregards the psychological aspect of economic life, treating it as irrelevant, compared to the fact that individuals have to bend to economic necessity, no matter what their feelings might be. This is certainly not correct. Integration of individuals in the system of production relations is a complex process, in which psychology plays an important part. Marxism refuses to reduce all explanations of social events solely or primarily to psychological facts.[1] It does not, on the other hand, fail to register the importance of human psychology as a link in the chain of forces that hold together (or disrupt) a mode of production.

The transition from simple commodity production to capitalism is one area where a change in psychology, in the motivation of a certain class of decision makers, acquires basic importance. The more fundamental material and ownership changes are closely associated with a change in psychology. The simple commodity producer is, presumably, motivated by desires no more complex than those of an ordinary need for goods and services which, under the division of labour, he cannot himself produce. He tries to place his own commodities on the market as a means of acquiring other commodities, for the sake of their use-values. The aim of his economic activity (summarised in the formula $C - M - C$, or Commodity–Money–Commodity) is use-value. Naturally, to acquire command over the commodities of others, the producer has to sell his own commodity first. It might, therefore, be argued that, as far as the economy is concerned, his aim is exchange-value, while the enjoyment of use-value is his private business. Formally this is so, but in substance demand for money, as such, does not assert itself, as long as the dominant preoccupation of producers is the acquisition of use-value in the most direct manner possible.

With the consolidation of exchange as the form typical of economic intercourse, circulation of commodities (defined as a continuous chain of acts of purchase and sale) itself begins to educate the producers to the virtues of an independent demand for money. The intermediation of money has freed the act of exchange from barriers of space and time. The sale $(C - M)$ may be separated from the purchase $(M - C)$. A producer who has sold is under no obligation to simultaneously buy something else on the spot. He may save his money for a purchase in a different market or at a different time. During the interval, he holds on to the money he has earned and can be said to have acquired an independent demand for it. More significantly, the separation of purchase and sale may lead to a situation where the second step (the purchase) precedes the first (the sale). Individuals buy before selling when they buy on credit. In such cases their future activity will not be directed to the acquisition of use-value – this they have already acquired and consumed – but of exchange value to place themselves in a position to discharge their debts. Finally, ownership of a sum of money, not earmarked to specific purchases, is the best security available against the consequences of some future trading failure that might leave one insolvent in the future. Accumulation of a hoard for this purpose is one additional reason for demanding money for its own sake.

In all these various ways circulation automatically promotes money from a mere medium to a final aim of economic activity. The transaction motive and the precautionary motive for holding money as an asset are easily recognisable in the preceding discussion. But the reasons which confirm money as the supreme aim for producers go deeper. Possession of money places the individual in a position of strength towards society. His own productive contribution has received the seal of social approval, in the form of the money paid to him for his goods. He is now able to command the labour of other producers, in whatever form suits him best. Possession of money encapsulates for him a moment of freedom, the tantalising possibility of free choice, which he would like to cling on to, permanently if possible. The capacity of money to place its possessor in a position of this kind gives a solid psychological basis to an independent, separate demand for it.

The character of the psychology involved has very far-reaching consequences for the evolution of the capitalist mode of production. From the point of view of its possessor money has both a qualitative and a quantitative aspect. Qualitatively it opens up to choice a practically infinite number of possible alternatives, because money is convertible to any one of the great multitude of goods available in a reasonably well-stocked market. Even non-readily available goods, existing possibly only in the imagination of the buyer can often be made on order if someone is willing to pay for them.

The qualitative open-endedness of an infinity of choice finds its limitation in the quantitative aspect of money. For the possession of money to open up to the buyer the full range of possibilities available on the market, an amount of it must be at hand, capable of covering the price of the most expensive items extant. Most individuals never lay their hands on sums of this magnitude. Second, the mercurial power over commodities, qualitatively inherent in a sum of money, lasts only so long as the amount has not been spent. After it has been used to purchase something, the fleeting moment of freedom it made possible to the individual vanishes, with the consumer restricted from an infinite horizon of choice to the enjoyment of just one good. To restore the open-endedness of choice a second amount would be needed, a third, a fourth and so on.

The conflict between the qualitative and the quantitative aspect of money could only be resolved by the possession of a virtually infinite stock of money. Only a stock of such dimensions would lead the desire for money to the point of satiety. In the case of other commodities satiety is ordinarily based on the observation that the capacity of enjoyment of the consumer for any one good is finite. A person can eat only so much steak in the meals of the week, he can only sit on one chair at a time, sleep in one bed etc. It is only scarcity which keeps most people's consumption below the level of satiety, not any inherent psychological boundlessness of desire. Demand for money on the other hand cannot be brought under the same rules. It is not directed to anything specific because, through money, individuals are in fact aiming at the totality of goods and services, present and future. The same reasoning, which establishes the possibility of satiety in the case of the individual good, should lead to the conclusion that there can be no satiety for the demand of a continually renewed expanding totality. Moreover, it is very doubtful whether, in the antagonistic conditions of class-divided society, any finite limits can be placed on the need for a feeling of freedom or of command over society that possession of money makes possible.

Possession of a stock of money of infinite dimensions is clearly impossible. Each individual is placed under a budget constraint. The only way of escaping from it is the continuous addition of fresh supplies, preferably larger than the also continuous inevitable outflows from the original stock. The unattainable aim of forming an infinite stock of money is thus transformed to demand for money as an infinite flow; a boundless desire for money making. An infinite sequence of finite sums (an infinity in time) becomes the substitute or the form of satisfying the desire for an infinite stock (a timeless infinity). Marx's remarks on hoarding are relevant here:[2]

The desire after hoarding is in its very nature insatiable. In its qualitative aspect, or formally considered . . . [i.e. disregarding the fact that every individual operates under a budget constraint] money has no bounds to its efficacy, i.e., it is the universal representative of material wealth, because it is directly convertible into any other commodity. But at the same time, every actual sum of money is limited in amount, and, therefore, as a means of purchasing, has only a limited efficacy. This antagonism between the quantitative limits of money and its qualitative boundlessness, continually acts as a spur to the hoarder in his Sisyphus-like labour of accumulating. It is with him as it is with a conqueror who sees in every new country annexed, only a new boundary.

From hoarding to industrial capitalism

In hoarding the effort to accumulate an infinite fund of purchasing power appears in its primitive, ineffectual form. On the other hand accumulation of a hoard of finite dimensions is a necessary accompaniment of the circulation of commodities. It smooths out the flow of goods by bridging the gap between payments and receipts (transactions demand for money). Presence of such gaps implies various temporary stoppages of the circulation process, various leads and lags in the sequence of purchase and sale. During such leads and lags money stays idle in some hands, so that the formation of the first hoards is virtually automatic. Individuals are not slow to infer from this that hoards can both be formed and increased if money is not allowed to return to the stream of circulation, where it originally came from; if a purchase $(M - C)$ is avoided after a sale $(C - M)$ has been effected. Some commodity producers, therefore, take it upon themselves to limit as much as possible their purchases for the sake of accumulating money. They renounce use-value for the sake of exchange value in its independent form; they become, in other words, misers.

Being a miser is to adopt a depriving, unnatural and, in the long run, even possibly self-defeating attitude. The miser is forced to abstain from social life, cut himself off from the network of social relations and may, because of this, even miss a number of opportunities of making profits.

Merchants have shown a better way of accumulating monetary wealth: buying cheap, selling dear and pocketing the difference. Their activity takes the form $M - C - M'$, where profit, $(M' - M) > 0$, can be set aside for the formation of a hoard. Better still, it can be used for expanding business, in order to make still more profit (the demand for an unlimited stock of money being converted to demand for an ever-widening flow).

Pursuing money-making by ordinary trade, however, presents two short-comings, one of them being both theoretical and historical, the second mainly historical. First, it presupposes opportunities of unequal exchange. Although early capitalist merchants have been able to amass vast fortunes from conducting trade, such opportunities are neither very widespread nor very lasting. Second, the scope for conducting trade is restricted by the fact that, historically, it interposes itself between socio-economic formations where production is not mainly but only residually commercial. In the epoch of early trade, goods are not produced mainly for sale, not as commodities, but for direct use. They become commodities only when a residual part of production is offered for exchange. The scale of commercial operations and in consequence the scale of profits is restricted to this residual. Trade cannot penetrate the self-sufficient sector, which predominates quantitatively, particularly in the countryside. By imposing on producers division of labour and thereby disrupting the pattern of self-sufficiency, manufacturing (and agrarian) capitalism manage to make sufficient inroads into traditional production sectors that, eventually, the area of profit-making trade is expanded over the whole of economic life. Only when all types of production are transformed into commodity production is there an adequate basis created for making the pursuit of money, for its own sake, the predominant aim of economic life. In Chapter 4 the source of such money-making was traced back to the exploitation of labour. All that remains to be said here is that extraction of surplus-value through the process of production solves the dilemmas confronting both the miser and the trader. Regarding the first, industrial capitalism shows how money can be thrown back from a hoard into the stream of circulation and yet not only not be lost for ever, but even be recovered with an increment. Regarding the second, it demonstrates how trade can continue to the point of equal exchange, without destroying the basis for money-making. Here again Marx has given one of his striking characterisations of capitalist mentality and mode of operation:[3]

> The simple circulation of commodities – selling in order to buy – is a means of carrying out a purpose unconnected with circulation, namely, the appropriation of use-values, the satisfaction of wants. The circulation of money as capital is, on the contrary, an end in itself, for the expansion of value takes place only within this constantly renewed movement. The circulation of capital has therefore no limits.
>
> As the conscious representative of this movement, the possessor of money becomes a capitalist. His person, or rather his pocket, is the point from which the money starts and to which it returns. The expansion of value, which is the objective basis or mainspring of the circulation $M - C - M$, becomes his subjective aim, and it is only in so far as the appropriation of ever more and more wealth in the abstract becomes the sole motive of his operations, that he functions as a capitalist, that is, as capital personified and endowed with consciousness and a will. Use-values must therefore never be looked upon as the real aim of the capitalist; neither must the profit on any single transaction. The restless never-ending process of profit making alone is what he aims at. This boundless greed after riches, this passionate chase after exchange-value, is common to the capitalist and the miser; but while the miser is merely a capitalist gone mad, the capitalist is a rational miser. The never ending augmentation of exchange value, which the miser strives after, by seeking to save his money from circulation, is attained by the more acute capitalist, by constantly throwing it afresh into circulation.

Repercussions on the production process

Capitalism subjects every sphere of production to the aim of acquisition of exchange value. By so doing it introduces into the historical development of society a sharp break of continuity which divides traditional, non-growing or slowly-growing from fast-growing economies.[4] Logically, the separation corresponds to the different dominant aim that provides the driving motive for economic activity in the two categories of economic systems. In pre-capitalist economies, even where trade had managed to make certain inroads, use-value remained the prevailing aim of economic activity. Needs for use-value being satiable, the ruling-class in pre-capitalist modes of production lacked, after a point, the motivation to push for an expansion of the productive effort beyond all bounds. Of course, it was not merely a question of exchange value. Just as, in capitalism, the emphasis on exchange value, dictated by the relations of production, generates the psychology of greed, of money-grubbing and the productivist ethos of the bourgeoisie, the predominance of use-value in pre-capitalist societies was reinforced by an attitude of aristocratic disdain for material cares – expected to solve themselves at the expense of the actual producers. Sluggishness in economic development permitted the relations of production, and the whole social edifice resting on them, to settle down to a given form and (responding to the conservative instincts of every ruling class) to be reproduced over the ages without much strain. The relatively relaxed character of social reproduction enabled the ruling class sometimes to cultivate its mode of existence to the point of excellence, even of perfection. That is why, in pre-capitalist economies, we observe the simultaneous presence of low levels of productivity together with very high achievements in art, literature (classical Greece), law, administration (Rome). Despite its high degree of perfection, development in such societies, lacking the dynamism of economic growth, remained one-sided, unadventurous and restricted.

With exchange value becoming the central aim of production in capitalism, the characteristics described above, as pertaining to the psychology of money making, spread through the whole of the productive and, by extension, of the total social effort. The infinite demand for money as a stock is translated into a requirement for unlimited production. As such, it is, of course, non-operational, just like the demand for an infinite money hoard. When the latter is transformed into demand for an infinitely expanding flow of finite sums of money, however, it finds an easy counterpart in the capitalist imperative of a continually expanding reproduction process. This correspondence of the stock with the flow approach is in Marxist economics expressed as the identification of the accumulation of capital (accumulation of a stock) with expanded reproduction (a flow concept). It is worthwhile exploring this idea a bit further.

The process of capitalist production has been schematically presented in Chapter 4 as

$$M - C \mathrel{\mathop{-\!\!\!-\!\!\!\!<}} \begin{array}{c} MP \\ LP \end{array} \ \dots \ P \ \dots \ C' - M'$$

Obviously, the capitalist's effort does not end with the achievement of profit 'in one single transaction' (see above); it must be repeated continually. The same schematic presentation, with time subscripts attached to its various constituents, is sufficient for describing the process of simple (i.e. non-expanded) reproduction. Finally, with a small modification, it can also describe the process of expanded reproduction. All that is needed is to split M' into M and $m(= \triangle M)$, (original money capital and surplus value).

Assuming that consumption by capitalists is relatively to total output small enough to be neglected (assumed equal to zero) the circuit of money-capital will then take the following form:

$$\text{First Period:} \qquad M - C \longleftarrow \begin{matrix} MP \\ LP \end{matrix} \dots P \dots C' \longleftarrow \begin{matrix} C \\ c \end{matrix} \dots M' \longleftarrow \begin{matrix} M \\ m \end{matrix}$$

$$\text{Second Period:} \left\{ \begin{array}{l} M - C \longleftarrow \begin{matrix} MP \\ LP \end{matrix} \dots P \dots C' \longleftarrow \begin{matrix} C \\ c \end{matrix} \dots M' \\ \\ \\ m - c \longleftarrow \begin{matrix} mp \\ lp \end{matrix} \dots p \dots c' \dots m' \end{array} \right.$$

where upper-case letters represent the circuit of the original capital and lower-case ones the circuit of surplus value. In the second period total original capital is equal to $M + m$, total labour force is $LP + lp$, total means of production $MP + mp$, so that increased stocks of capital have accumulated everywhere along the path of the circuit. But they have accumulated only by virtue of being parts of a moving whole, moments in the process of expanded reproduction. Accumulation of capital stock is, therefore, dependent on the recurrent increase in the scale of the production process, and vice versa. An unquenchable thirst for exchange value pushes capitalists towards ever-increasing capital accumulation and this sets in motion an ever-expanding process of reproduction. The extraordinary dynamism which exchange value, by replacing use-value as the aim of production, imparts to economic growth in capitalism is thus explained. Growth is, however, conditional on the continuing capitalisation of surplus-value, and ultimately on the expansion of labour exploitation. In capitalist conditions, the lust for exchange value is transformed into a drive for surplus-value.

In addition to providing a dynamic motive, the predominance of exchange value enhances the productive effectiveness of capitalism in various other ways. First, it provides a homogeneous and consistent system of cost-accounting which allows every step in the production process to come under scrutiny, to have its cost compared to the alternative of purchasing the relevant item directly from the market (rather than having it in store or making it in the factory). Historical costs are thus continually revised and tend to be reduced to the level of replacement costs. Given the propensity of capitalist production to lower costs over time, this tendency exercises unflagging pressure on producers to expedite their activities in the shortest possible time, for fear of getting caught before they have fully recovered their original money advances. Second, the re-emergence, at the end of each circuit, of the amount of money originally spent, enables the producer to change the technical structure of production by purchasing labour power and means of production in different proportions or by purchasing altogether different types of labour and equipment. The absorption of new techniques in the production process is thus greatly enhanced. Flexibility in reinvesting one's money earnings may reach the point where money migrates from one industry to another or even starts up an entirely new venture. The profile of technological possibilities, as well as the range of all possible products, is thus continually probed into for new opportunities of profit.

This feverish activity in production imposes on social relations under capitalism strains of an altogether different order than those to be met with in pre-capitalist societies. Commercialisation becomes the enemy of perfection both in the production of goods and services and in the cultivation of higher aspects of life. On the other hand, by constant expansion, by exploring ever new production avenues, capitalism prepares the ground for the development of the individual human being in a free manner, uninhibited by tradition and external coercion. During the initial epoch of capital accumulation, however, expansion and enrichment of the productive basis is achieved at the expense of those contingents of workers increasingly brought under the sway of capitalist exploitation, but sharing only minimally in the material gains achieved under the new mode of production. It was stated earlier that the extraction of surplus value presupposed a supply both of work and of 'waiting' or 'abstention', on the part of the labourers. The capitalist mode of production therefore represents a device whereby the self-ordained deprivations of the miser are forced upon an unwilling working class. The dynamism of the production process in capitalism is purchased at the expense of the stultification and the inhibited life-style of the majority of the population.

The enormous productive potential, creation of which is sparked off and, for a certain period, maintained by the drive for surplus-exchange-value, suffers from an inherent contradiction. It provides the conditions for a multidimensional development of the individual, while at the same time, because of exploitation, it deprives the vast majority of individuals of the possibility of such development. To the extent that capital accumulation, via expanded reproduction, calls forth the higher levels of productivity which reduce, often to the vanishing point, the urgency of man's economic problems, exploitation loses its historical justification. Capitalism can, therefore, be seen as an epoch of transition from modes of production giving rise to societies that allow only limited scope for individuals, to a society of free individual development. In this society, use-value becomes again the aim of production, not, however, in the fixed, frozen form of a pre-packaged way of life, as in primitive or classical society, but endowed with the full versatility made possible by the enormous range of productive potential achieved in the historic capitalist breakthrough. This aspect of the role of capitalism Marx summed up in the following:[5]

> Except as personified capital, the capitalist has no historical value, . . . But, so far as he is personified capital, it is not values in use and the enjoyment of them, but exchange-value and its augmentation, that spur him into action. Fanatically bent on making value expand itself, he ruthlessly forces the human race to produce for production's sake; he thus forces the development of the productive powers of society, and creates those material conditions, which alone can form the real basis of a higher form of society, a society in which the full and free development of each individual forms the ruling principle.

A Keynesian parallel

The grand vision of society led forward from primordial scarcity to a state of affluence through a desert of exploitative deprivation, under the compulsion of money-making, is explicit and central but it is not exclusive to Marx. Keynes expressed himself along similar lines, admittedly in minor writings, the echo of which, however, resounds distinctly through the pages of the *General Theory*.

Starting with satiable and non-satiable needs, the distinction is clearly adopted by Keynes,[6] in the form of that between absolute and relative needs. Absolute needs are those needs which people feel whatever the situation of their fellow human beings; relative needs are those which satisfy the desire for superiority over one's fellows. Keynes accepted only the second class of needs as insatiable, 'for the higher the general level the higher still they are', while he expected satiability to be a feature of the first. This is not quite the distinction between use-value and exchange-value; it is, however, very reminiscent of it, in particular as there is nothing like money to raise one above one's fellows in a market economy.

Keynes himself established no explicit connection between relative needs and the desire for money as such. Indirectly, however, there is a whole multitude of such linkages in his works. He perceived that the possession of money can become an end in itself, leading to an unnatural situation where avarice and usury become socially legitimised activities. From there on the pursuit of growth of one's wealth (expressed by its monetary value) at compound interest is raised to the position of the highest 'virtue'. Economic activity becomes an aim in itself, rebounding into production for the sake of production rather than of consumption, (a characteristic of obvious Keynesian significance).[7]

The love of money as a possession – as distinguished from the love of money as a means to the enjoyments and realities of life . . . is a somewhat disgusting morbidity, one of those semi-criminal, semi-pathological propensities which one hands over with a shudder to the specialists in mental disease.

However, for all its distastefulness, love of money is the essential driving force of accumulation at compound interest. Such accumulation is in the process of solving man's economic problems, thus making room for him to confront his deeper, abiding problem of[8]

how to use his freedom from pressing economic cares, how to occupy his leisure . . . to live wisely and agreeably and well.

Capitalist practices culminate in an outcome beyond capitalism:[9]

The strenuous purposeful money-makers may carry us all along with them into the lap of abundance . . . But beware! The time for all this is not yet . . . Avarice and usury and precaution must be our gods for a little longer still. For only they can lead us out of the tunnel of economic necessity into daylight.

Large-scale production

To Marxist insistence on the importance of capitalist ownership over the means of production for keeping the proletariat in the dependent position of a hired factor of production, it is sometimes objected that the issue of ownership is irrelevant. In production, capital needs labour just as much as labour needs capital. Institutions could be devised whereby labour could hire capital, without any change in the ownership structure or any effect on the allocation of resources, the level of output or even on the distribution of income.

Logic working in a historical vacuum could no doubt consistently produce some such scheme. This kind of logic is not very useful in the analysis of economic systems. Looking at the matter outside its historical context, owners of the means of production could indeed, by the hiring-out method, spare themselves the toil and trouble of organising, and directly exploiting, labour. They could invite the direct producers to become tenants of the means of production and delegate organisation of the production process to them. The owners then could sit back and relax, living off the rents that the working class would pay to them. Whether they were able to maintain their exploitative position for long in this manner is questionable. Absentee landlords find it hard, after some time, to hang on to their property, let alone their incomes. Even if they could, the type of production activity or the output levels that would emerge would have very little relation to production under capitalism. Looking at the matter historically, the only technology available to producers in the early period of capitalism, in the sixteenth and seventeenth centuries, was small-scale artisanal production, or small-scale, low-productivity, peasant farming. Under these conditions, allowing direct producers to hire the means of production from their owners would at most universalise small commodity production, creating a kind of petty-bourgeois capitalism with the incubus of a tithe-drawing aristocracy installed on the backs of producers. It would never lead to anything even remotely similar to capitalism as it actually developed in history.

A system like that, if it could be maintained, would be in strident opposition with the expansionary logic and psychology of money-making. Petty-commodity producers are not accumulators of exchange-value, they are use-value oriented. Under their management, the flow of exchange-value is not likely to expand very much. Capitalists, on the other hand, are not merely exclusive owners of the means of production, they are also money-makers. To achieve the aim of continually expanding reproduction of exchange value (of capital), they have to enlarge and keep on enlarging the scale of their production activities. In the early stages of the capitalist mode of production, when mechanisation had yet to be discovered, the only way of enlarging the size of firms was by drafting in additional contingents of workers. This could not be done by the method of forced labour, which had supplied the few centres of collective work effort (public works, ships) in pre-capitalist modes of production. For very good reasons, both logical and historical, capitalism is normally premised on individual freedom of occupation for all citizens. Under these rules, the only way to form a team of workers under one command is for one master to hire them all (to buy their labour-power). Buying and selling of labour power is thus not merely the market technique of exploitation; it also acts as the mechanism for labour centralisation, operative under capitalist conditions of freedom of work. This is why the hiring relationship between labour and capital is not freely reversible. If capitalism is to be the outcome, capital must hire labour and not vice versa.

One final question might be asked: why is it not possible for owners of the means of production to hire them out to workers individually, while satisfying their urge for accumulation by reinvesting their incomes into more means of production, which they will hire out to more workers and so on? The answer to this question must be that the rate of growth of capital achievable by this method will inevitably be lower than under direct capitalist command of labour. For reasons to be discussed immediately, in the latter case accumulation depends on two factors: reinvestment of surplus-value, and increasing productivity generated by the capitalistic reorganisation of the labour process. In the former case, on the other hand, only one of these two sources of economic growth is still operative: reinvestment of surplus-value. *Ceteris paribus* the resulting growth rate cannot but be proportionately lower.

In the crucial period of the emergence of capitalism in Europe (in the sixteenth to eighteenth centuries), historical conditions were such as to activate all the potentialities inherent in the logic of capitalist relations and the psychology of money-making. The revival of international trade following upon the reopening of the route to the East (Vasco da Gama, 1498), the expansion of the frontiers of trading by the discovery of the New World and its subsequent colonisation, the sudden leap in the demand for goods and services in Europe resulting from the influx of gold and silver from the American mines between 1550 and 1660, all contributed to imposing on the production capacity of late medieval European society a kind of strain that traditional methods could not meet. Exploding demand could not be satisfied by artisanal methods. For the challenge to be met, labour productivity had to increase by leaps and bounds. Capitalism lived up to the challenge by replacing small-scale, artisan methods by large-scale, manufacturing production. The centralising tendencies inherent in money-making received an additional, possibly decisive outside stimulus from the sudden trading euphoria of the centuries of great geographical discoveries. The result was modern capitalism.[10]

Individual and collective labour

For vindicating the claim that capitalist centralisation of labour raises productivity, the starting point is a study of cooperation. A group of workers cooperating under unified command can physically achieve results bound to remain inaccessible to the individual worker, no matter how high the degree of his exertion. Ten men, pulling together, will easily move a weight which ten successive heaves by the same number of isolated individuals will not make budge even an inch. In terms of brute force the group is unquestionably superior to the individual.

Brute force is just one of the requisites of production. The other is skill. Artisanal production in the pre-capitalist era was based almost exclusively on skill. Gathering together under one command, and eventually one roof, a group of more or less equally skilled artisans does not increase the skill, hence the productivity, of any one of them. Some productivity gains may, even so, be achieved as a result of the possibility of supervision. An artisan working domestically (assuming he works on order with materials supplied to him) may slacken off or waste and embezzle materials and tools. Such wastage is not tolerated under the discipline of the capitalist manufacturing workshop. But the basic force of production, the worker's skill, is still not increased thereby.

The first great breakthrough in this area is achieved with the introduction of the division of labour. This division is no longer the phenomenon extensively discussed in Chapter 2, as providing the basis of commodity production and exchange (*division of labour in society*). There each individual producer turns out a finished product, not necessarily in the technical sense, but finished from the economic point of view, i.e. saleable. The product is a complete commodity, belonging to its maker, which other commodity producers will purchase.

The division of labour introduced by capitalism (*division of labour in the workshop*) differs in the sense that each individual worker no longer produces a complete commodity but merely one part – often a very small part – of the finished article. The dramatic increases in productivity achieved by this method have been described so often as to make repetition here superfluous. For the purposes of the present argument the point that needs to be made is the establishment of the superiority of the group over the individual, not simply in the area of strength but in the area of dexterity as well. No artisan, no matter how skilled, can ever hope to outdo, in terms of productivity per head, a group of workers each performing partial operations under a well-coordinated scheme of division of labour. (In terms of artistic perfection of the finished item, individual skill may, of course, continue to reign supreme.)

Using the criterion of the division of labour inside the workshop Marx identified a whole epoch in the development of the capitalist mode of production, the epoch of Manufacture (dated from the middle of the sixteenth to the last third of the eighteenth century). By comparison with the dramatic transformation in the methods of production that occurred immediately after that epoch (in the period of the Industrial Revolution) Manufacturing is a still rather undeveloped stage of capitalism. Even so, a crucially important characteristic of the system has already taken shape. The product is no longer the result of the identifiable efforts of any single individual worker. It is the product of a team. Production methods have become social. The productive power of organisation has arrived to displace for ever the power of the individual.

Science and mechanisation

The next big step in the development of the forces of production is mechanisation. It makes its first massive appearance in Britain in the period of the Industrial Revolution (roughly 1750–1850). Thereafter it becomes so closely identified with capitalism as to virtually totally eclipse, in the common mind, several other, equally important features of capitalist production methods. Yet, for the argument presented here, its derivation from capitalist production relations is considerably more problematic than in the case of division of labour in manufacturing. For the latter, the connection between mass employment, the inherent need of capital to expand, and the organisation of the labouring team along principles of efficiency is straightforward. Capitalism operates both on the demand side, by confronting existing technology with the problem of expanding output, and on the supply side, by increasing productivity through methods (centralisation of labour) naturally emanating from the logic of its economic structure.

With mechanisation, the need of capital to expand is still operative on the demand side. On the supply side, however, the picture is considerably more complicated. *Ex ante* there is nothing obviously capitalistic about the use of machinery in production. Hence the puzzlement of historians over the non-emergence of some kind of mechanisation in societies like that of classical antiquity or of Byzantium, or indeed that of China in the sixteenth century, where scientific and technical knowledge, sufficient to make a start with the invention of machines, were not lacking. Hence, also, the wide variety of influences identified as causes of the Industrial Revolution in Britain, only some of which are directly traceable to the peculiarly capitalistic structure of the economy, while some others (freedom of thought and expression, practical mind) are features common to capitalism and to other social formations. (The Romans were famous for their practical spirit, while freedom of thought and expression, as a privilege, naturally, of the free citizenry, was prevalent in classical Athens and the Ionian part of the Greek world.)

Obviously one might still try to defend the necessity and sufficiency of capitalism for mechanisation by arguing that capitalist relations of production were the indirect cause of the phenomenon; that they worked through various cultural and social mediations, the rise of which were, in turn, caused by capitalist changes in the base of the social structure. This, however, would tend to strain the idea of causality almost to the point of tautology. The line of attack which seems preferable to the present author is to follow Marx in distinguishing two technological epochs in capitalism: the epoch of manufacture (16th to last third of 18th century), characterised by the rise of multiperson establishments applying the division of labour (manufactories); and the epoch of modern industry, characterised by mechanisation, which begins with the Industrial Revolution in Britain. The significance of capitalist relations of production for technological development varies between the two epochs. In the first it is arguable that the institution of buying and selling of labour-power, with its centralist tendencies, explained above, plus the very fact that labour is treated as a commodity, are instrumental in paving the way to the kind of technology which emerges. Capitalist relations of production take an identifiable lead over the forces of production.

In the second epoch this, more or less clear-cut, precedence of production relations recedes. More basic social forces, concerned with the development of human thinking and with the confrontation of man and nature, achieve a breakthrough and acquire a momentum, to some extent, of their own. Originally these new forces are successfully harnessed into capitalist institutions and carry capitalist production to its well-known unprecedented heights. They also, however, maintain their own independent momentum, which gives them the capacity to grow beyond capitalist limitations, eventually posing a challenge to the whole mode of production in which they were originally conceived.

Leaving aside, for the moment, the potential of mechanised production to transcend capitalism, mechanisation can at first be seen to strengthen the capitalist characteristics already apparent in the economy in the manufacturing epoch. The main areas of such progress are the following:

(a) The scale of the firm is vastly expanded. Numbers of workers employed in the typical enterprise pass from the few score to the hundreds and for the larger ones to the thousands. Concentration of labour on that scale has continued to our days, the really big corporations counting their labour force by the hundred thousand. Both output and the absolute amount of surplus value produced have, correspondingly, increased (although, in the case of surplus value, probably not in proportion to the labour force).

(b) Mechanical installations give to capitalist ownership an impressive and effective material form. Exclusion from ownership of means of production can now be literally enforced by locking-out from the factory. This cannot but reinforce the authority of capital over labour.

(c) Mechanisation breaks the last hold of skill on production. Deskilling had already begun with the division of labour, as a result of the fragmentation of the process of making a complete object into a sequence of simple repetitive operations. Even so some parts of the work still required the special attention of particularly skilled operatives who, because of that, found themselves in a position of some strength *vis-à-vis* their employers.

Mechanical production substitutes for the skill of the hand the efficiency of a mechanical instrument. The worker no longer makes anything, either as a whole or as a part of an object. He is reduced to the role of a minder of a machine. Of course, even in machine-minding there can be a hierarchy of necessary qualifications. There is no reason to expect a car-driver, or indeed an aeroplane pilot, to be any less skilled than a coachman. But, on the whole, mechanisation has inevitably reduced the level of conscious participation of the labourer in the production effort. Machinery harnesses to the tasks of industry natural forces, the introduction or the mere supervision of which cannot be left to practical experience acquired on the job. Science has to take charge of production; in fact science becomes one of the major, perhaps increasingly *the* major force of production. But, for social class reasons, science is not accessible to the typical ordinary worker. It rests in the hands of a social elite which is not necessarily an integral part of the capitalist class, but is more often than not in close and conscious alliance with the bourgeoisie. Mechanisation consolidates capitalist control not only over the instruments of production but also over the knowledge of production. In the eyes of the worker productivity and technical progress appear now as attributes no longer of labour but of capital.

The development of capitalist technology through division of labour and mechanisation can thus be described as a process of progressive separation of manual from intellectual labour. While the latter grows in importance, the former becomes increasingly trivialised. The culminating point of the process is reached when the worker loses control of the movement of his own limbs. This takes two forms. Either the worker is forced to adapt the rhythm of his work to the speed of machinery (e.g. in conveyor belt work). Or he is made the subject of a time and motion study, after which he is trained to execute a specific sequence of movements that minimises the time of work per unit, even when no machinery is involved (e.g. in shovelling, loading and unloading weights, digging etc). Increase of efficiency under time and motion studies might be mistaken for an increase in skill, but in fact it is not. The worker does not acquire any conscious ability; he is trained to perform as an automaton. The skill remains with the industrial engineer who analyses a task and maps out the most efficient way of going about it.

(d) Originally mechanisation was introduced in response to increasing demand which production based on the division of labour could no longer cope with. At that stage it was not yet antagonistic to labour in terms of employment. A point, however, was reached when, because of fluctuations which the capitalist system itself induces, demand was no longer sufficient to keep constantly fully employed the whole of the capacity that had been installed. From that point (placed by Marx in 1825[11]) onwards, the capacity of machinery to reduce costs by replacing a certain part of the labour force came to be increasingly appreciated. Capitalist expansion ceased to be synonymous with an increase in employment; it could proceed even with diminishing total numbers of men at work. By breaking the link between expansion of output and employment of labour, by moreover making redundancy an ever-present possibility, mechanisation increased the degree of independence of capital from labour. The capacity of management to impose discipline at work and resist the wage claims of employed workers was correspondingly enhanced.

Modern automation brings the tendencies of mechanisation to their logical conclusion. From being trivialised and permanently insecure in the epoch of mechanical industry, labour sees in automation the beginnings of its total elimination as a factor of production. (See below, Chapter 10.)

(e) The overwhelmingly higher productivity of capitalist production methods, compared to the small-scale production that preceded it, has been attributed to its capacity to release the power of social (i.e. team versus individual) labour. For the manufacturing epoch, the validity of the claim is obvious. Under division of labour a team of cooperating performers of various specialised tasks constitutes an organic whole which is manifestly a social entity replacing individual workers. With mechanisation, on the other hand, numbers of workers attached to a certain firm increase dramatically – and in that sense production becomes even more social – but the new entity that makes all the difference is no longer an organic group of people but an organic collection of machines. Moreover, trivialisation of the role of labour makes it appear as if the social (human) element of production is actually receding before the purely mechanical one. Can it still be maintained that mechanisation constitutes one step further on the way to the greater socialisation of the production process?

Leaving the counter-socialising effect of machinery on the productive contribution of labour for separate examination (in Chapter 10), the answer must be in the affirmative. It rests on the observation that, through mechanisation, scientific thinking, which for long ages had remained a virtually exclusively theoretical preoccupation, becomes an immediate production force. An important and very interactive section of society, its specialists in higher thinking, from being cut off from material production, become directly involved in it. This is certainly a new and important step in the direction of increased socialisation but, on its own, it may appear not totally convincing. It could be argued that the drafting into the army of production of one new social group (the scientists and technologists) is more than compensated by the trivialisation of the role of a much more numerous one (the manual labourers). For its social character to be properly assessed, the process of mechanisation has to be considered as a whole.

The basic production unit of mechanical industry is the factory. Compared to the workshop of the manufacturing period the factory is manifestly much more of a social organisation. Not only does it bring together scientific and manual labour, it also recruits for the task the abilities and talents of a whole army of administrators, linking up with the rest of the economy by developing specialist buyer, marketing and finance departments. Even the regulatory and eventually the planning agencies of the state acquire a role in it. While the manufacturing workshops operate as separated specialist organs of an economic body, it would be no exaggeration to say that the factory is a microcosm of the whole economy. Factories represent the beginnings of an integrated production process, in which the whole of society takes part.

By unleashing the potential of direct social cooperation in production, capitalism achieves an unprecedented development of the forces of production. This development is partly a direct consequence of the influence of capitalist social relations (division of labour, accumulation of productive wealth), partly a consequence of other forces for which capitalism provides, for a certain period, a favourable environment (science and mechanical invention).

This increasing industrial might goes side by side with an increasing capacity of capital to dominate labour, hence with an increasing potential for exploitation (as long as organised labour does not enter into the scene). Given that exploitation is a specific effect of the mode of appropriation of the product (despite the social character of work, the product passes into the hands of a class of private owners), any reaction against it must ultimately challenge capitalist ownership in the name of society as a whole. Thus the final outcome of the colossal development of the forces of production under capitalism is the need and the demand for socialism.

PART II

THE FETTERING OF THE FORCES OF PRODUCTION

CHAPTER 6

Capitalism and crisis

It is now time to consider how capitalist relations of production, from forms of development of the productive forces turn into their fetters. To this effect, the concept of 'fettering' will be examined first, followed by an explanation of the mechanisms which bring it about. For the original development of these ideas the writings of Marx, Engels and Lenin will be surveyed briefly, in the spirit also of whatever shifts of emphasis have been registered in Marxist writing subsequently to the works of the original contributors. It is useful at this point to recall the distinction, attempted in the preface of this book, between an old and a new Marxist model. Of the laws of motion of capitalism, which make up the old model, two – the law of increasing severity of cyclical crises and the law of the falling tendency of the rate of profit – have clear 'fettering' implications. Their discussion in this and the following two chapters pave the way to the consideration of the transition from the old to the new model in Chapter 9. In parallel, the definition of fettering itself undergoes, as argued below, an evolution from classical to neo-Marxist notions.

The concept of fettering

What happens when capitalist relations of production start acting as fetters on the development of the forces of production? In what specific way is the development of productive forces arrested? For Marx, as early as 1848, before he had yet plunged into the exhaustive study of Political Economy from which *Capital* was to emerge in 1867, the answer had become obvious. Fettering had begun to operate in contemporary capitalism, manifesting itself mainly in the phenomenon of the economic crisis. In the *Communist Manifesto* (1848) he wrote:[1]

Modern bourgeois society with its relations of production, of exchange and property, . . . is like the sorcerer, who is no longer able to control the powers of the nether world whom he has called up by his spells. . . . It is enough to mention the commercial crises that by their periodical return put on its trial, each time more threateningly, the existence of the entire bourgeois society. In these crises a great part not only of the existing products, but also of the previously created productive forces are periodically destroyed. In these crises there breaks out an epidemic that, in all earlier epochs, would have seemed an absurdity – the epidemic of over-production. The productive forces at the disposal of society no longer tend to further the development of the conditions of bourgeois property; on the contrary, they have become too powerful for these conditions, by which they are fettered, and so soon as they overcome these fetters, they bring disorder into the whole of bourgeois society, endanger the existence of bourgeois property . . . And how does the bourgeoisie get over these crises? On the one hand by enforced destruction of a mass of productive forces; on the other by the conquest of new markets, and by the more thorough exploitation of the old ones. That is to say, by paving the way for more extensive and more destructive crises, and by diminishing the means whereby crises are prevented.

Marx even went so far as to set a precise date for the beginning of the 'fettering' process in Britain; this was 1825, the year of the first general crisis of a capitalist economy of which classical economists took any notice. His comments, brief but crucial for an understanding of his views, justify one more quotation:[2]

One can say that up to the year 1825 – the period of the first general crisis – the demands of consumption in general increased more rapidly than production, and the development of machinery was a necessary consequence of the needs of the market. Since 1825, the invention and application of machinery has been simply the result of the war between workers and employers. But this is only true of England.

The main points in Marx's description can be classified as symptoms and as elements of the mechanism of fettering. Among the symptoms are:

(a) The periodic breakdown of the process of capital accumulation. No permanent stoppage is envisaged: the engine of capitalist growth does not cease to function, it begins to malfunction.
(b) Periodic breakdowns are not mere stoppages; they involve a temporary regression, leading to partial physical destruction of output and of accumulated productive equipment.
(c) Unemployment of labour, surprisingly perhaps, is not included by Marx among the fettering symptoms. He does notice the correlation between fluctuations in output and in employment but explains unemployment mainly by mechanisation, which is an indication of progress in productivity not a symptom of fettering. In addition he treats the unemployed reserve

army as a condition of the development of productive forces in a capitalist regime. It would be inconsistent of him simultaneously to present it as evidence of the fettering of the forces of production. Whether and in what way unemployment can be integrated with the destruction of capital in the wider context of fettering is discussed in Chapter 10 below.

In the texts quoted Marx has given, in addition to symptoms, also the main rudiments of an explanation of the mechanics for the onset and maintenance of fettering. He perceives fettering as an immediate consequence of productivity catching up and overtaking the growth of markets. In what sense does the growth of markets prove to be insufficient? On the basis of some other of his texts[3] the answer must be: demand is insufficient to absorb full capacity output at prices yielding to capitalists their expected rate of profit. (It is useful to recall at this point that exchange value rather than satisfaction of needs is the aim of capitalist production.) Since profits are but another form of surplus value derived from the exploitation of labour, it follows that, in moments of crisis, the whole system, based on extraction and realisation of surplus-value (on capitalist production *and* trade) breaks down as an engine of growth. From being a source of capital accumulation, exploitative acquisition of exchange value turns into an obstacle to further enrichment.

With all their destructiveness, crises for Marx are recurrent transient events. The downturn is succeeded by recovery, which leads the capitalist economy to higher levels of productive performance. Marx considers the 'conquest of new markets' as essential to the mechanism of recovery. These, however, by expanding the area of the economy over which the laws of motion of capitalism hold sway, do not resolve any problem permanently; they simply lay the basis for future, more extensive crises.

The economic crisis was not the only manifestation of fettering singled out by Marx. In *Capital*, Vol III he made the point that the collision between the development of productive forces and production relations appears in economic crises only 'partly'.[4] Nevertheless, his most persistent references to specific examples of fettering are drawn from the incidents of the trade cycle. After his death Engels, his lifelong friend and collaborator, in the Preface which he contributed to the first English edition of *Capital*, advanced one step further in the development of the concept. Writing in the midst of what economic historians have named 'The Great Depression' (1874–1895?) and indeed in a year described as one of the worst years for unemployment, Engels ventured on a new idea which, in the work of certain Keynesians half a century later, became known as the theory of secular stagnation. This is how Engels expressed its nucleus:[5]

> While the productive power increases in a geometric, the extension of markets proceeds in an arithmetic ratio. The decennial cycle of stagnation, prosperity, over-production and crisis, ever recurrent from 1825 to 1867, seems indeed to have run its course; but only to land us in the slough of despond of a permanent and chronic

depression. The sighed-for period of prosperity will not come; as often as we seem to perceive its heralding symptoms, so often do they vanish into air. Meanwhile, each succeeding winter brings up afresh the great question 'what to do with the unemployed'; but while the number of unemployed keeps swelling from year to year, there is nobody to answer that question; and we can almost calculate the moment when the unemployed losing patience will take their own fate into their own hands.

Engels does not differ basically from Marx in his diagnosis; he simply de-emphasises the periodic nature of the setbacks and launches the idea of a possibly long-lasting period of recession. He also relates unemployment to the stagnation of production forces much more unambiguously than Marx. As to the mechanism generating these negative effects he restates Marx's thesis, surprisingly clothed in Malthusian garb: productive power increases in a geometric ratio, markets in an arithmetic ratio.

Engels's market Malthusianism, combined with his stagnationist thesis, can be seen as the bridge to Lenin's more uncompromising formulation of the exhaustion of the room for capitalist expansion.[6] Lenin's position is by no means absolute; he is aware that even his contemporary, early-twentieth century, capitalism is still capable of spurts of considerable growth. At the same time he bases an important part of his analysis on the assumption that the areas of economic space (defined as a combination of outlets for products and sources of raw materials) globally available to capitalism become fixed, incapable of further increase. He combines this point with a new emphasis on conflicts among the capitalist ruling classes in the various industrial nations. His perception is of a world parcelled out among the leading capitalist countries, with each one of them protecting its share not mainly by economic but by political means (colonial administration, tariff barriers, trade prefer-ences etc.).

Distribution of space among the chief imperialist powers, a result of past history and the current balance of military power among them, is by no means correlated with their respective potential for enlarging productive capacities. In this respect some capitalist economies grow much faster than others. Fast growth of production potential in the context of a small or non-existent colonial empire (the case of Imperial Germany) constitutes a special case of fettering.[7] To escape from being asphyxiated for lack of outlets, imperialistic capitalism in the more dynamic nations seeks to redress the distribution of control over markets and resources by violent means, culmina-ting in wars, of which the First World War was, for Lenin, the paradigmatic example. The burden of armaments, together with the recurrent destruction from military operations, is thus added by him as a consequence of fettering to the relatively milder ravages of the trade cycle.

Against this line of thinking one obstacle, discussed at greater length later in this chapter, must be mentioned. It is an accepted characteristic of capitalist expansion that, as the economy grows, each one of its (expanding) sectors has the potential to provide a market for the increasing output of other sectors. In such a case why should capitalism display such crucial need of conquering extraneous markets rather than depend on its endogenously generated market potential?

The objection has particular force in the case of Lenin who, at the beginning of his political career, made extensive use of the argument about the self-generating character of capitalist markets in his polemics against the *Populists* (a Russian progressive party, which preceded the Social-democrats (Lenin's party), and preached a kind of agrarian, rather than industry-based, socialism).

An attempt at explaining the need for extraneous markets as 'shock-absorbers' for capitalist growth is made in the last section of the chapter. That explanation is based essentially on the idea of desynchronisation, of a time-lag, between the increase of productive potential and the emergence of the corresponding endogenous markets.

Another explanation, more in line with Lenin's theory of imperialism, might be sought along the lines of the law of the falling rate of profit. Capitalists in advanced industrial countries, for which the law predicts declining levels of profitability, could find internal outlets for their products if they were prepared to accept lower profit-rates. Rather than accept that, however, they opt for the conquest of fresh markets, where superprofits are still possible. Probably consistent with the development of Lenin's theorising, this explanation has to stand or fall with the 'law' of the falling rate of profit itself (discussed in Chapter 8).

The development of the idea of fettering from Marx to Engels and on to Lenin displays a certain regularity. It rests on the diminishing availability of market outlets, ascertained by each successive author to have become more restrictive. Increasingly heavier bouts of destruction of productive wealth succeed one another as a result, acquiring, in the case of World Wars, a viciousness out of all proportion to the degree of economic imbalance at the origin of the conflict. But the contribution of these successive authors is not limited to registering a continuously deteriorating trend. Each of them contributes some new explanatory element. To the idea of periodic destructiveness Engels adds secular stagnation. Lenin, using the concept of uneven development, takes up the stagnationist thesis but adds to it an original twist of his own. Under the influence of Hobson,[8] with Britain as his typical case, he argues that the early capitalist nations have reached a point in the accumulation of funds such that their ruling classes can earn a substantial part of their income by simply investing abroad, transforming themselves into international rentiers. The international dimension of exploitation begins to win, over the internal one. Productive investment in the metropolitan country suffers a decline, symptoms of de-industrialisation make their appearance, employment at home is restructured towards luxury and leisure industries, while an increasing proportion of productive work is shoved onto the shoulders of cheaply available immigrant workers. Capitalist financial maturity is thus accompanied by the onset of an economic *parasitism* which, in advanced countries, infects not only the capitalist but to some extent also the working class. The latter, or at least a section of it (described by Lenin as 'the aristocracy of labour') finds itself under reduced pressure to sell its labour power on conditions as unfavourable as those prevailing earlier. The ruling class, confident in its overseas earnings, allows the workers to improve their position by the devices of a welfare state and even takes the lead in creating such a state. To their somewhat improved position workers respond by reducing their offer of labour. Avoidance of employment, under these conditions, gives to a section of the working class (of revolving, probably, membership) the character of a lumpen-leisure-class, indirectly subsidised by worldwide over-exploitation.

Economic crises with their violently destructive effects, wars, and the long-drawn-out attrition of productive strength resulting from stagnation or parasitism, constitute the main instances of fettering adduced in evidence by classical Marxist authors. The causes of such disasters are sought in the obsolescence of capitalist relations of production, which constitute the highest form of exploitative class relations in history, up to and including the emergence of capitalism. From a broader point of view, therefore, the whole structuring of the work process dictated by class division, the manner of rewarding, the very structure of class privilege are called into question when capitalist society begins to exercise, after a point, dysfunctional effects on productivity. The idea of the surplus product is crucial in this part of the argument. In early societies based on exploitative relations of production, surplus product is barely sufficient for sustaining the material existence of a minority ruling class, who exempt themselves from productive labour. This class creates for itself and its retainers conditions of life which allow some of them to concentrate on the general tasks of social organisation – politics, law, administration, the letters, science. It is not suggested that ruling classes do any of these things in a purely public-spirited manner or with optimal efficiency; rather the opposite. They are self-serving, terribly wasteful managers of public affairs. But, in conditions of heavy scarcity, this heavy-handed, wasteful, ruthless centralisation of surplus in the hands of a few leads, in some cases, to socially beneficial developments in the very long run. Classical Greeks were slave-owners who laid down the foundations of many a science that lightens human toil, preparing the ground for socialism even today. But, side by side with one Euclid, thousands of useless exploiters prospered on the sweat and agony of the slave population.

Having brought the effects of class-privilege to their climax, the capitalist class continues to defend it long after its economic rationale has vanished. The margin of surplus, over and above the needs of subsistence achievable by modern industry is sufficient to allow a significant degree of leisure, hence of opportunity for the higher forms of social activity, to the totality, rather than to a minority of the population. Capitalist distribution, by preventing the self-development of the exploited working population, blocks the creativity of the vast majority. In conditions of a fair degree of material affluence an uncreative population, alienated from the work it is doing, is less productive than one liberated from the trammels of class-exploitation. From being a means of centralising a small amount of surplus, exploitation has become a fetter on the process of achieving even more surplus. This is the wider, but also rather unspecified, way in which relations of production fetter the forces of production in the view of classical Marxist authors.[9]

It is at this point that the classical Marxist comes closest to the modern Marxist formulation of the idea of fettering. For some important modern Marxist writers,[10] the idea that capitalist relations of production present increasingly unsurmountable obstacles to pure productivity is no longer tenable. Capitalism manages to overcome its crises and resume the process of growth to ever-rising levels of output. Its problem is not in failing to increase the amount of surplus, but in using an increased surplus in a manner destructive of the lives of people and of values of social intercourse.

The neo-Marxist formulation of the fettering concept differs from the classical one in adopting a criterion from outside rather than from inside the capitalist mode of production in order to evaluate its results. While stoppages of the production mechanism, destruction of productive wealth and of the product, de-industrialisation, unemployment and parasitism can all (with the possible exception of parasitism) be seen as negative developments even by bourgeois standards, the critique of the way surplus is used presupposes the positing of an alternative (socialist) regime that would use surplus differently. For this reason, further discussion of this line of argument is postponed until the third part of the book, where the emergence of socialist preconditions inside the context of capitalist institutions is discussed. The rest of this chapter will concentrate on the cyclical crises of the capitalist economy.

The cyclical character of the process of capitalist growth, pioneered by Marx, has by now become an integral part of economic theory. His inference, on the other hand, that it constitutes a manifestation of the fettering of the forces of production is by no means universally accepted. The destruction of wealth which often accompanies recessions is put down as one of the inevitable costs of progress, having even been graced by Schumpeter with the euphemism of 'creative destruction'.[11] Keynes, on the other hand, viewing the stagnationist proclivities of modern capitalism with genuine concern, comes much closer to Marx's spirit. He perceives that a mechanism conducive to capital accumulation at earlier times (saving based on wealth and income inequality) becomes, under the changed conditions of mature capitalism, an obstacle to further accumulation and growth:[12]

> Thus our argument leads towards the conclusion that in contemporary conditions the growth of wealth, so far from being dependent on the abstinence of the rich, as is commonly supposed, is more likely to be impeded by it.

The similarity between Marx and Keynes on this issue goes further. In their analysis of the mechanism which brings about recession and crisis in capitalism, the two coincide in attributing the problem to a lack of markets (Marx), a shortfall of effective demand (Keynes). Lack of effective demand is nothing else but a lack of markets, with the difference that Keynes places the emphasis on markets internally generated, by the process of capital accumulation itself (investment is a market for capital goods which, via the multiplier effect, creates a further market for consumer goods). Classical Marxist authors, on the other hand, convey the strong impression that they are thinking of markets additional to those self-generated by capital, in its circular movement $(M - C - M' - C' \ldots)$. They seem to be thinking of new markets, the result of, say, geographical discoveries, conquest of new colonies, elimination of pre-capitalist producers, abolition of tariff barriers, of self-sufficient closed economies etc.

Such outside stimuli, or external shocks, were important also for Keynes,[13] but he always internalised them, treating them as opportunities for additional investment, a sufficient amount of which would stabilise the capitalist market. Marx was conscious of the capacity of capital itself to create the market for its own expansion. The way in which he attempted to deal with this 'Keynesian' point is the first that must be cleared up in an exposition of his theory of crisis.

Simple and extended reproduction

Marx began his analysis by setting up a static two-sector (or two-department, to use his expression) model of the economy. The first department produces means of production (or, in more modern language, capital goods), the second means of consumption (wage and luxury goods). Exchange takes place between the two. Under totally static conditions (zero investment, no technical change, no change in tastes, zero population increase) there exists some structure of output consisting of consumer and capital goods in the right proportions which, in every period, reproduces exactly the original state of the economy, while the market between the two sectors remains permanently in equilibrium. Marx demonstrated this case, which he described as that of simple reproduction, by an arithmetical example; modern reconstructions of his doctrine proceed algebraically. The structure of industry is described, in a very elementary manner, in labour theory of value terms, under the assumption that all means of production and, naturally, all labour power are completely used up in a one-period production process, with their value, but not their physical forms, reappearing in the final product. This means that durable production goods (plant and equipment) are not represented in Marx's basic schema, a limitation of which he was not unaware.[14]

Using C, V and S with their usual meaning (constant capital, variable capital and surplus value), W to represent the value of total output, and subscripts 1 and 2 to indicate the relevant departments, Marx's model of simple reproduction can be written as a system of two simultaneous equations:

$$C_1 + V_1 + S_1 = W_1$$
$$C_2 + V_2 + S_2 = W_2 \qquad (1)$$

Exchange between the two departments takes the following form. Department 1 supplies with constant capital goods the needs of both departments. For supply to equal demand the following relationship must hold:

$$C_1 + C_2 = C_1 + V_1 + S_1 = W_1 \qquad (2)$$

Department 2 supplies consumer goods to both itself and Department 1. Again for equilibrium the following relationship must be satisfied:

$$V_1 + V_2 + S_1 + S_2 = C_2 + V_2 + S_2 = W_2 \qquad (3)$$

Using either (2) or (3) (and assuming, obviously, either that each department consists of one firm only, with Firm/Department 2 paying labourers and capitalist *in natura* from its own product, or, slightly more realistically, that intra-departmental equilibrium is automatically guaranteed) the equilibrium condition

$$C_2 = V_1 + S_1 \qquad (4)$$

is derived. Therefore, at first sight, static capitalism (capitalism in a state of simple reproduction) can generate its own markets, maintaining itself in perpetual equilibrium.

Simple reproduction serves Marx as a mere starting point, a first step towards the analysis of a growing capitalistic economy, much more consistent with his general approach. He describes the relevant model as one of *extended reproduction*.

An attempt may be made to formulate an equilibrium condition for extended reproduction similar to the one above, applying to the case of simple reproduction. Using the additional symbols $\triangle C$, $\triangle V$ and F to indicate the increase in constant capital, the increase in variable capital and consumption by capitalists (keeping in mind that F may also increase from period to period to the extent that the economy grows, so that in a more explicit statement it would have to be written as $F = f + \triangle f$) the two equations of (1) may be rewritten as:

$$W_1 = C_1 + V_1 + S_1 = C_1 + V_1 + \overbrace{\triangle C_1 + \triangle V_1 + F_1}^{S_1}$$
$$W_2 = C_2 + V_2 + S_2 = C_2 + V_2 + \underbrace{\triangle C_2 + \triangle V_2 + F_2}_{S_2} \qquad (5)$$

The modification refers to the surplus value terms of equations (1) and signifies that capitalists no longer consume the total amount of surplus value accruing to them, but use one part of it to invest in additional means of production ($\triangle C$), and another to pay for the additional labour force they have to employ ($\triangle V$). The equilibrium condition between the two sectors can now be expressed as:

$$C_1 + \triangle C_1 + C_2 + \triangle C_2 = C_1 + V_1 + \triangle C_1 + \triangle V_1 + F_1 \qquad (6)$$

or

$$V_1 + \triangle V_1 + V_2 + \triangle V_2 + F_1 + F_2 = C_2 + V_2 + \triangle C_2 + \triangle V_2 + F_2 \quad (7)$$

Either (6) or (7) will yield

$$C_2 + \triangle C_2 = V_1 + \triangle V_1 + F_1 \qquad (8)$$

as the interdepartmental equilibrium condition. Equation (8) contains, as one should expect, the equilibrium condition of simple reproduction ($C_2 = V_1 + f_1$) together with some additional terms, needed for maintaining balance in a growing rather than a stationary economy. Simple and expanded reproduction appear thus to obey very similar rules. But the similarity is only formal and somewhat deceptive. For a stationary economy to maintain its balance, once it has somehow hit upon the behavioural pattern required, is really rudimentary – everybody has simply to go on behaving as in the past. For a growing economy this is no longer so. Maintaining equilibrium may require adaptive, changing behaviour while mere repetitiveness may have destabilising rather than stabilising effects.

Marx's demonstration of equilibrium in expanded reproduction makes use of a mixture of adaptive and repetitive behavioural patterns, which achieves its effect only at the cost of very considerable artificiality. On the repetitive side of behaviour Marx assumed that technology (presumably also tastes) remained unchanging, while investing capitalists always placed their money in the department of their origin, never crossing inter-departmental lines. Those of Department 1 were in addition expected always to accumulate (save and invest) one half of their surplus value. Adaptive behaviour was reserved for capitalists in Department 2, who were supposed to vary their needs for constant capital in such a way as always to take up the slack in the supply of capital goods flowing in their direction from Department 1.

To convey the flavour of Marx's difficulties at this point, a part of his arithmetical tables is reproduced (his numbers represent value aggregates). He begins with his table for simple reproduction (a stationary economy). The relationship between the two departments stands as follows:

$$
\begin{aligned}
&1.\quad 4000c + 1000v + 1000s = 6000W\\
&2.\quad 2000c + 500v + 500s = 3000W
\end{aligned}
\tag{9}
$$

The equilibrium condition of simple reproduction can be verified ($1000v_1 + 1000s_1 = 2000c_2$). No capital accumulation takes place. To get accumulation started, Marx proceeds in three stages. First he modifies, arbitrarily, the organic composition of capital in Department 2. (Readers may think of the organic composition (the ratio c/v) as a capital/labour ratio expressed in value terms. The main importance of the concept in the present discussion is in indicating the proportions in which a certain investible amount of capital will be divided up between additions to plant and equipment ($\triangle C$) and additions to the labour force ($\triangle V$). The concept of organic composition is further discussed in Chapter 8, which may be used for reference here). Marx's modification, a mere arithmetic manipulation, reflecting no theoretical principles, leads from

$$
2000c + 500v + 500s = 3000 \left(\frac{c}{v} = 4\right)
$$

to

$$
1500c + 750v + 750s = 3000 \left(\frac{c}{v} = 2\right)
\tag{10}
$$

Then, faithful to his hypothesis that capitalists in Department 1 accumulate always one-half of the surplus earned by them, Marx rewrites the equation relating to Department 1 as:

$$
4000c + 1000v + 500_s^i + 500_s^c = 6000
\tag{11}
$$

where 500_s^i is the amount of surplus value intended for investment in Department 1, while 500_s^c is earmarked for consumption by capitalists. He remarks that the amount of constant capital used up in Department 2 ($1500c$ in equation (10)) is just sufficient for exchanging against $1000v_1 + 500_{s1}^c$ (in equation (11)). So far, no accumulaiton has taken place. The condition $1500c_2 = 1000_{v1} + 500_{s1}^c$ is nothing but the condition for simple reproduction. The use of the 500_s^i, intended to be accumulated, remains to be settled.

In the second stage of his iteration, Marx transfers the 500_{s1}^i to the capital account of Department 1. According to the organic composition (capital/output ratio) prevailing there, of the 500_{s1}^{i}, 400 will be invested in the form of additional constant capital (leading to $4400c$), while 100 will be spent on hiring additional labour (leading to $1100v$). The 400_{c1}^{i} (the additional constant capital) is supplied by Department 1 itself; hence 400_{c1}^{i} never appears in the interdepartmental balance. The 100_{v1}^{i} corresponding to variable capital will, however, have to be exchanged against consumer goods produced in Department 2. This leads to the third stage of the iteration.

At that stage Department 2 accumulates just enough of its surplus value to take up the slack in the supply of means of production from Department 1. It devotes 100_{s2}^{i} for exchanging against the 100_{v1}^{i}, which makes its constant capital rise to 1600_{c2}. Given its organic composition of $c/v = 2$ it must invest another 50_{s2} in hiring additional labour to work with the 100_{c2} Therefore its total accumulation of surplus-value is 150_{s2}, split into 100_{c2} and 50_{v2}. This 150_{s2}^{i} is subtracted from the 750 units of surplus value, intended for capitalist consumption in Department 2, so that consumable surplus value there falls to 600. Correspondingly, constant and variable capital increase to $1600c$ ($1500c + 100_{c}^{i}$) and $800v$ ($750v + 50v$). The final picture which emerges, taking both departments together, is the following:

$$\text{Department 1: } 4400c + 1100v + 500_{s}^{c} = 6000W$$
$$\text{Department 2: } 1600c + 800v + 600_{s}^{c} = 3000W \tag{12}$$

What has taken place between equations (10) and (11), and equations (12) is a reallocation of value, earned in the previous period, from the sectors to which it was imputed, when first earned, to those sectors of the economy which must expand, in certain given proportions, for output to grow.

The stage has now been set for a self-sustaining process of expanded reproduction (of economic growth, in the language of modern theory). This growth is obvious on the right-hand side of equations (13), where value of output increases by 600 units, for Department 1 and 200 for Department 2.

$$\text{Department 1: } 4400c + 1100v + 1100s = 6600W$$
$$\text{Department 2: } 1600c + 800v + 800s = 3200W \tag{13}$$

On the left-hand side of the equations, however, things are less straightforward. Certain items, present in equations (12) vanish altogether on the way to equations (13). These are the 500_{s}^{c} and 600_{s}^{c} which represent capitalist consumption, consisting of luxury items, that are used up and drop out of the productive cycle without leaving any trace.

The amounts of value representing constant capital, on the other hand (4400 units in Department 1 and 1600 units in Department 2), do not vanish, but reappear in equations (13), having exactly the same size as in equation

(12). The significance of this entry is that equipment, machinery, raw materials, all physical objects that make up constant capital, used up during production have been reproduced so as to be available again for the next round. Their value, however, has not increased. According to the labour theory of value only living labour, represented by variable capital, has the capacity not merely to replace but also to expand its value, to create new, additional, value, in the production process. The mere replacement of the value of labour power is represented by the entry of $1100v$ in Department 1 and $800v$ in Department 2. New value, finally, is represented by the surplus-value entries, $1100s$ in Department 1 and $800s$ in Department 2, assuming a rate of surplus-value (rate of exploitation) of 100 per cent. Surplus-value newly produced minus capitalist consumption in the previous period, ($1100s - 500\substack{c \\ s}$ for Department 1 and $800s - 600\substack{c \\ s}$ for Department 2) give the net increase of the value of total output (600 in 1 and 200 in 2) from one period to the next. Total output in value terms has increased by 10 per cent in Department 1 and 6.6 per cent in Department 2. Items in equation (13) are then reclassified by the same rules as those applied to transform equation (9) into equation (12) and, after one more production period, a system along the lines of equation (13) is presented as follows:

$$\text{Department 1:} \quad 4840c + 1210v + 1210s = 7260W$$
$$\text{Department 2:} \quad 1760c + 800v + 800s = 3520W \tag{14}$$

Between equations (13) and (14) total output in each department, as well as all other terms of the two equations, has increased by 10 per cent. Repetition of the method yields a similar 10 per cent expansion ever after. Thus Marx's scheme of expanded reproduction displays a very strong tendency to converge onto an equilibrium growth path. Disequilibrium behaviour, with the two departments growing at different rates, lasts only one period. After that, both sectors and the economy as a whole grow together at a common rate of 10 per cent for ever. This result is not dependent on the actual numbers Marx has chosen for his arithmetical example. Morishima has shown that it follows from the very peculiar assumptions made by Marx about investment.[15] He has also shown that with some different, more natural, assumptions about the investment behaviour, Marx's scheme produces either explosive oscillations around the growth path, or monotonic divergence from it. Morishima argues, very convincingly, that the artificiality of Marx's own solution derives from his lack of mathematical equipment adequate for dealing with a problem, the full complexity of which was only realised in the twentieth century.

Reproduction schemes, circuits of capital and Say's Law

One cannot know how various modern attempts at modifying his extended reproduction schemes, to make them generate endogenous cycles, would have been received by Marx. Given the critical bent of his mind and his commitment to a continuing effort towards developing theory, he would probably have welcomed such attempts, subject to their remaining consistent with what he felt to be the crucial institutional characteristic of capitalism. From this point of view it must be stressed that he viewed his reproduction models as demonstrating not the tendency of the capitalist economy towards equilibrium but rather the problematic nature of the conditions necessary for it ever to attain such equilibrium. In fact, only an overview of the whole economy, at a very high level of abstraction, permits one to ascertain the structure of output and of exchanges guaranteeing equilibrium at full employment. The horizon of individual capitalists is far too narrow to allow them even to perceive the problem. A central authority, the state, might perceive it but, under the institutional set-up of private capitalism, it would not have the means of enforcing the right proportions on economic activity. Only planning at the level of the whole of society can safeguard the proportionate development of the economy, but capitalism is not a planned economy. To the question raised at the end of the first section of this chapter (whether capitalism can generate its own markets internally rather than always seek new markets outside the boundaries of any existing capitalist economy) Marx's answer – on the strength of his reproduction schemes – was, yes, but the process is unstable. In fact, on his analysis, what has to be explained is not why the capitalist economy goes off the rails once in a while. Lack of central coordination is sufficient for that. The problem is, rather, how it manages to stay on the rails for as long as it does, in between economic crises. Although Marx did not formulate it explicitly, this question is strongly suggested by his emphasis on the persistently anarchic character of capitalist reproduction.

An answer to this question is needed and one will be proposed immediately below. First, however, the diametrically opposite argument must be confronted, that in his more rigorous attempts Marx, despite his acknowledged opposition to it, had in the end to succumb to Say's Law (the theorem that, under free market conditions, supply creates its own demand, so that no state of general overproduction, in essence no depression or crisis, is ever possible). The mainstay of this argument is provided by the formal structure of the reproduction schemes.[16] By contrast, the second of the main schematisations of the capitalist production process to be found in *Capital*, the three circuits of capital, typified by the circuit of money capital

$$M - C \overset{MP}{\underset{LP}{\diagdown}} \ldots P \ldots C' - M'$$

has been treated as a basis for the formal rejection of Say's Law.[17] The present author will maintain that, although the formal structure of the reproduction schemes is not, perhaps, very helpful, Marx clearly intended these as well to serve the rejection of Say's Law. Evidence to that effect will be presented after the argument based on the circuits of capital is examined first.

The most characteristic symptom of a crisis is a generalised collapse of trading in 'all' (which, in practice, means 'very many among the more important') markets in the economy. The classical economists tried to deny the possibility of a generalised paralysis of this kind. They freely admitted that disproportions may occur in certain markets, because of mistaken past decisions, but these would be balanced by compensating opposite disproportions in some other markets, so that overall a uniform state, particularly a state of excess supply, of universal overproduction, could never occur.

Marx replied that commodity producers, having sold their commodities, are by no means constrained automatically to buy other commodities immediately. Supply and demand are identical only in the case of barter exchange. When money intervenes to effect the circulation of commodities, as in the $C - M - C$ circuit, a supplier who has acquired money may choose not to complete the cycle. $C - M$ and $M - C$ are two separate steps, the second of which may be postponed. In such case, other producers (the ones who have not yet sold) will see their markets vanish; they will be unable to make further purchases themselves and a chain reaction will be set off. Under certain conditions it is quite possible that all traders, pressed by their expiring obligations, will, as a matter of priority, try to acquire money rather than commodities. They will all try to be sellers, not buyers. A state of universal excess supply or universal overproduction of all specific commodities is thus quite possible, despite Say's Law, if excess demand prevails for the general commodity, money.

Marx formalised his argument that crises are always possible in a monetised economy by pointing to the fragility of the $C - M - C$ chain. But he did not particularly press this point. The $C - M - C$ exchange is typical of simple commodity production, in which disproportions are not likely to build up to the point of disrupting markets. Simple commodity production contains the possibility of crisis, but it takes capitalist commodity production and circulation, formalised in the

$$M - C \underset{MP}{\overset{LP}{\longrightarrow}} \ldots P \ldots C' - M'$$

circuit to make crises inevitable. Marx even set out a whole morphology of economic crises, classified according to the part of the circuit which they affect:[18]

Capital describes its circuit normally only so long as its various phases pass uninterruptedly into one another. If capital stops short in its first phase $M - C$, money capital assumes the rigid form of a hoard; if it stops in the phase of production, the means of production lie without functioning on the one side, while labour power remains unemployed on the other; and if capital is stopped short in its last phase $C' - M'$, piles of unsold commodities accumulate and clog the flow of circulation.

Subsequent research on the circuits, as a theory of crisis, has concentrated on discovering more points, additional to the three mentioned by Marx. These points can be increased further if exchanges not simply among the subsections of the bourgeoisie, but also between capitalists and workers as consumers, are also taken into account. (Part of C' appears in the form of means of subsistence; it must therefore be purchased by working class households.) More rigorous formulations, introducing time explicitly as a mathematical variable crucial for the proper articulation of the various moments of the circuits, have also been recently proposed.[19]

Multiplying the points at which the circuit may break down or bringing to the surface the conditions on time-delays (time for which capital can be allowed to stay immobile in any one form) necessary for maintaining the circuit in regular operation do not, in themselves, demonstrate the necessity of crises. They show that the circuit of capital is more precarious than the simple exchange chain $C - M - C$, not that the circuit is doomed to break down periodically at certain intervals. To achieve a demonstration of this last point a special theory of destabilising capitalist behaviour is needed. A suggestion towards such a theory is made in the following section. It is interesting, however, to notice that the first step towards this suggestion can be attempted with the help of a careful reading of Marx's comments on the reproduction schemes (sometimes considered as an implicit, though unwilling, endorsement of Say's Law).

Adherence to Say's Law may be given one of two interpretations: (a) that markets actually tend to absorb any overall excess supply of goods, quickly and efficiently, so that it makes practical sense to talk about an identity of supply and demand (Say's Identity).[20] (b) Alternatively, Say's Law may be interpreted as a condition of equilibrium, not necessarily achieved by actual markets (Say's equation) but true only for some specific values of the variables. Given Marx's emphasis on the unplanned, anarchic character of capitalist production and exchange, any suggestion that he may have endorsed Say's Identity is simply ridiculous. On the other hand, the reproduction schemes do appear to subscribe to some version of Say's equation.

Yet the appearance is deceptive. For Marx the equilibrium of the capitalist economy, even in the context of the reproduction schemes (simple reproduction included), is not merely a matter of a current exchange in the right proportions between the two departments (e.g. $C_2 = S_1 + V_1$, as in the case of simple reproduction). The exchange condition does not stand isolated; it relies on appropriate saving and investment behaviour which determines the actual (not necessarily equilibrium) exchange proportions, without being determined by them.

In the process of capitalist reproduction (both simple and extended) Marx observes the occurrence both of leakages from the circular flow of income as well as of injections into it. Some capitalists have to sell without buying; they are those who must form a hoard either for replacing in the future capital assets that become worn out and fully depreciated, or for net investment. Other capitalists must buy without selling; they are those who have to currently make replacement or net investment purchases, by spending their previously accumulated hoards. The first group (the As, as Marx calls them[21]) obviously generate leakages of purchasing power; the second (the Bs) make injections. Only if the amounts hoarded by the As are just balanced by the amounts injected by the Bs (or if saving, as defined here, is equal to depreciation plus net investment) does the balance between the two Departments obtain. The balance of supply and demand ($c_2 = v_1 + s_1$ in simple reproduction, or $c_2 + \triangle c_2 = v_1 + \triangle v_1 + f_1$ in extended reproduction) which might be seen as an instance of Say's Law, is thus purely derivative of the prior equalisation of saving and investment – a thoroughly Keynesian condition. Marx does not indeed use the terms 'saving' and 'investment' but, in the context, the correspondence is unmistakable. Talking about the leakages of purchasing power from circulation, he writes:[22]

> Money is withdrawn from circulation and stored up as a hoard by selling commodities without subsequent buying. If this operation is therefore conceived as a general process, it seems inexplicable where the buyers are to come from, since in that process everybody would want to sell in order to hoard, and none would want to buy. And it must be conceived generally, since every individual capital must be in the process of accumulation.

This dilemma he resolves further on in what has by now become the classic Keynesian fashion:[23]

> But inasmuch as only one-sided exchanges are made, a number of mere purchases on the one hand, a number of mere sales on the other – and we have seen that the normal exchange of the annual product on the basis of capitalism necessitates such one-sided metamorphoses – the balance can be maintained only on the assumption that in amount the value of the one-sided purchases and that of the one-sided sales tally.

Marx proceeded to investigate the consequences of inequality between these two aggregates (saving and investment). In cases where saving exceeded investment, an overproduction crisis, resulting from a shortfall of aggregate demand, would follow. In the opposite case of investment exceeding saving, the present author would maintain that Marx, implicitly assuming a state of full employment, had discerned the rudiments of an inflationary gap analysis. The relevant passage, which comments on the implications of excessive aggregate demand, is as follows:[24]

> True, the same labour can . . . turn out a greater product through increasing productivity, extension or intensity, and the deficit could thus be covered in that case. But such a change would not take place without a shifting of capital and labour from one line of production of [Department] I to another, and every such shift would call forth momentary disturbances. Furthermore (in so far as extension and intensification of labour would mount) [Department I] would have for exchange more of its own value for less of II's value. Hence there would be a depreciation of the product of I.

Far from resting on an implicit acceptance of Say's Law, Marx's reproduction schemes constitute an advanced anticipation of Keynes's basic theorem about saving and investment. The comparison could be pursued further, but enough has been said to discount suggestions that there may be substantive dependence on Say's Law in Marx's reproduction schemes. Returning now to the question raised at the beginning of this section, if absence of any central coordinating authority in capitalism makes it impossible for the correct macro-economic proportions (either of exchanges between the two departments or of aggregate saving and investment) to be established otherwise except by chance, how is even that degree of order which prevails in practice possible in the capitalist economy? Why does it not collapse in perpetual chaos? Alternatively, why is it that the crises, which punctuate its career, display very broadly a regular periodic pattern, rather than being totally random?

The answer to this question is that capitalist development relies on various shock-absorbers which even out its inherent anomalies. But it is also part of the nature of the system to stretch the tolerance of its shock absorbers to the breaking point. Whenever they do break down they take some time to mend; hence the periodic recurrence of the boom and slump episodes of the trade cycle. With the expansion of the capitalist economy, however, shock absorbers become increasingly less effective. The capacity of the capitalist system to renovate and extend them dwindles. As a result, difficulties of reproduction increase to the point where capitalist institutions turn into fetters of the production forces, impeding their further growth.

The term 'shock-absorbers' does not occur in Marx but the idea, implicit in his analysis, develops through various stages. Initially Marx observes that for accumulation to proceed on his assumptions (i.e. with Department 1 accumulating 50 per cent of its surplus value) the condition of simple reproduction ($c_2 = v_1 + s_1$) has first to be violated. Department 1 is now reinvesting in itself one half of the surplus value which it was previously spending on purchases of means of consumption from Department 2 (see equation (11) on page 137 above and the comments there). Given this discrepancy, Department 2 has to readjust the structure of its spending, so as to take up any supplies that Department 1 has to offer in order to acquire the means (the wage-goods) for its own expansion. Therefore Department 2 is cast in the role of shock absorber at the front line: shock absorber no. 1.

It is, however, a theoretical shock absorber only. Marx is fully aware of the fact. Not for a moment does he entertain the illusion of the ideal proportions being in any way maintained. Rather he continuously experiments with figures which reflect various imbalances, leading to overproduction or shortages in the economy. When these arise he mobilises what can be described as shock absorber no. 2: real life outlets (or inlets) for goods, which take up the slack of the malfunctioning system. This way of proceeding may give the impression of an exercise in theoretical 'ad-hocery', but it is not that at all. Marx is groping towards a general disequilibrium system (which he was unable to formalise mathematically), and explains its relative stability by reference either to external balancing factors or to its internal flexibility. An instance of the former is foreign trade:[25]

> Foreign trade could help out in either case: in the first [shortages] in order to convert commodities [of Department] I held in the form of money into articles of consumption, and in the second case [overproduction] to dispose of the commodity surplus. But since foreign trade does not merely replace certain elements (also with regard to value), it only transfers the contradiction to a wider sphere and gives them greater latitude.

The last, somewhat cryptic, sentence of the quotation indicates Marx's awareness of the exhaustible character of the shock absorbers. His idea about the role of foreign trade can be generalised. Writing in an era of virtual British monopoly of capitalist production, Marx viewed foreign trade essentially as an exchange between a developed capitalist economy and a group of non-developed, or even totally non-capitalistic nations. Their economies could easily be dominated by the capitalist centre and saddled with certain (in the wider sense) costs of capitalist economic growth, that might otherwise threaten to overwhelm the metropolitan economy. In such countries new markets could be opened up, for large-scale capitalist industry, to the detriment of local pre-capitalist producers; the classic example is the elimination of Indian handloom weavers under the impact of competition from British mechanically produced textiles. A part of the expanding supply of British textiles, which might have led to overproduction and unemployment in Britain, was thus offloaded onto India, so that, in this particular episode, the benefit of capitalist expansion remained with the metropolitan country while one of the costs was shouldered by an underdeveloped, peripheral, nation.

The general tenor of these remarks is that capitalist expansion can continue more or less unimpeded (despite the inevitable disproportions which its unplanned character generates), as long as a non-capitalist environment exists to function as a shock-absorber. As capitalism expands, however, it either totally destroys pre-capitalist economies or it changes them according to its own image. In either case the shock-absorber zones become reduced, so that, eventually, the capitalist economy has to bear the full brunt of its inherent difficulties alone.[26] Fettering begins at some point along that course.

CHAPTER 7

Growth, acceleration and credit

The previous chapter surveyed the Keynesian-type mechanism of leakages and injections which underpin Marx's reproduction schemes and hinted at the consequences of a loss of balance between them. It also outlined the idea of shock absorbers that tend to stabilise the capitalist economy, despite the anarchic character of its operation and development. These same ideas will be considered again in the present chapter from a slightly different point of view: that of the interplay among the various specialised sections of capital and among the strata of the bourgeoisie which represent capital by owning it. (For the idea of people representing social relations incorporated, 'reified', in objects the reader might wish to refer back to the section on commodity fetishism in Chapter 2.) An explanation of the periodicity of the economic cycle will be attempted along these lines.

The structure of the capitalist class

The economic type of the individual capitalist assumed so far combines in one person three main functions: money-owner, industrialist and merchant. Logically these functions can be separated and assumed by different persons. Historically some such separation of roles precedes the capitalist era. Money-owners (originally usurious money-lenders, later money-capitalists) and merchants practised their trade long before the dawn of modern times. Capitalism inherited them from previous epochs and drafted them into the service of its own characteristic creation, the industrial capitalist. In addition to their functions of direct employers, members of that category developed also subsidiary banking or commercial capacities.

Cutting across this threefold division of the capitalist class there runs an implicit two-fold classification into money-capitalists (or rentiers) and entrepreneurs (industrial or commercial).[1] Entrepreneurs are then subdivided by Marx further into production managers and pure speculators. It will be

147

argued below that this last distinction is particularly useful for analysing behaviour which sparks off economic crises.

Underlying the money-capitalist/entrepreneur division, Marx perceived the distinction between capital functioning as a social privilege and capital as an organising principle of production. For an individual capitalist to represent capital in its former capacity no active behaviour was required, merely a passive assertion of ownership rights. Representation of the productive aspect of capital, on the other hand, did involve effort, both actively to enforce exploitation on workers and to supply the leadership and coordination indispensable to any collective undertaking, under any social system. Marx therefore accepted that an element of productive labour is not absent from the functions of the active capitalist, nor an element of wages from his profits.[2] It follows that this aspect of the role of capitalist can be delegated to a hired employee, a professional manager, who will undertake the coordinating and supervisory functions not for profit but for a salary (thus spreading an aura of respectability over the whole phenomenon of capitalist profit, which may be presented as just a special kind of wage). Marx's own formulation of these points, being particularly felicitous, is well worth quoting:[3]

> [To] represent functioning capital is not a sinecure, like representing interest-bearing capital. On the basis of capitalist production, the capitalist directs the process of production and circulation. Exploiting labour entails exertion, whether he exploits it himself or has it exploited by someone else on his behalf, therefore, his profit of enterprise appears to him as distinct from interest, as independent of the ownership of capital, but rather as a result of his function as a non-proprietor – a *labourer* . . . so that the labour of exploiting and the exploited labour both appear identical as labour . . . The social form of capital falls to interest. The economic function of capital falls to profit of enterprise, but abstracted from the specific capitalist character of this function.

The separation of the capitalist class into active and non-active capitalists constitutes the starting point for the development of the credit system. Non-active capitalists can enjoy the social privilege of capital ownership only if they lend their money-capital to active capitalists. Active capitalists will then use the loaned funds to extract surplus value from labour, which they share with the lenders by paying them interest. This creates the basis for a certain antagonism between active and passive capitalists, who have to compete for a given total amount of surplus value. With the development of the capitalist mode of production the ranks of passive capitalists become more numerous as a result of both voluntary and involuntary enlistment of new recruits. There exist capitalist rentiers-by-choice and capitalist rentiers-by-necessity. The former are the product of increasing prosperity. Formation of large fortunes enables an increasing number of scions (and daughters) of big bourgeois families to live on their inheritances, or, at least, to retire from business earlier than they would if they had to start accumulating from zero.

Leisure, being a normal good, becomes more desirable at higher levels of income.

Rentiers-by-necessity are sociologically a more interesting case. They also emerge as the product of the development of the capitalistic economy; structural changes are, however, necessary in it before they start making their impact felt. It is a feature of the capitalist mode of production – one which in Marx's day existed mainly in his predictions but has been amply vindicated since by events – that, in the process of expansion, capitalism changes from a system based on small firms to one based on large firms. The consequences of this are twofold: first, the minimum amount of capital required for setting up an independent business keeps on increasing. Smallish sums of accumulated money capital cease to be sufficient for establishing their owner as an independent businessman. He can only participate in the distribution of surplus value by lending out his money at interest, or by joining forces with others in a company. This leads to the second consequence of large-scale enterprise. Given the centralised structure of command in the capitalist firm, the number of top management posts does not grow in proportion to the size of the firm. Only one or two among the shareholders of a company can be managing directors. Hence again the number of inactive capitalists, rentiers-by-necessity, is bound to increase.

Many small capitals, each one of them incapable of independent action, can be joined together to form a critical mass sufficient for the launching of new independent business ventures. The initiative for this cooperation may come from the individual owners themselves, as in the case of company formation. Alternatively, institutions gradually develop which specialise in collecting funds from various sources and making them available, in one lump sum, to business entrepreneurs. Banks are the most obvious case in point. They will obviously not limit themselves to small depositors. Big capitalists will also need their services, not only as borrowers but also as depositors of money-capital sums they happen to be keeping idle at the moment. Small independent sums plus temporarily idle fractions of larger capitals are the main sources of capitalist bank deposits. However, given a banking system, depositors need no longer be limited to capitalists. All kinds of people acquire the habit of saving with the banks, the working-class included. To quote Marx:[4]

> The depositors consist of the industrial capitalists and merchants and also of workers (through savings-banks) – as well as ground-rent recipients and other unproductive classes.

This generalisation of the habit of saving to the level of the whole of society brings about further mutations in the functions of the archetypal capitalist. While originally he combines in his person the role of both saver (out of his own profits) and investor, the rise of the credit system frees him, in whole or at least in part, from the burden of saving. On the other hand, the development of professional management lifts from his shoulders the burden of day-to-day supervision of production or trade. Relieved from these duties, the capitalist remains a pure speculative entrepreneur, free to specialise in the pursuit of profitable financial combinations. He does not even have to carry the risk of personal financial loss. He is playing with other people's money. Marx comments that:[5]

> Equally sordid becomes the phrase relating the origin of capital to savings, for what [the capitalist] demands is that *others* should save for him.

and describes capitalism at that stage as:[6] 'private production without the control of private property.'

In disassociating entrepreneurship from accumulation through saving, in substituting in place of saving the credit system, in perceiving the entrepreneur as subject to no own-property risk, Marx has been followed step-by-step by Schumpeter. For the latter, however, the entrepreneur is essentially a creative individual who leads society forward in the process of innovation. For Marx innovative activity is subordinate to financial speculation:[7]

> [There] appears swindling and a general promotion of swindling by recourse to frenzied ventures with new methods of production, new investments of capital, new adventures, all for the sake of securing a shred of extra profit which is independent of the general average and rises above it.

Entrepreneurs, investment and acceleration

The aim of capitalist production is the continuous expansion of exchange value, accumulated in the form of capital, by each particular capitalist. The appetite for exchange value, in its independent money form, has been seen above (Chapter 5), to be insatiable. It never ceases prodding capitalists on to further accumulation and expansion. At the same time, exchange value becomes an end in itself. It is not pursued for the sake of the use-value of the goods it can buy, but for the sake of the additional exchange value (surplus value) it can call forth. That is why the circuit, where the end is always the beginning, gives such an incisive characterisation of the capitalist economic process. The means for increasing exchange-value is the extraction of surplus-value in the production process. It follows that, for the appropriation of surplus exchange-value to continue to grow, production must also cease-lessly expand. The insatiable, self-contained character of the aim of capitalist production (the appropriation of surplus exchange-value as an end in itself) becomes transferred to the means by which the aim is pursued: the production process. Capitalism becomes a system of production for the sake of production. This is one of the most important corollaries of the labour theory of value.

Marx's capitalists are assumed to operate this system under a peculiar type of deficiency of perception. Having discovered, or stumbled upon the fact, that the way to make money bear more money is to spend it productively, they concentrate their efforts on the (from a long historical perspective new-found) method of industrial expansion, piling up capacity and increasing output while they happily assume that sufficient demand will always be available at the end to redeem any ventures. Their spirit of enterprise is evidently strengthened by the fact that the credit system enables them to risk other people's money rather than their own. This does not imply that capitalist entrepreneurs are either indifferent with regard to the outcome of their efforts or criminally irresponsible. They naturally wish their businesses to succeed. But they act in a less inhibited, less circumspect manner than if they were at each and every step of the way taking a life-or-death risk with their personal property.

The assumption of a deficiency in perception as an explanatory device for economic behaviour may seem unusual, but it is by no means unique to Marxist economics. Neoclassical competitive general equilibrium analysis is premissed on agents who are blindly led by profit to positions that make all (extra-normal) profit zero. Also in Keynes the psychology attributed to entrepreneurs bears some resemblance to the surfeit of speculatory optimism under which they labour in Marx. In the presence of uncertainty about demand, investment decisions depend on instinct and faith:[8]

> If human nature felt no temptation to take a chance, no satisfaction (profit apart) in constructing a factory, a railway, a mine or a farm, there might not be much investment merely as a result of cold calculation.

Or, as Keynes put it in the *General Theory*, in a turn of phrase that has become famous:[9]

> Most, probably, of our decisions to do something positive, the full consequences of which will be drawn out over many days to come, can only be taken as a result of animal spirits – of a spontaneous urge to action rather than inaction, and not as the outcome of a weighted average of quantitative benefits multiplied by quantitative probabilities.

Both the Keynesian and the Marxian entrepreneur take action in disregard, to some extent, of the possibility of failure. But important differences between the two cases do remain. Keynes, when appealing to the creative urges of human nature in general, de-emphasises the importance of the profit motive. Marx depends on a type of psychology which is socially, not naturally, conditioned: the compulsive urge of money-making in the context of capitalist production relations. Keynes's entrepreneurs believe that luck will not let them down. Marx's businessmen believe that the well-tried exploitative methods of capitalism will not let them down. What for Keynes are animal instincts are, for Marx, social instincts.

Animal instincts, social instincts, insatiable urge towards surplus-value, reinforced and cushioned by the relaxation of the disciplines of risking one's own property, are all very good for explaining the expansiveness, the investment aggressiveness of entrepreneurs. They are less suited to explain why entrepreneurs should ever hold back from capital accumulation through production, precipitating a crisis. If their irresistible force of industrial expansion came up against some irremovable obstacle, a damaging crash would indeed follow. As stated at the beginning of Chapter 6, Marx, and those of his main followers reviewed there, located that obstacle in the exhaustion of available market outlets for an ever-increasing flow of products. The question which Marx, despite his insight into the mechanism of leakages and injections (discussed in the previous chapter) did not confront as emphatically as modern macro-economic theory sensitivities would require, was the following: how can markets ever become exhausted while productive investment continues, since the investment process itself constitutes an expanding market?

It emerges from various parts of his writings that, whether he had grasped the full significance of this aspect of investment or not, Marx was by no means unaware of its existence. His analysis of machinery, in chapter 15 of *Capital*, Vol. I, is there, among other things, to testify clearly to this effect. Although he does not refer explicitly to demand, supply and markets, he describes a chain of events, sparked off by the mechanisation of certain productive sectors, which could easily be reinterpreted in terms of any modern multiplier-accelerator model capable of dealing also with technical change. This is a relatively neglected aspect of Marx, and it is therefore worth shedding some more light on it, even at the expense of a rather lengthy quotation:[10]

A radical change in the mode of production in one sphere of industry involves a similar change in other spheres. This happens at first in such branches of industry as are connected together by being separate phases of a process, and yet are isolated by the social division of labour, in such a way, that lack of them produces an independent commodity. Thus, spinning by machinery made weaving by machinery a necessity, and both together made the mechanical and chemical revolution that took place in bleaching, printing and dyeing, imperative. So too, on the other hand, the revolution in cotton-spinning called forth the invention of the gin, for separating the seeds from the cotton fibre; it was only by means of this invention, that the production of cotton became possible on the enormous scale at present required. But more especially, the revolution in the modes of production of industry and agriculture made necessary a revolution in the general conditions of the social process of production, i.e. the means of communication and transport . . . The means of communication and transport handed down from the manufacturing period soon became unbearable trammels on Modern Industry, with its feverish haste of production, its enormous extent, its constant flinging of capital and labour from one sphere of production into another, and its newly created connexions with the markets of the whole world. Hence, apart from the radical changes introduced in the construction of sailing vessels, the means of communication and transport became gradually adapted to the modes of production of mechanical industry, by the creation of a system of river steamers, railways, ocean steamers and telegraphs. But the huge masses of iron that had now to be forged, to be welded, to be cut, to be bored, to be shaped, demanded, on their part, cyclopean machines for the construction of which the methods of the manufacturing period were inadequate.

If production sectors are as mutually supportive and mutually stimulating as Marx describes them: if, moreover, entrepreneurs, under the spell of surplus-value, are always opening up further areas to capitalist investment, what is there to stop markets growing? After Keynes, the answer which has become almost traditional is that, on the assumption of unflagging investment, the only thing that can put a brake on economic growth is the constraint of full employment or full capacity utilisation.

In the Marxist context, economic prosperity is consistent with the virtually permanent presence of an unemployed reserve army. The dimensions of this 'army' are fluctuating, depending on the nature of technical progress and the extent of investment activity (the rate of capital accumulation). However, if, under the coincidence of exceptional circumstances, unemployment ever goes down to zero, the capitalist process of expanded reproduction begins to malfunction. There are two main reasons for this.

(a) Unemployment exercises a restraining influence on wage demands (helping to keep the price of labour power close to its value) and a disciplining influence on labour at the place of work. Some unemployment is, therefore, one useful way, and, in the last resort, perhaps the only way, of maintaining control over the working class.

(b) Unemployment provides a pool from which additional contingents of labour can be drawn quickly whenever the sudden appearance of profitable opportunities dictate either an urgent redeployment of the balance of activity among the various sectors of production, or an acceleration of the rhythm of work, or both. The establishment by Marx of the existence of a linkage between unemployment and acceleration, rather than growth at a constant rate, is again not very often stressed and must be supported textually:[11]

[A] surplus labouring population is . . . a condition of existence of the capitalist mode of production. It forms a disposable industrial reserve army, that belongs to capital quite as absolutely as if the latter had bred it at its own cost . . . With accumulation, and the development of the productiveness of labour that accompanies it, the power of sudden expansion of capital grows also; it grows not merely because the elasticity of the capital already functioning increases, not merely because the absolute wealth of society expands, of which capital only forms an elastic part, not merely because credit, under every special stimulus, at once places an unusual part of this wealth at the disposal of production in the form of additional capital; it grows, also because the technical conditions of production themselves – machinery, means of transport, etc – now admit of the rapidest transformation of masses of surplus-product into old branches of production, whose market suddenly expands, or into newly formed branches, such as railways, etc, the need for which grows out of the development of the old ones. In all such cases, there must be the possibility of throwing great masses of men suddenly on the decisive points without injury to the scale of production in other spheres. Overpopulation supplies these masses. The course characteristic of modern industry, viz., a decennial cycle (interrupted by smaller oscillations), of periods of average activity, production at high pressure, crisis and stagnation, the greater or less absorption, and the re-formation of the industrial reserve army or surplus-population.

The interest of this lengthy quotation is not only in the light it throws on the function of the unemployed in capitalism. It also lies in the emphasis on acceleration of production (understood as speeding-up in existing sectors with the old ones retaining undiminished activity) as a source of enrichment and an outlet for entrepreneurial initiative. Marx's great success in explaining the presence of surplus value under normal general equilibrium conditions tends sometimes to overshadow the fact that the great moments of capitalist enrichment, as well as of technological breakthrough (development of the forces of production), occur in states of disequilibrium rather than equilibrium. Profit-making in capitalism always rests partly on equal, partly on unequal exchange. One form of unequal exchange takes place when substantial disequilibrium occurs. Theoretical analysis must correspondingly proceed in two steps. Distinguish, first, a settled core of old-established industries, capable of equilibrium growth, on the pattern of the reproduction schemes and, second, superimpose on it economic activity typical of entrepreneurs, who rush after every important opportunity of extra-normal profit, without heeding the constraints imposed by the requirements of proportionate development. As long as internal or external margins (shock-absorbers) exist to bear the brunt of disproportionate acceleration, the system operates relatively smoothly and is very effective in developing the forces of production.

Acceleration, however, pushes the economic mechanism to its limits. At these points various things may go wrong. Costs, in particular wage costs, may explode, eating into profits in such a way that they disappoint entrepreneurial expectations. Additional wage incomes certainly call forth additional demand, representing an expansion of certain markets. It cannot, therefore, be maintained, in this case, that the direct cause of the stoppage of capitalist expansion is a market barrier. However, the decline in profitability discourages further entrepreneurial activity. Investment capital is held back and/or is withdrawn from production. As soon as such retrenchment begins, investment no longer provides a market for expanding output. Simultaneously demand from wage income drops, since deceleration of activity increases unemployment. The restriction of markets is derived from the prior decline of profitability but, once it sets in, it becomes an obstacle in its own right to further capital accumulation.

It is true that an organised, well-planned capitalism ought to find it possible to accept the reduction in the rate of exploitation, not on grounds of generosity but simply because a crisis brought about by an 'investment strike' would cost much more in terms of profit forgone than an organised retreat to a position of lower profits. This sort of restraint, however, fits ill with the impulsive, essentially opportunistic, character of entrepreneurial activity. It has never been seriously tried and probably would not succeed even if it were.

Acceleration of production, stimulated by persistent entrepreneurial pressure, need not lead to an explosion of costs that terminates the boom. Marx's perceptive remarks in the last quotation above show that the production mechanism in a capitalist economy displays elasticities which may allow production to expand without raising unit costs. To illustrate this idea an extreme example will be proposed. Assume that all costs are direct or indirect wage costs, that supply of effort from a given number of workers is perfectly elastic at a given wage-rate, and that it responds to changes in the degree of capitalistic pressure. It is then perfectly possible for capital to increase output without raising unit costs (the rate of exploitation would, obviously, rise). Assume also that both consumption and investment spending by capitalists has reached an absolute maximum, a ceiling above which it cannot possibly rise, even though profits increase.

These are all unnatural assumptions, to be understood as limiting cases of tendencies to such behaviour. Under them it is possible for output to go on increasing without a corresponding increase in spending, hence in incomes, hence in effective demand. Why should output be increased in such cases? Because, despite the saturation of the internal market, there may be foreign markets still capable of absorbing output. Indeed, new sudden opportunities may arise in these markets, stimulating the production of output for which no home demand is possible.

Acceleration would, in this case, have proceeded without additional investment, hence without creating its own demand via a multiplier process. It would nevertheless remain possible by virtue of a foreign market acting as a shock absorber. However, there is no reason to expect its absorbing capacity to be endless. When it is saturated, then producers (who, as a result of the anarchy of production are in no position to foresee this event) find themselves with unsaleable stocks that they have to get rid of at home or abroad. To save transport costs they prefer to dispose of the goods at home, sparking off a price collapse that raises real wages and depresses profits. Entrepreneurs then react by cutting back on their previous level of investment, and the downward spiral of output and unemployment sets in.

It is therefore conceivable that, on the basis of an elastic production mechanism, acceleration may bring on overproduction without any prior cutback of investment. This would be a case of typically Marxist overproduction; production blindly pushed by entrepreneurs beyond the limitations of the market, or of the capitalist system generally. These limitations would not operate via the psychological medium of flagging entrepreneurial spirit (as in Keynes or in Schumpeter) but by setting up tangible, objective barriers to demand.

Of course, with Marx's definition of overproduction, interpreted broadly in his spirit, an overproduction crisis still exists even if it were sparked off by a drop in investment first. Overproduction, in Marx's sense, is production beyond the point which the economy, hemmed in by the narrowness of capitalistic institutions, can sustain. The peculiarly strong economic position of the entrepreneur is undoubtedly a feature of a developed stage of the capitalist mode of production. When he brings about a depression by cutting back on investment, the implication is that output has grown beyond the point which he can capitalistically (i.e. on the basis of adequate profit) sustain. Broadly conceived, even the typically Keynesian case of depression-causation is a case of overproduction.

Whatever, on the other hand, its cause, a depression is unlikely to become considerable unless it spreads widely through most production sectors. In an economy with a high degree of interdependence, as under-developed commodity production, such spread becomes certain when the financial system itself is attacked by the diseases, i.e. when the chain of payments is broken at various points by an increase in the number of bankruptcies. Collapse of the whole edifice is then precipitated by the mass defensive reactions of the capitalist class, the 'animal instincts' of which push it in this case to an animal panic. The instrument of such panic is readily at hand, consisting of exchange value in its independent form, money. With exchange value being the aim of capitalist economic activity and with business in a depression losing rather than making money, those lucky enough to be in possession of, or able to acquire the general commodity by selling goods hold on to it rather than re-spend it. The result of this choice is to generalise the breakdown in the sequence of payments started by the onset of bankruptcies.

The insatiable character of the desire for surplus value does not always act as an impulse for productive expansiveness. In a depression it reverts to the primitive form of an insatiable desire for money in its direct form. Keynes might describe this case as one of infinite liquidity preference, while Marx, without giving it a special name, has painted a most vivid image of it.[12]

On the eve of the crisis, the bourgeois, with the self-sufficiency that springs from intoxicating prosperity, declares money to be a vain illusion. Commodities alone are money. But now the cry is everywhere: money alone is a commodity! As the hart pants after water, so pants his soul after money, the only wealth.

Speculation, interest and credit

The withdrawal of entrepreneurial capital from production was seen in the previous section to be the result either of (a) a fall in profitability, due to rising costs, particularly wage costs or (b) the exhaustion of outside, additional, foreign markets. Withdrawal of capital from production ventures implements, in these cases, an essentially negative, defensive policy. Capital may also, however, be withdrawn from production as a result of a positive entrepreneurial choice. Entrepreneurs may decide to invest their capital in speculation rather than production.

The distinction drawn in the first section of this chapter between the roles of the capitalist as a production manager and a pure profit-seeker (a pure speculator) becomes relevant here. The development of the capitalist class, together with the increase of wealth in capitalist societies, has, by a process of division of functions, thrown up two complementary types of capitalist – the rentier and the speculator. Their common characteristic is that of seeking profit without necessarily promoting production. They differ in so far as the rentier is passive while the speculator is an active businessman. As such he may freely alternate his activities between production and speculation, moving capital from one sphere to the other according to his judgement as to where the highest profit opportunities arise.

If speculators move capital out of production they may provoke or contribute to the outbreak of a crisis even before other causes (fall in the rate of exploitation due to rising wage-rates, exhaustion of exogenous markets) start making an impact. Speculative capital typically finances the acquisition of already existing assets which show a tendency to appreciate (shares, real property, objets d'art, stocks of commodities). Most of these assets constitute elements of already existing wealth in the hands of people interested in reshuffling assets of various degrees of liquidity rather than engaging in productive activities. An increase in speculative activity will, therefore, most of the time reduce the level of effective demand for current output; it represents one additional leakage out of the circular flow of income (to use the modern macroeconomic concept) or out of the circuit of capital (in Marxist terms).

It may, of course, be argued that such leakage need not be accompanied by an outburst of overproduction, since output would also be reduced, together with demand, to the extent that investment capital is withdrawn from production. Depression and unemployment would certainly appear, but their cause would be the typically Keynesian mechanism of under-spending rather than the Marxian one of overproduction. This would only be correct if analysis were to discount the elasticity of capitalist production, to which, as argued earlier in the chapter, Marx attached great importance. In this case, if a significant proportion of formerly industrial capital is drawn into speculation, the remaining industrial capitalists may, nevertheless, for some time keep up the existing level of production by having recourse to credit. The division of the capitalist class into money capitalists, industrial capitalists and wholesalers demonstrates its operational character here. To supplement the gaps created by the 'defection' of a part of industrial capital into speculative activity, industrial capitalists may turn to money capitalists (i.e. to banks) and increase their borrowing. Alternatively, if the speculative leakages have already started to tell on final demand, industrialists may ask wholesalers to hold larger stocks (wholesalers will then probably turn to the banks seeking additional finance).

In either case, additional demand for loanable funds will exercise upward pressure on the rate of interest to the point where interest starts eating into the profits of industrial capital. At some stage, industrial capitalists will find it preferable to switch as much of their capital as they can set free from production into lending or speculation, restricting further the basis of effective demand for current output. Restrictions of this kind eventually spell the end of a boom.

There remains the question whether entrepreneurs (their positive preference for speculation having, in the last example above, been hypothetically taken as the first event in the sequence which breaks the boom) have any special reason to turn to speculative choices just as economic activity is approaching a peak. The answer has to be affirmative. With industrial and general activity pushing capacity to its limits, supply bottlenecks start making a sporadic appearance.

Commodities in the supply of which bottlenecks have appeared acquire a privileged position in terms of the market power of their owners. The market value of stocks under their owners' control begins to multiply rapidly, a fact that makes them both a target and an enticement for speculative attack. Capital begins to be transferred to finance holding of such stocks in the hope of their further appreciation. To the extent that the number of bottlenecks increases and the speculative fever spreads, transfers of capital become insufficient. The banking system is mobilised to supply additional credit; additional demand for loans leads to higher interest rates; these interest rates eat into the profits of industrial capital, discouraging its productive recycling.

Some industrial capitalists may then curtail their activities, with their suppliers discovering as a result that formerly secure outlets for their product begin to vanish. In their turn they may seek credit to hold stocks of their own goods or may agree with wholesalers (for a consideration, obviously) that the latter will be the ones who will hold the stocks. Either way, additional pressure is put on the loans market, with interest rates rising further. At some point a significant group of speculators or wholesalers or industrialists discover that, to face up to their obligations falling due, they have to liquidate stocks at a loss. With such sales, various markets start collapsing. Bankruptcies escalate until they attain the banking sector itself, so that the inevitable bursting of the speculative bubble carries the economy along into a crisis and into the subsequent depression.

Acceleration and theoretical inconsistencies

The scenario of the boom–crisis sequence outlined above may be useful in shedding some light on and in helping reconcile certain theoretical inconsistencies attributed to Marxist crisis theory. Two such inconsistencies can be identified, a broader and a narrower one. The former arises out of the coexistence in Marx's analysis of a reproduction scheme, leading almost immediately to an equilibrium growth path, with a theory of persistent and pronounced economic fluctuations. The latter consists of the alleged simultaneous adopting both of an overproduction and an underconsumption theory of crisis.

These fundamental inconsistencies are, in the present author's opinion, more apparent than real. The first can be reconciled if a non-capitalist environment is superimposed on a capitalist economy evolving along some full-employment equilibrium growth path, in accordance with the scheme of extended reproduction. The non-capitalist environment, combined with some elasticity of the production potential even along the full employment growth path, provides to entrepreneurs the means of accelerating activity beyond the balanced growth rate. In this construction the reproduction scheme is no obstacle to overexpansion, which eventually turns into collapse, as soon as the exogenous market is exhausted.

Is there any evidence that Marx actually thought along these lines? The evidence is not massive, but it does exist. In his various references to foreign trade he consistently associates it with the need for an infinite (or rather ever-receding) horizon for expansion. 'Capitalist production does not exist at all without foreign commerce,' he reminds his readers in the course of the very discussion of extended reproduction.[13] And in his study of the rate of profit he expands on the idea further:[14]

> [The] expansion of foreign trade, although the basis of the capitalist mode of production in its infancy, has become its own product, however, with the further progress of the capitalist mode of production, through the innate necessity of this mode of production, its need for an ever-expanding market.

The second alleged inconsistency of Marx (the co-existence in his crisis theory of both an overproduction and an underconsumption scenario) can also, in the present author's opinion, be reconciled along similar lines. Underconsumption by the masses is fundamental in capitalism. This is not meant in the sense either of any peculiar psychology, inherent in the system, which prompts workers to consume less than they need, or to restrict their very needs, before they ever plan their consumption. On the contrary, capitalist institutions are, if anything, biased in the direction of stimulating, e.g. by commercial advertising, new needs in people – needs that most workers find hard, if at all possible, to satisfy. Nor is it meant in the Keynesian sense of a decline in the marginal propensity to consume as income increases. The term 'underconsumption' simply means the inability of workers, constrained, as they are by the value of their labour power, to buy back from the market the full volume of consumption, investment and luxury goods they produce. Thus defined, underconsumption does not provoke permanent stagnation because of the injections of additional demand through investment (and the luxury consumption of the ruling class). A combined balance of spending by (under-consuming) workers and (investing) capitalists could ideally maintain the capitalist economy on an equilibrium growth path for ever. This, however, would be inconsistent with the tendency of entrepreneurs to accelerate the process of expansion above equilibrium growth on every opportunity. Such acceleration can be supported only by outside markets. As long as the outside markets continue to expand, underconsumption leading to a deficiency of effective demand remains latent. After the external outlet has been closed, the deficiency of demand asserts itself.

The three circuits of capital

The idea that the relative stability of the capitalist system in non-crisis periods can be explained by the presence of 'shock-absorbers', capable of smoothing out the more-or-less continuous disturbances arising from the anarchic character of the capitalist market, was introduced at the end of the previous chapter. The point was made there that Marx had studied both purely theoretical and also practical forms of shock-absorbers, but of the latter the only example mentioned was the world market.

In the course of the present chapter two main internal rather than external shock-absorbing mechanisms were introduced, without being described explicitly as such, namely: credit and wholesale trade. For a more formal presentation of their function the discussion must now turn to the three circuits of capital defined by Marx. The concept of the circuit of capital has been used repeatedly so far, but only in one of its forms, that of the circuit of money capital, schematically presented as

$$M - C \overset{MP}{\underset{LP}{\longrightarrow}} \ldots P \ldots C' - M'$$

It must be noticed that, at the two ends of this circuit $M' > M$, so that money has expanded itself, fulfilling the aim of capitalist production. The circuit of capital can be presented in another two forms: that of the circuit of productive and that of commodity capital. Schematically these two circuits are represented by the following sequences:

$$P - C' - M' - C' \longrightarrow\!\!< \begin{array}{c} LP \\ MP \end{array} \ldots P' \qquad \text{(Productive capital)}$$

and

$$C' - M' - C' \longrightarrow\!\!< \begin{array}{c} LP \\ MP \end{array} \ldots P' \ldots C'' \qquad \text{(Commodity capital)}$$

In all the above schemes, primed symbols are greater than non-primed ones, as in the case of money capital.

It must be stressed that, basically the circuit of capital is only one. A certain capital sum must assume successively all three forms of money, industrial and commodity capital in order for the aim of capitalist production to be achieved. It must be spent as money in the purchase of constant capital and labour power, these two must be joined to form productive capital, their commodity output must be sold for money, and so on. The distinction of the three types of the circuit depends on the starting point chosen for running round it one full circle. From a less formal point of view, each circuit type corresponds to one of the three subsections of the bourgeoisie listed earlier – the money, industrial and commercial capitalists. The success of the aims of each subsection depends on the circuit of capital completing each time a full cycle, so that the money capitalist can receive back his funds with interest, the commercial capitalist replenish his stocks with profit, and the industrial capitalist expand his equipment while making profit himself. It does not follow, of course, that the subsections of the bourgeoisie are conscious of the fact that capital, in the specific form owned by each one of them, must go through every other form, in order to return to its original owner increased by the addition of surplus value. Money capitalists in particular observe just one thing: that they lend out money which returns to them augmented ($M \ldots M'$), as if by magic. The fact it has to be used in production in order to expand escapes their field of vision. On misapprehensions of this kind, resulting from the limited horizons of practical businessmen, the myth gradually takes root that capital has some inherent value-generating capacity, separate from labour.

If the circuit in any of its three forms were examined in pure isolation, as a once-over, not a repetitive, event, one could never observe capital in all its three forms simultaneously. At the beginning, only a sum of money could be observed. After that money would vanish and only means of production and labour power would exist. In their turn they would vanish and only the product, in the form of commodities would remain. These, when sold, would drop out of the circuit, and money would reappear, to start the process anew.

But, at the single instant of time, not more than one moment of the circuit could be observed.

By contrast, if the circuit is examined in its more realistic state of a perpetual progression from one stage to the next, as soon as one tranche of money capital has been converted into means of production and labour power, a second one queues up to keep production going. The spending of more money capital, at the beginning of the circuit, is not conditional on the receipts from the sale of the product flowing back into the original reservoir. Money is spent all the time, constant and variable capital are used and reused without idle intervals, commodities are stored up and sold off continuously, in other words a part of capital is simultaneously present in all its forms at the various points of the circuit. Given that production and exchange take some time, the simultaneous presence of capital at all points of the circuit implies the formation of certain stocks to support the process at its various stages, before it becomes self-supporting from the flow of its own output. A fund of money capital is required in the hands of the money capitalists, stocks of materials, foodstuffs and finished products in the hands of wholesalers and, assuming that durable capital goods are also used, a stock of equipment (fixed capital) in the hands of industrialists.

Of all three sub-sections of the bourgeoisie, only industrialists are directly engaged in the extraction of surplus value from labour, because only labour employed in the production (as distinct from exchange and circulation) of commodities is productive of value, hence also of surplus value. The circuit of productive capital is, therefore, the focus of the whole process, with the circuits of money and commodity capital functioning alongside it in an auxiliary capacity. This does not mean that money and/or commercial capitalists do not strive all the time, often with success, to cut for themselves, to the detriment of the industrialist, a bigger slice of surplus value in the form of interest and commercial profit. This kind of competition is always present. It does mean, however, that without productive capital prospering, the other two forms are also condemned to eventual atrophy.

For productive capital to prosper, industrialists must have some leeway for unhindered acceleration of their production, over and above any prevailing rate of growth, in pursuit of sudden opportunities, without being continually restrained by demand barriers. The division of functions among the sections of the bourgeoisie (reflected in the distinction of the three circuits) does provide some such scope. Marx has put this point very incisively:[15]

[As] soon as C′ has been sold, been converted into money, it can be reconverted into the real factors of the labour-process, and thus of the reproductive process. Whether C′ is bought by the ultimate consumer or by a merchant for resale does not affect the case. The quantity of commodities created in masses by capitalist production depends on the scale of production and on the need for constantly expanding this production, and not on a predestined circle of supply and demand, on wants that have to be satisfied. Mass production can have no other direct buyer, apart from other industrial capitalists, than the wholesaler. Within certain limits, the process of reproduction may take place on the same or on an increased scale even when the commodities expelled from it did not really enter individual or productive consumption . . . So long as the product is sold, everything is taking its regular course from the standpoint of the capitalist producer.

Money-capitalists have also been seen by Marx to join forces with merchant capitalists in enlarging the margins of action of industrial capital:[16]

[Merchant] capital . . . under the modern credit system . . . disposes of a large portion of the total social money-capital, so that it can repeat its purchases even before it has definitely sold what has previously been purchased . . . [By] virtue of its independent status [merchant capital] moves, within certain limits, independently of the bounds of the reproduction process and thereby even drives the latter beyond its bounds.

Acceleration beyond the limits of expanded reproduction is, therefore, possible even without an external non-capitalist environment as long as the 'division of labour' between the various sections of the bourgeoisie creates internal margins to the action of industrial capital, setting up in the form of credit and wholesale trade internal shock absorbers for disproportionate, excess, supply. And, just as in the case of the non-capitalist environment, when the potential of internal shock-absorbers becomes exhausted, the deluge of an economic crisis breaks loose. The circuit of capital cannot proceed forever by dividing itself up in its three constituent forms, incestuously multiplying supply and demand among capitalist traders by merely inflating financial assets, without an opening to the mass of final consumers or investors in the real economy. When the limits of 'intra-capitalist' trading are reached, Marx observes that:[17]

Now one stream of commodities follows another, and finally it is discovered that the previous streams had been absorbed only apparently by consumption. The commodity-capitals compete with one another for a place in the market. Late-comers, to sell at all, sell at lower prices. The former streams have not yet been disposed of when payment for them falls due. Their owners must declare their insolvency or sell at any price to meet their obligations . . . Then a crisis breaks out.

And again, in a clearer reference to the temporary, somewhat artificial, character of internal shock-absorbers he repeats:[18]

This internal dependence [between merchant capital and the bounds of extended reproduction] and external independence push merchant's capital to a point where its internal connection is violently restored through a crisis.

Conclusion

In his original writings Marx pioneered the idea of a cyclical development of capitalism, punctuated by crises. For Marxist economics the inevitability of crises has remained almost axiomatic ever since. Even many non-Marxists would presumably agree that, despite the theoretical insights and the policy prescriptions of Keynesianism, the behaviour of the capitalist system has so far on the whole vindicated the Marxist prediction.

The idea of cycles in growth has struck a sympathetic chord with many non-Marxist economists. Not all of them would, however, agree with Marx that the cycle is a symptom of capitalist morbidity, of the fettering of the forces of production, and hence a symptom heralding the end of the capitalist system. Most Keynesians, while very critical of the human and material wastage caused by depressions, would argue that unemployment and other attendant phenomena are curable by reforming rather than totally rejecting capitalism. Others, like Schumpeter, would argue that the cycle has dominated the economy right from the beginning of the capitalist era, that it is not a symptom of senility but the typical form which economic development assumes under capitalism, that it constitutes a normal, basically healthy, phenomenon.

Marx's argument, at least as interpreted in this volume, makes the following distinction. In the capitalist mode of production it identifies a hard-core section, already established by previous periods of capital accumulation, capable of being expressed as an equilibrium system along the lines suggested by the reproduction schemes. (With the tools created in the meantime by mathematical economics, the reproduction schemes could, nowadays, be cast in the form of input–output tables, while extended reproduction could be presented as a multisectoral growth model along an equilibrium (probably 'golden age') path.)

On this core of a regularly growing economy (or, rather, an economy theoretically capable of equilibrium growth) Marx has superimposed economic activity of a typically capitalist kind, as he perceives it. His capitalists rush after opportunities of extra-normal profit, as these appear on the horizon, by accelerating production beyond the constraints of proportionate development. As long as there are internal or external margins which allow disproportionate acceleration to continue, the system operates at full capacity, dramatically developing the forces of production. After acceleration reaches its limits, the economy bounces back, with the crisis carrying in its wake not only the accelerating fringes but also the (theoretically) equilibrated core.

At the beginning of the capitalist era, the margins for uncoordinated acceleration were still very wide. The development of productive forces could proceed uninhibited and the economy could grow without deep cycles and prolonged depressions. By the early nineteenth century, however, as a result of the enormous rise in productivity achieved during the Industrial Revolution, the margins for free acceleration began to shrink, crises started to occur periodically and, from then on, growth continued in a fitful manner, accompanied by vast wastage of resources.

For Marx, this change was one main aspect of the historical vindication of his theoretical, historical materialist, prediction of a 'fettering' process setting in during the later stages of the capitalist epoch. The economic key to this historical mutation he perceived in free-wheeling capitalist acceleration becoming increasingly difficult. With the gradual exhaustion of the non-capitalist environment, possibilities of acceleration, supported by the opening up of hitherto unconquered territories, became increasingly rare. With acceleration becoming problematic, the development of the forces of production finds no encouragement and fettering begins. Capitalist entrepreneurs gradually realise that they cannot assume an endless horizon for their initiatives. But in order to give full vent to the productive potential implicit in the achievements of science, technology, education and accumulation prior to the modern epoch, capitalism needs this assumption (and the reality which underpins the assumption). It must proceed as if no barriers of production anarchy, social privilege, exploitation, class division etc. existed, as if production could genuinely aim at the greatest possible satisfaction of needs for the greatest number of people. This assumption is indeed possible, but only in periods when acceleration has sufficient scope. In such phases the trammelling aspects of capitalism with regard to the development of productivity become momentarily suspended. To the extent that the capitalist system loses the schizoid capacity putatively to abolish and actively suspend its own limitations, it ceases to serve the purpose of economic progress. It enters the phase of historical decline when, as Marx perceived, it becomes its own obstacle:[19]

> The *real barrier* of capitalist production is *capital itself.* It is that capital and its self-expansion appear as the starting and the closing point, the motive and purpose of production; that production is only production for *capital* and not vice versa, the means of production are not mere means for a constant expansion of the living process of the *society* of producers. The limits within which the preservation and self-expansion of the value of capital resting on the expropriation and pauperisation of the great mass of producers can alone move – these limits come continually into conflict with the methods of production employed by capital for its purposes, which drive towards unlimited extension of production, towards production as an end in itself, towards unconditional development of the social productivity of labour. The means – unconditional development of the productive forces of society – comes continually into conflict with the limited purpose, the self-expansion of the existing capital. The capitalist mode of production is, for this reason, a historical means of developing the material forces of production and creating an appropriate world-market and is, at the same time, a continual conflict between this its historical task and its own corresponding relations of social production.

CHAPTER 8

The falling tendency of the rate of profit

Introductory remarks

At present, the theory of the falling tendency of the rate of profit is, quite possibly, the most controversial part of Marxist economics. Its empirical validity has been repeatedly tested statistically, without conclusive results.[1] In more recent discussions its logical validity has also come under heavy challenge.[2] Disagreements about the very meaning of the theory are many and hard to resolve by reference to the original sources. Marx's statement in *Capital*, Vol III[3] of what he called 'the law of the tendency of the rate of profit to fall' is fraught with deliberate, quite explicit ambiguities. He presented his 'law' in two parts. First, the reasons for maintaining that the development of the forces of production in capitalism would bring about the very opposite of what capitalists intended – a fall, instead of an increase in profitability. Second, a number of 'countervailing influences' which tended to hold back and even reverse the main tendency. As a result, the basic theory produces no logically necessary prediction as to whether the rate of profit must be expected to rise or to fall, although it is clear that Marx, presumably on grounds of whatever empirical evidence was available to him, had resolved the ambiguity to his own satisfaction, in favour of a progressive decline. From the point of view of empirical testing, this state of the theory can raise insuperable obstacles. Any set of statistics brought forward to testify against the hypothesis of declining profitability can be refuted by means of the claim that, in the period in question, one or other of the 'countervailing influences' were successfully offsetting the main trend.

   In the present author's opinion, the ambiguity of the original formulation, while undoubtedly onerous, is not necessarily fatal. In some respects (although emphatically not by offering an eternal alibi to empirical refutation) it may be turned into an advantage. It generates a certain conceptual tension which may lead to further theoretical developments. A suggestion of possible progress in this direction will be made in the last section of this chapter.

A different set of difficulties associated with the 'law' consists of problems of exposition. In the overall structure of Marx's work, the part concerned with declining profitability occupies a focal place. It weaves into a single pattern the three main themes of Marxist economics: the epoch-making development of the forces of production under capitalism; the idea of fettering of the forces by the relations of production; and the idea of the emergence of the objective preconditions of a socialist society in the midst of capitalism, by virtue of capitalist development itself. It is, therefore, hard to decide under which main heading the 'law' should appear in the present book. Its inclusion in the part dealing with the fettering of the forces of production is due to the way its importance has been assessed by most commentators and by Marx himself. On the other hand, in this topic more than in any other, it should never be forgotten that Marxist theory constitutes a very tightly knit body of reasoning which must be taken as one coherent whole, although, for purposes of exposition, it has to be presented under different headings.

The last difficulty to be mentioned here concerns the quantitative terms in which the law is formulated. It has already been stated above, that Marxist economic theory operates with two sets of quantitative concepts: values and prices of production. So far in this book it has been possible to present the analysis purely in terms of values, without going into the problem of consistency of the two accounting systems (the transformation problem). This has been attempted in the belief, stated earlier, that an introduction to Marxist economics best achieves the purpose of arousing interest and offering insight into the theory if all its main points are first stated in terms of a pure value regime, to be placed under the grid of the price regime only afterwards.

However, the recent spate of criticism against the logical validity of the law of the falling rate of profit cannot possibly be summarised in value terms. It is crucially dependent on the assumption of a price-of-production regime. To get round this difficulty, the law will, in this chapter, be presented in two stages. The traditional presentation, in labour theory of value terms, will be given first, followed by a separate, price-regime discussion, where new concepts will be explained as they are introduced.

Technical, value and organic composition

Keeping firmly in mind that the mere algebraic statement of a relationship is far from equivalent to a proof of its validity, the law of the falling tendency of the rate of profit can be stated, very simply and elegantly, by the use of three ratios, all expressed in labour value terms: the rate of profit, the rate of surplus value and the *organic composition of capital*. The rate of profit, both as $r = s/(c + v)$ and as $v = (s/v)/((c/v) + 1)$, (where c is constant, v variable capital and s surplus value) has already been introduced in Chapter 4. Of the two ratios in which the rate of profit can be analysed, s/v, (the rate of surplus-value) and c/v, the first has been discussed in Chapter 7. It remains to consider c/v.

The two value magnitudes in the numerator and in the denominator of this fraction, are respectively constant and variable capital. Taken on its own, before its determinants are considered, the ratio is described as the *value composition* of capital (where total capital is, of course, $c + v$). Behind the value composition stands the technological relationship of a certain quantity of means of production to a certain number of men (or a certain quantity of means of subsistence). This relationship is described as the *technical composition* of capital. Although men (or their means of subsistence) and means of production, both measured in the physical units naturally corresponding to each, are not commensurable, and hence cannot be represented by one index,[4] it does make sense, as long as the type and quality of the means of production do not change too much, to describe the technical composition as rising or falling. More machines (e.g. more power looms) per operative signify a rising technical composition, provided the looms added on are roughly similar to the pre-existing ones. Difficulties would of course arise if many small looms per worker were replaced by fewer, larger ones, if steam-operated power looms changed into electrically operated looms, and so on. Such qualitative transformations, even if they made fully rigorous exact numerical measurements impossible, should not prevent broad assessments of the direction of change, when in the nature of things this direction is sufficiently clear-cut.

It was on broad assessments of this kind that Marx based his thesis of the evolution of the technical composition. His life overlapped with a century of great upheaval in production techniques, known as the Industrial Revolution, so that he could hardly avoid the generalisation that capitalism was opening up an era of increasing replacement of human labour by mechanical methods. Fewer workers would set in motion an increasingly large stock of mechanical equipment; they would also process vastly larger quantities of materials in any given period of time. The culmination of such trends would be total replacement of manual productive labour by automated factories – a visionary forecast of Marx's that seems to be coming into its own in this latter part of the twentieth century.

Significant increases in the technical composition are one of the two forces singled out by Marx as acting on the value composition. In so far as the latter is determined by changes in the technical composition, it is described as the *organic composition* of capital.

The second force acting on the value composition is technical progress, particularly of a kind that would reduce the cost of elements of constant capital. If the stock per man of mechanical equipment and materials, measured in physical units, increased the ratio c/v would, assuming v constant, rise. Technical progress, however, could reduce the value-unit-cost of c sufficiently to compensate for the physical increase. In pure logic, technical progress makes the change in the total value-magnitude of *c* indeterminate. No one can exclude *a priori* the possibility that technology may evolve fast enough even to reduce the total value of *c*, although equipment etc, in physical terms, is increasing.

Marx did perceive these possibilities but concluded, on what must have been, to his mind, incontrovertible empirical grounds, that technical progress, while slowing down the rise in the total value-magnitude of *c*, was not sufficiently strong to reverse it altogether. This, obviously, leads to the result that, as long as *v* does not change, the organic composition rises, though not as fast as the technical composition.

Given, however, that technical progress may seize hold of the sector producing wage-goods, the assumption of a constant *v* cannot be sustained. For completeness, the effects of technical progress on *c* and *v* must be considered jointly. Any fall in *v*, due to the cheapening of wage goods, will raise *c/v*. For technical progress in the production of *c* to reverse this rise it would have to satisfy two conditions: (a) be fast enough to offset the physical increase in mechanical equipment and materials and (b) having satisfied (a) remain sufficiently powerful to offset any cheapening of *v*, due to increased productivity in the wage goods sector.

Alternatively, the condition of an equal rate of technical progress in the sector producing capital and the one producing wage goods might be formulated. Under this condition (which might be given the name of 'Marx-neutral technical progress') relative unit values (Marx's exchange value) of all commodities would remain fixed, allowing the effect of changes in technical composition to be fully reflected in the organic composition of capital. Subject to rising technical composition, organic composition would then rise unambiguously, only by virtue, however, of the assumption of 'Marx-neutrality'.[5]

The rate of exploitation

With rising organic composition, the definition of the rate of profit immediately predicts its own falling tendency, provided that the rate of exploitation remains constant. Simple inspection of the fraction

$$r = \frac{\dfrac{s}{v}}{\dfrac{c}{v} + 1}$$

shows that if the numerator (*s/v*) does not change while the denominator (*c/v*) rises, the fraction as a whole will become smaller.

The elegant simplicity of this demonstration should not be mistaken as a proof of validity of the proposition involved. Such proof depends not on the algebraic statement of the relationship but on the logical consistency and empirical robustness both of the assumptions and of the analysis based on them. Early criticisms of the law of the falling tendency of the rate of profit consisted of a joint logical–factual challenge, with the logical element predominating. It was argued,[6] in particular, that the assumed constancy of the rate of surplus-value was inconsistent with the basic premise of mechanisation, hence of increasing productivity, in the economy. Such developments would reduce the value-cost of wage goods leading, *ceteris paribus*, to a fall in v and an increase in s, and hence to a rise in the rate of profit.

Marx was aware of the possibility of an increase in the rate of surplus-value counteracting the main trend of his 'law'; he had included it among the 'countervailing influences'. The mechanism relevant for him was not the cheapening of wage-goods, via productivity increases, but the reduction of wages, through increased aggressiveness of the capitalist class against the workers on the wages front. Taking the idea to its ultimate logical conclusion – that of variable capital sinking virtually to zero, the workers consuming nothing – he argued that this method of compensating for the rise in organic composition was bound to come up against the insurmountable barrier of the natural length of the day. Even if workers did not do any necessary labour (for themselves) but performed only surplus labour (for the capitalist), and even if their working day was prolonged indefinitely, they could not toil beyond the theoretical maximum of 24 hours. Once this was reached the compensation of the falling rate of profit by a rising rate of exploitation would come to an end. Well before approaching the theoretical maximum (the infinite rate of exploitation), this kind of compensation would become increasingly difficult. It can be demonstrated arithmetically that, even for keeping the rate of profit constant, the rate of exploitation has to increase at an increasing pace.[7] It is to be expected that workers will put up mounting resistance against accelerating encroachments of the bourgeoisie on working-class living standards. The flavour of Marx's argument can be tasted in the following quotation:[8]

> Inasmuch as the development of the productive forces reduces the paid portion of employed labour, it raises its rate; but inasmuch as it reduces the total mass of labour employed by a given capital, it reduces the factor of the number by which the rate of surplus-value is multiplied to obtain its mass. Two labourers, each working 12 hours daily, cannot produce the same mass of surplus-value as 24 who work only 2 hours, even if they could live on air and hence did not have to work for themselves at all.

Marx's point is valid, but it cannot be formalised on the basis of the algebraic expression given to the rate of profit for the purpose of demonstrating the separate impact of the rate of exploitation and the organic composition of capital. In the fraction

$$r = \frac{\dfrac{s}{v}}{\dfrac{c}{v} + 1}$$

if v becomes zero, both numerator and denominator become infinite and the whole expression is indeterminate. The equivalent form

$$r = \frac{s}{c + v}$$

has therefore to be used for studying the maximum rate of profit. It then becomes obvious that, with v shrinking to zero while s expands to engulf the whole length of the working day, the profit rate becomes

$$r = \frac{\bar{s}}{c}$$

With $\bar{s}$ now bounded from above by the natural duration of 24 hours of the day, any further increase in c will necessarily lead to a reduction in r.

   To show explicitly that $\bar{s}/c$ is an upper bound for the rate of profit, this result can be restated as:

$$r = \frac{s}{c + v} < \frac{s + v}{c} = \frac{\bar{s}}{c}$$

Formally, this inequality is established by noticing that v, a positive quantity, is transferred from the denominator of $s/(c+v)$ (when labour is treated as costing nothing in terms of capital advanced) to the numerator (because even when costing nothing to the capitalist, labour still creates value). Since the other quantities (s and c) in the original fraction do not change, the fraction $(s+v)/c$ has a larger numerator and a smaller denominator than $s/(c+v)$, it is, therefore, a larger fraction. Upper-boundedness follows from the inequality, thus established.

   The response to the rising rate of surplus value argument has subtly shifted the ground of the discussion from the trend in the *actual* to the trend of the *maximum* rate of profit. There can be no doubt that this weakens the original Marxian position. It should be obvious that the two rates do not have to move in the same direction over any definite period of time, although it could, perhaps, be maintained that, at some undetermined point in time, the trend in the maximum rate of profit will come to dominate the actual rate.

Figure 8.1 illustrates a case where a fluctuating actual rate of profit first rises and then, having reached the trend of the maximum rate of profit it turns down and starts falling.

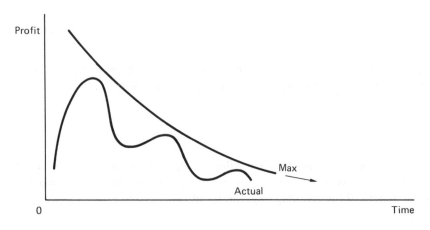

FIGURE 8.1

It must be noticed that the maximum rate of profit $\bar{s}/c$ is simply the inverse of the organic composition of capital, when all current labour has become surplus-labour. Therefore the demonstration of a falling trend in the maximum rate of profit is strictly equivalent to the assumption of a rising organic composition of capital.

It is exactly this assumption that a second line of criticism has chosen to attack. The substance of the relevant arguments follows directly from the discussion of the effects of technical progress above. Admittedly, if technical progress is sufficiently faster in the production of elements of constant capital than in the production of wage goods, the actual rate of profit will rise. The maximum will rise even further because there is no longer a wage-goods sector to counterbalance economies in c by cost reductions in its own sphere.

The possibility that even the maximum rate of profit may rise in response to technical progress, leaves open only one escape route. It has to be argued that some areas of production come up against diminishing returns which stubbornly refuse to yield to human inventiveness. It is interesting to notice that this ultimate refuge was not missed by Marx. In the *Theories of Surplus Value, Part III*, he asked and answered the following rhetorical question:[9]

One may ask with regard to raw material: If, for example, productivity in spinning increases tenfold, that is, a simple worker spins as much as ten did previously, why should not one Negro produce ten times as much cotton as ten did previously, that is why should the *value ratio* not remain the same? . . . To this it is quite easy to answer that some kinds of raw materials, such as wool, silk, leather, are produced by animal *organic* processes and capitalist production has not yet succeeded and never will succeed in mastering these processes in the same way as it has mastered purely mechanical or inorganic chemical processes . . . As far as coal and metal (wood) are concerned, they become much cheaper with the advance of production; this will however become more difficult as mines are exhausted, etc.

Although this passage occupies a rather peripheral place in Marx's opus, it contains the only possible ultimate answer to the technological objection mentioned above. It is, however, an answer less of Marxian, more of Ricardian inspiration. It traces the cause of the falling rate of profit not to rising organic composition but back to the niggardliness of Nature, possibly ill-treated in the hands of capitalism, but niggardly nonetheless. If that were to become the main reply to the technological objection, the critical power of Marx's 'law' would be shaken to the roots.

In basing his 'law' of the falling tendency of the rate of profit on rising organic composition, Marx attempted a very daring theoretical break with classical Political Economy. The latter, in the person of Ricardo, had already formulated a similar law, based, however, on rising rents due to diminishing returns in agriculture. This made capitalism a naturally, not a socially bounded system. By contrast the rising organic composition, premissed as it was upon the antagonism of the machine, and hence of capital, against the worker, linked the decline in profitability, and hence in the weakening of capitalist incentive and source of enrichment, to features intrinsic to the capitalist relations of production. The point was not simply that capitalism found itself embroiled in an unresolvable contradiction: the undermining of the incentives and rewards of capitalists by the very means (mechanisation) through which they strove to support profits. A contradiction between profits and diminishing returns in agriculture is equally unresolvable. However, the second case implies that the forces of production have been developed within their capitalist integument to the limit of what is humanly and naturally possible, no less. No room is left for a successor mode of production to carry forward the conquest of nature beyond what capitalism was inherently able to achieve. Therefore, on the principle of historical materialism, there will be no successor mode of production. Capitalism is eternalised.[10]

The first contradiction, on the other hand (the one between mechanisation and profitability) drives capitalist economic activity into the dead end of a stationary state – an economy where no growth takes place – before nature-imposed limits are reached. Hence the system belongs to the 'prehistory' of humanity and will be replaced, by means of social class struggle, by one capable of expanding further to satisfy more amply human needs.

It is therefore crucial for Marx to be able to avoid borrowing from Ricardian economics on this point. To the extent that he is not able to avoid it, a very important part of Marxism, as a theory of social revolution, is jeopardised. The flaw is not, in the present author's opinion, fatal, but it is a serious one.

The new critical wave

Criticisms examined so far represent what one might call the enlightened Marxism of the older generation. There can be no doubt that they shake Marx's law profoundly. At the same time they have remained within the basic frame of reference of Marx's formulation: a struggle between a main tendency and a set of counter-tendencies. In a sense the overall drive of older criticism was to insist that not one but two main tendencies of indeterminate relative strength could be identified, so that the outcome, in terms of the rate of profit, became uncertain. But that a struggle was taking place, that the two opposing forces had been correctly identified and that a falling tendency of the rate of profit remained a distinct possibility – these propositions never became an issue.

The radical character of the recent spate of criticism consists of exactly this: it challenges the two-opposite-forces framework. According to the new critics, who have in fact revived and restated a very old criticism going back to Tugan-Baranowsky and von Bortkiewicz at the turn of the century, choice of techniques in competitive capitalism is such as to leave no room for two tendencies; it allows only one possibility for the rate of profit, that it rise.

As mentioned in the introductory remarks, the new criticisms are formulated not in value but in price of production terms. The concept of the price of production has been introduced in Chapter 4. To repeat briefly: the starting point of the definition of the price of production is the concept of the value of a commodity:

(1) $W = c + v + s$

In (1) s is then replaced by the expression $r(c + v)$, where r is the going rate of profit. This substitution is justified on the basis that capitalists neither know nor are interested in the distinction between constant and variable capital or the claim that only variable capital generates surplus value. In practice they spend a sum of money both on equipment, materials etc. and on wages (they buy elements both of constant capital and of labour power), aiming at getting a return on their money investment as a whole, not just on the wage bill. Hence they charge a certain markup, r, on their total costs $(c + v)$, as their profit per unit of output. Whether the ultimate source of this profit is surplus value from workers or a return on capital equipment, they neither understand nor want to know. Nor would they behave any differently even if they did know. The price of production is accordingly written as:

(2) $p = c + v + r(c + v) = (1 + r)(c + v)$

Expression (2) is a hybrid between the price and the value regimes; c and v are measured as values, p is expressed as a price. But, then, the elements of constant capital and the wage goods are themselves traded on the market not as value but as their prices. To determine these, a system of two simultaneous equations, one for the capital-good one for the wage-good, are needed:

(3) (I) $p_I = (1 + \varrho)(p_I k_I + w l_I)$

(II) $p_{II} = (1 + \varrho)(p_I k_{II} + w l_{II})$

p_I and p_{II} are prices of production, k_I and k_{II} capital inputs measured in physical units per unit of output, l_I, l_{II} hours of work per unit of output, w is the wage rate, and ϱ the *price rate of profit* (defined below).

In this very elementary system, one of the two goods will be used as accounting money (as a *numéraire*), (so that its price will be equal to one unit of itself). Taking the wage good as the *numéraire* (3) can be rewritten as:

(4) (I) $p = (1 + \varrho)(pk_I + w l_I)$

(II) $1 = (1 + \varrho)(pk_{II} + w l_{II})$

where p is a relative price expressing a unit of the capital good in terms of a quantity of the wage good. Making the additional assumption that workers consume a quantity w of the wage good and no units of the capital good, w can be taken as the real wage in the system. Fixing w exogenously (say at subsistence level), the system can be solved for the remaining two unknowns, ϱ and p.

Typical of systems of this kind is that the rate of profit, ϱ, in them is not predetermined but emerges, simultaneously with prices, as a result of the solution of the system. This ϱ is known as the *price rate of profit*, to be distinguished from the *value rate of profit*, $r = s/(c+v)$. The value rate of profit is not found as part of the solution of any system of equations. Aggregate c and v invested in the economy as well as aggregate s are assumed to be known, so that the value rate of profit for the whole of the economy is found as

$$r = \frac{\Sigma s}{\Sigma c + \Sigma v}$$

and is then applied to the costing of each particular commodity (as in equation (2)). In general the value and the price rate of profit are not the same.

While Marx, in formulating his 'law', used the value rate of profit, the new critics use the price rate of profit. This is not inadmissible, because choice of techniques (the decision to introduce either more or less mechanised methods) is taken by practising capitalists, who operate in a price not in a value context. It is also accepted that no capitalist ever introduces innovations likely to reduce his current rate of profit. For the rest, capitalists proceed in the same manner as under the value regime described by Marx. Some of them discover a new technique, which, if introduced by one or two firms will not affect the market price of the good or the general profit rate, while it will yield extra-normal profits to the pioneering firms. The question is, again, what happens to the rate of profit after the new technique has become generalised, costs have been reduced throughout the industry, and a correspondingly new price level has been established.

On these premisses plus the assumption that the real wage remains fixed, argue the new critics, the rate of profit can only increase. To convey the flavour of their argument system (4) above will be used. For the purposes of the demonstration in the text, it will have to be assumed that technical progress is 'Marx-neutral' (costs and prices drop by the same proportion in each sector). In general no such assumption has to be made. Selecting equation I of system (4) the argument proceeds as follows: Some innovating firm in sector I introduces the new technology (k', l'). It can take advantage of existing prices while reducing its costs and realising extra-normal profits; so for this firm the price-cost situation appears as:

(5) $p > (1 + r)(pk' + wl')$

After the new technology becomes generalised, with the formation of new prices and a new rate of profit, prices fall in line with costs again and (5) reverts to an equation:

(6) $p' = (1 + r')(p'k' + w'l')$

for all firms in an industry, since by assumption, $w = w'$ (constant real wage) and $p = p'$. ('Marx-neutral' technical progress; recall that $p = p_1'/p_2 = p_1'/p_2'$). Although $p_1 \neq p_1'$ and $p_2 \neq p_2'$, expressions (5) and (6) differ only with respect to the rate of profit. It follows immediately that $r' > r$.

It is important to state carefully exactly what modern critics of the 'law' of the falling tendency of the rate of profit have demonstrated. They have shown that *in conditions of an established general equilibrium*, choice of techniques, which allow super-normal profits for some firms, leads to higher profit rates for all firms, when some new technology (introduced just by a few firms and originally not strong enough to disturb the old equilibrium) becomes generalised and a new general equilibrium set of costs, prices, quantities and rate of profit is reached. Constancy of the real wage (the bundle of goods consumed by workers) is crucial to this demonstration. The method used is that of comparative statics, which reaches its conclusions by comparing the values of the variables in two equilibrium states, differing from each other in some of the original equilibrium parameters. (In the present case, the parameter which changes is the technological form of the production functions). This again is a legitimate analogue to Marx's procedure on this topic. He also compares equilibrium states where one set of values succeeds another. (Value accounting presupposes equilibrium.)

The difference in method between the critics and Marx is that they formulate their analysis in terms of production prices, while he studies the problem in terms of values. In this the critics are certainly more realistic: capitalists who choose the techniques, operate in a price not in a value world. Marx would reply that lack of realism is not a relevant objection here. Values help to clarify relationships without distorting the picture in the aggregate. When all industries are aggregated, the main relationships (rate of surplus value, rate of profit) do not differ between the price and the value regime. Given his own solution of the transformation problem, he would be right to say this. But his solution, when rigorously restated, cannot be depended upon to maintain the crucial relationships invariant. There is no reason, in general, for the value rate of profit to coincide with the price rate of profit.

For the broader, sociological and political, conclusions which Marx wished to derive from his 'law', the value regime, even granting him his own solution of the transformation problem, does not give him any decisive advantage. It would only do so if it could establish the logical necessity for the rate of profit to decline as a result of the development of the forces of production. In that case the existence of an inherent barrier in the capitalist system, would have been vindicated. It has been seen, however, that 'counteracting influences', in particular the cheapening of the elements of constant capital, are sufficient to make the outcome of the 'law' indeterminate even when all magnitudes are expressed as values.

It is also important to clarify what the critics of the 'law' have *not* established (or, indeed, not tried to establish). They have not shown the non-existence of an upper limit to the rate of profit. With given methods of production and a zero wage rate, the rate of profit has an upper bound: the maximum rate of profit in the production-price system. System of equations (4) can be used to demonstrate this. In (4) the assumption of zero wage implies dropping equation 4,I from the system altogether. If no wages are paid, no sector producing wage goods (and represented by 4,II) functions any longer. 4,I is then rewritten as

$$p_I = (1 + \varrho)\, p_I k_I$$

(since $w = 0$, the second term on the right-hand side of 4,I vanishes). Solving the above expression for ϱ, the maximum rate of profit is found as

$$(7) \quad \varrho_{max} = \frac{1 - k_I}{k_I}$$

which is obviously finite, since k_I is a technologically given constant. (A more general proof of this result is given in the Appendix to this chapter.)

Will the maximum *price* rate of profit fall in response to a rise in the organic composition of capital? The answer is again affirmative. Keeping in mind that k_I (or k_{II}) are capital inputs per unit of output, the expression $1 - k_I$ in (7) can be interpreted as the net unit output in the capital good sector (or output after unit capital good inputs have been subtracted). In other words it is the surplus output, measured in physical units, in the capital goods sector. A rise in the organic composition (which now coincides with the technical composition of capital) implies an increase in k_I. It follows that r_{max} will fall in consequence, because in the expression

$$\varrho_{max} = \frac{1 - k_I}{k_I}$$

a rise in k_I will make both the numerator smaller and the denominator larger. Hence the conclusions about the maximum rate of profit in the value regime remain valid for the price rate of profit.

The response to the new critics

Those who have tried to confront the new critics fall into two camps. One (Anwar Shaikh) has attempted the confrontation on the critics' own ground, granting them all their assumptions but criticising the scope of their definitions. Others have replied by presenting models which abandon one or another of the assumptions to reach a different result. Anwar Shaikh[11] has suggested that if *fixed capital* is taken into consideration Marx's result can be made consistent with rational choice of techniques by capitalists under competitive conditions. So far, fixed capital (defined as that part of capital, corresponding to producer durable goods, which transmits its value to the commodities not all in one period but over a number of periods of production) has not been explicitly introduced. In the value expression $c + v + s$, or the alternative price of production expression $(1 + r)(pk + wl)$, the elements of constant capital (c or pk) have been tacitly assumed to be fully depreciated in one period only. Shaikh argues that if fixed capital were introduced, then a distinction could be made between the rate of profit, estimated now over total fixed and *circulating* capital ($c + v$ in each current period – c in this case would stand mainly for materials currently used and current depreciation) and the *margin of profit*, estimated over current costs only (either in value or in price terms). Symbolically, the rate of profit could be written as:

$$r = \frac{s}{F + c + v} \quad \begin{array}{l} \text{(value regime)} \\ \text{(F–fixed capital)} \end{array}$$

or

$$\varrho = \frac{p - (pk + wl)}{(pk + wl) + p \, \alpha \, K} \quad \left(\begin{array}{l} \text{price regime;} \\ \text{where } K \text{ is total capital} \\ \text{stock and } \alpha \text{ is an output/} \\ \text{capital-stock coefficient} \end{array} \right)$$

while the margin of profit would be

$$r = \frac{s}{c + v} \quad \text{(value regime) or} \quad \varrho = \frac{p - (pk + wl)}{pk + wl} \quad \left(\begin{array}{l} \text{price} \\ \text{regime} \end{array} \right)$$

Given these definitions the following can be argued. Capitalists introduce new techniques which increase the margin of profit, because they reduce current costs, but possibly reduce the rate of profit, because increased mechanisation raises F, or $(P \, \alpha \, K)$. The first part of this statement satisfies the requirement of capitalist rationality; the second vindicates Marx's prediction, based on the internal (contradictory) logic of capital, viewed as an impersonal, overpowering social relationship. Shaikh appears to have squared the circle. His argument seems all the more incisive because he extended it to explain competitive behaviour. He argues that the innovating capitalist, who achieved a higher profit margin at the cost of higher mechanisation, can sacrifice a part of it in order to compete his rivals out of existence. To defend themselves in this price war they are forced to adopt his innovations reducing the rate of profit throughout the affected industry.

The new critics have replied to Shaikh's objections[12] that, if fixed capital is to be explicitly taken into account, its financial costs must also be reckoned. Capitalists will have to pay for it in instalments including interest over a certain period of time. They will, therefore, be comparing their total outlays (on fixed and circulating capital) with a stream of expected future incomes (from the sales of the product). They will introduce a more mechanised technique only if the stream of expected incomes yields overall a rate of profit at least equal to, and preferably higher than, the currently available one. Therefore, the original point of the new critics about the effects of the choice of techniques by rational competitive capitalists remains valid.

Whatever the justice of the critics' reply on the level of a strictly microeconomic argument, where they firmly place themselves, explicit intro-duction of fixed capital considerations cannot but shake the broader impli-cations of their argument. Their case must now rest on rational choices of techniques involving not only actual, current, but also expected, future, receipts. The future, however, is fraught with natural uncertainty which, in a capitalist mode of production, is compounded by the anarchical character of the economy. It is very doubtful whether any methodical algorithm of rational choice can tame this kind of uncertainty; whether, therefore, the theory of rational choice of techniques is at all relevant to the problems at hand. A comment by Keynes is particularly apt in this connection.[13]

> If we speak frankly, we have to admit that our basis of knowledge for estimating the yield ten years hence of a railway, a copper mine, a textile factory, the goodwill of a patent medicine, an Atlantic liner, a building in the City of London amounts to little and sometimes to nothing; or even five years hence . . . Investment based on genuine long-term expectation is so difficult today as to be scarcely practicable.

The new critics might reply that Marx himself, in formulating his 'law', did subscribe to some form of rational choice theory. It can hardly be denied that Marx was over-optimistic, perfectionistic even, in this application of the labour theory of value. He never, however, lost sight of the fundamental systemic irrationality of investment, behind the facade of rational individual decision-making in capitalistic conditions. In this he and Keynes stand as one, although for different analytical reasons. By their insistence on the microeconomic (or Walrasian general equilibrium) rationality of the choice of techniques in competitive capitalist markets, the new critics have ignored the far more interesting side of the issue: the inevitable irrationality of capitalist investment behaviour (choice of techniques included) generated by the aggregate functioning of the system. It is in the balance of relevance rather than the logic of their analysis that they fail.

Shaikh is the only one to have attempted to confront the new critics, granting them their assumptions. All other contributors, accepting the main point, have tried to bypass its consequences (the inconsistency of a falling rate of profit with cost-reducing, capital-using innovations) by changing some of the assumptions. The crucial assumptions which have been dropped are:

(a) The constancy of the real wage. That may be abandoned. In particular it may be replaced either by the assumption of constancy in the rate of surplus-value. This, with rising labour productivity, implies a rising real wage. Alternatively, what for some people is an acceptable price-regime counterpart – the constancy of the share of labour in value-added – may be used. It can be shown both that capitalists will choose capital-using, labour-saving techniques and that the rate of profit will fall.[14]

It has been argued in Chapter 4 that Marx did expect the real wage to increase with rises in productivity. It might, therefore, appear that the reformulation proposed above is in line with an important strand in his thinking. However, this is not so. First, Marx did not go so far as to suggest that the rise in the real wage would be sufficient to guarantee a fixed rate of surplus-value (which he *assumed* constant in formulating his 'law'). Second, more importantly, he insisted, for reasons that go deep in the structure of his analysis (reasons that, reaching beyond economics, pertain also to historical materialism) that he deduced, from his generalisation about the character of technical change in a capitalistic economy, a falling tendency of the rate of profit. In this generalisation the increasing substitution of men by machines – pressure on the wage-front, real or anticipated – was one of the ingredients. Only one, however. Marx would certainly not have wished to reduce the basis of such powerful conclusions, like those implicit in his 'law', merely to the conditions of the labour market. His argument ought to hold with constant as well as rising real wage.

(b) The second assumption to have been dropped is that of perfect competition. If an oligopolistic market structure is assumed it can be shown that a technique involving a rise in organic composition and a fall in the rate of profit can be chosen, on rational capitalistic grounds, pertaining essentially to the (higher) opportunity cost of alternative uses of capital. The possibility of lending at interest is blocked because of the imperfections of the market, so that firms are constrained to carry out real investment, even though at a lower profit rate. The scenario that has been proposed, as an illustration of this case is, however, highly implausible.[15]

(c) The third assumption dropped is that of perfect foresight (needed to evaluate the future stream of earnings in order to compare it with current costs). A very interesting construction has been proposed, according to which a sequence of projects, involving increasing levels of mechanisation, rapidly succeed each other, each more recent one making the previous one obsolete. Each newer project is introduced in view of its higher expected profitability (so that the rationality criterion is satisfied) but as it is very shortlived, the more distant terms of its stream of profits fail to materialise. A sequence of actual falling rates of profit, combined with one of rising expected profits can thus be generated.[16] The exact scenario is again rather implausible, but it has the great advantage of letting in some realism about the state of long-term expectation in capitalism – the realism of Keynes and, indeed, of Marx.

Equilibrium or disequilibrium analysis?

As they readily admit, the new critics have not demonstrated that the rate of profit does not fall, in actual capitalism, or that the organic composition does not rise. They have shown that under competitive conditions, with the real wage constant, with perfect foresight and equilibrium prices and quantities, rational choice of techniques will lead to a rising, not a falling actual rate of profit. It is not denied that things in actual capitalism, as it evolved historically, may be different, allowing greater scope for Marx's original intuition.

As already stated, Marx based his 'law' on a generalisation about the character of technical change in capitalism, which he saw as leading to an increased substitution of workers by machinery in production. The generalisation rests on his perception both of developments consciously pursued by capitalists, and of the unintended effects of capitalist behaviour. Following his lead in its broad outline, though not in every detail, four causes of mechanisation can now be listed:

(a) The increase in the level of output intended for the supply of new, extensive markets, which could not be achieved by any number of workers available, producing with existing techniques.

(b) The winning, by means of cost-cutting, of an edge over competitors producing similar products.

(c) The winning of an advantage over competitors producing different products (since all producers compete for a share of the consumer's income) by the offer of a new product that only machines can produce. The product in this case is itself often a new machine. Aeroplanes are not introduced in order to cut costs by reducing the number of manual workers who fly on wings to transport people and goods. In the context of human flying, only machines can fly through air. Television was not introduced to cut down the number of workers transmitting pictures at a distance by telepathy. Only machines can transmit pictures over a distance.

Marx never considered this cause of mechanisation explicitly, nor indeed is there anything specifically capitalistic about it. But it is a part of the whole complex of modern production carried on under capitalist auspices and, in view of its importance, it should not be omitted.

(d) The need to impose control on the workers, either by enforcing the rhythm of a mechanical operation on their movements or by breaking certain crucial monopolies of personal skill or simply of strategic location in the production process that the working class can use as weapons in its fight against capital. A recent example of this type is the development of nuclear-powered electricity generating stations, intended deliberately and explicitly to break the hold of the miners over the energy supply in Britain.

It should be noticed that resistance to the pressure of wage claims is not mentioned as a direct cause of mechanisation. The reason for the omission is that it takes time to mechanise, while wage disputes have to be settled quickly. On the other hand, sustained wage militancy, particularly if it culminates in rising labour costs, is undoubtedly one of the wider considerations prompting the replacement of men by machines.

The unintended effects of capitalist behaviour in the sphere of mechanisation are the following:

(a) The creation of an unemployed reserve army. No matter how much this may benefit capitalism as a system, it cannot be put down as an intended effect of individual capitalist action. Its presence, however, apart from exercising a disciplinary influence on labour has other important effects. As discussed extensively in Chapter 7, unemployment enables capitalists to accelerate production whenever conditions of demand are promising. But mechanisation supplies overpopulation. It may, therefore, be argued that mechanisation creates its own capacity not simply for expanding production, but also for accelerating it at the chosen moments. This is not something that individual capitalists can foresee; it must therefore be put down as an unintended consequence of their actions.

(b) The cheapening of wage-goods, and hence the creation of a powerful means for reducing the value of labour power or, at least, for putting a brake on its increase. Again, this cannot constitute the intended aim of any individual capitalist, no matter how much he welcomes it as a result. Capitalists engaged in the production of wage goods do not reduce their costs and prices in order to help other capitalists make profits, but for the usual competitive reasons of their own. Moreover, the emergence of cost-cutting mechanised methods applicable to the wage-goods industries is, up to a point, a matter of chance. Therefore the reduction in the value of labour power again cannot be an intended effect of individual capitalists. Yet for Marx, who based on it his theory of relative surplus-value, it was one of the strongest advantages of the capitalist system.

(c) The creation of a market for further mechanisation. Railways and iron create a market for the products of mechanised iron and steel industries. Mechanical production of consumer goods creates a market for the machine tool industries and so on.

It is evident that the intended effects of capitalist behaviour concerning technical choice do converge into one powerful stream of influence towards increasingly replacing workers by mechanical and eventually by automated means of production. The case is not so clear with respect to the unintended effects. Some of them, particularly (c), will certainly feed back and enhance the original decision to mechanise. To some extent (c) also makes mechanisation a self-sustaining process. The effect of the creation of an unemployed reserve army and of the cheapening of the means of subsistence is not as unambiguous. To the extent that these two effects throw a damper on rising labour costs or on working-class wage pressure and other militancy, they are likely to make cost-cutting mechanisation less urgent for capital. To the extent that the presence of unemployed workers facilitates acceleration of production, it is likely to encourage further mechanisation. On the whole one may conclude that sufficient feedback from the unintended effects should be forthcoming to strengthen, rather than weaken, the influence of intentional behaviour.

Whether intended or prompted by feedback effects, however, mechanisation, as an inspection of the list of its causes shows, is intimately associated with disturbances of any existing equilibrium. It is either prompted by or results in market imbalances, such as prevail either in a boom or in a slump. It is universally agreed that in a state of equilibrium nothing much happens. Possibly the best moment to introduce new mechanised technologies, from the point of view of securing future profits, is when the economy is just emerging from a slump. Choice of techniques on the basis of microeconomic profit-maximising might then appear vindicated by results, although such results would really flow from aggregate trends rather than from individual rationality.

Eventually recovery gives way to a boom. Production begins to accelerate and a competitive race for markets gets under way. In parallel with the absorption of unemployed workers, increasingly mechanised techniques are introduced to take as much advantage as possible of the good season. Being in an optimistic phase, capitalists assume that the boom will last longer than in fact it does. For as long as it does last, increasingly capital-intensive methods are justified by expected profits. When the boom comes to an end, however, it is the most mechanised techniques (the last ones to be introduced) that are confronted with the shortest streams of expected profits. It follows that actual profits fall in inverse proportion to the organic composition of capital.

An advantage of this explanation is that it ties the 'law' of the tendency of the rate of profit to fall in with the crisis theory outlined in the previous chapter. Both crisis and profit theory would then be conceived in the context of disequilibrium, while the theory of exploitation would still be firmly anchored in equilibrium analysis. This methodological dichotomy could well be the only way of capturing the combination of stability and motion, permanence and impermanence, which a mode of production as dynamic as capitalism presents.

Internal contradictions and countervailing influences: Marx revisited

Only large capitals can keep up with the financing needs of increasing mechanisation and reap economies of scale. This makes large total profits an important consideration if a fall in the rate of profit becomes inevitable. Capitalists might even be prepared deliberately to sacrifice a higher rate of profit if, by so doing, they could achieve the advantage of bigger size. They might, therefore, deliberately undercut a competitor, even harming their own profits permanently in order to bankrupt and absorb him. When size is crucial, the rate of profit may become a rather secondary consideration. This seems to be the meaning of Marx's remark that 'the river of capital rolls on . . . not in proportion to the rate of profit but in proportion to the impetus it already possesses'.

If the pursuit of bigness is one main response to the downward pressure on profit rates, control of 'countervailing influences' can be the reward of bigness. Advanced technology, capable of reducing constant capital costs, is available in priority to big industrial organisations that can afford either to purchase it ready-made, together with the machinery that embodies it, or to generate it by their own research. There is thus a convergence in the effects of downward pressures on the rate of profit and of 'countervailing influences'. Both pressure and counterpressure are resolved in the increasing size of the capitalist enterprise.

Modern criticism has established that there is no logical necessity for the rate of profit to fall as a result of the development of the forces of production in capitalism. As suggested in the first part of this chapter, a close reading of the labour theory of value formulation of Marx's 'law' also reveals as much. On the other hand, pressures on the rate of profit do build up and capitalists do engage in efforts to counteract them. Contrary to what one might infer from the uni-directional conclusions of the new critics, the methodological setting of the problem by Marx in the context of the struggle of two opposite tendencies remains valid. With Marx's 'law' reinterpreted as predicting not a declining rate of profit but a tendency to increasing bigness of the capitalist firm, the original conflictual analysis of the subject retains a large measure of its usefulness.

The implications of increasing bigness for the development of capitalism are examined in Chapter 9. There is, on the other hand, one important aspect of Marx's conclusions which cannot be maintained under the interpretation proposed here. Marx intended his 'law' to be the pinnacle of his analysis of the process of fettering of the production forces by production relations. There is something powerfully striking in the idea that capitalism destroys the objective target of its own agents, not because of their failure to pursue or maximise it but through their very success in doing so. Equally striking is the predicted destruction of productive forces not because of any failing to develop them but because the system is too successful in raising productivity of labour. As a vindication of the general historical materialist proposition, this thesis, if true, would indeed be conclusive. Crisis theory could then be made a simple appendix of the 'law': as the rate of profit falls capitalists either go bankrupt and have to close down, setting off a cumulative process of unemployment and economic stagnation, or they anticipate bankruptcy by withdrawing into periodic bouts of abnormal liquidity preference, with the same disastrous stagnation in business as an outcome.

Without the central mechanism of a persistent falling tendency of the rate of profit, crisis theory will have to rest on its other leg, the unplanned, anarchically accelerating character of capitalist production. Anarchy of the market, combined with the impulsive character of the investment process and the progressive exhaustion of a non-capitalist environment (the main shock-absorber of the system in its expanding phase), will then have to represent the chief causes of the fettering of the forces of production. The result is neither as neat, as powerful nor as satisfactory logically as the law of the falling tendency of the rate of profit in its original formulation. But it remains a very respectably defensible basis for the historical-materialist propositions that Marxist economics is designed to uphold in the special, but all-important, case of the capitalist mode of production. This is what matters.

Appendix

This Appendix outlines a general proof of the two propositions stated in the main text: (a) that the *maximum* rate of profit will fall, subject to rises in the organic composition of capital, and (b) that, subject to real wages remaining fixed, the rate of profit can only rise, following the introduction of cost-reducing innovations.
  A proof of (a) proceeds as follows:
Let,

(1) $\bar{p} = (1 + \varrho)\bar{p}(A + wBl)$

where $\bar{p}$ is a positive price vector (implying absence of free goods), A is a matrix of capital-input coefficients per unit of output, B is a matrix, each column of which represents a bundle of means of subsistence necessary to support one unit of each special kind of labour, w is the *real* wage rate and l is a vector of labour-input coefficients per unit of output. When $\beta = 0$ (the workers live on air), the profit rate by the Fundamental Marxian Theorem reaches a finite maximum and (1) gives:

(2) $\dfrac{1}{1 + \varrho} P_{max} = PA$

Since $1/(1 + \varrho_{max}$ is obviously positive, it emerges as the dominant characteristic root of the input coefficient matrix A. Assuming A indecomposable, its dominant eigenvalue, by a well-established theorem on non-negative square matrices, increases when any element of A increases. Greater capital intensity (rise in the technical composition of capital assumed to lead to a rise in the value composition also) presupposes increases in the elements of A, or, at least, sufficient increases to outbalance any decreases that may also occur. (Intuitively, this argument would be more convincing if A were defined as a capital stock coefficients matrix, a redefinition which can be made without doing violence to the results). For $1/1 + \varrho_{max}$ to rise, ϱ_{max} must fall; it follows that the maximum rate of profit will decline with rises in the organic composition of capital.
  With respect to proposition (b) to establish the claim that the rate of profit can only rise when some capitalists introduce cost-cutting innovations which become subsequently generalised (1) is rewritten as

(3) $P = P[(A + \omega\beta l) = \varrho(A + \omega\beta l)]$

When a new technology (A', l') is introduced, real wages $\omega\beta$ remaining the same, more profits will be generated for its users if

(4) $P \geqslant P[(A' + \omega\beta l') + \varrho(A' + \omega\beta l')]$

In (4) the expression in square brackets can be seen as one non-negative square matrix (say matrix M) and P as a strictly positive vector (since all prices are positive). By the theorem on non-negative square matrices it follows from (4) that M has a dominant positive eigenvalue $s < 1$.

When a new equilibrium, profit and price structure (ϱ', P') is established, then

(5) $P' = P'[(A' + \omega\beta l') + \varrho'(A' = \omega\beta l')]$

Let M^* be the square, non-negative matrix in brackets in (5). Then M^* is associated with an eigenvalue $s' = 1$. It follows that $s < s'$, or that the eigenvalue of M^* is greater than the eigenvalue of M. But M^* differs from M only by ϱ' being different from ϱ. Since the dominant eigenvalue of matrices of the type considered is a rising function of the elements of the matrices, and since between (4) and (5) the two matrices involved differ only by ϱ and ϱ', it follows that $\varrho' > \varrho$. Therefore cost-reducing technical progress can only raise the rate of profit.

PART III

THE TRANSITION TO SOCIALISM

CHAPTER 9

The rise of collective capitalism

On historical-materialist principles, the transition to socialism presupposes two main developments: (a) the accumulation of a set of material preconditions. To quote the *Preface to the Contribution to the Critique of Political Economy* 'new, higher relations of production never appear before the material conditions of their existence have matured in the womb of the old society itself'. (b) The emergence of a social force, a social class who, in the achievement of this social transformation, perceive the way of asserting their interests. Consequently they adopt the aim of socialism as their long-term, historic mission. Needless to say, Marx identified this social force as the working class. Material preconditions constitute the topic of the present chapter, while the role of the working class is left for Chapter 10.

The character of the material preconditions

Marxist theory is opposed to laying out any very detailed outline of the organisation and institutions of a future socialist society. The reason is methodological. As explained in Chapter 1 of this book, historical material-ism's main concern is not with predicting the future development of the forces of production. It is with unravelling the correspondence-contradiction links between already existing production forces and their contemporary production relations, in the context of a given mode of production. In the case of capitalism it is possible to trace most of these links, because the character of the production mechanism of society has by and large crystallised. With socialism (which Marx expected to continue developing the forces of produc-tion, indeed to increase them dramatically) most of the basis for historical-materialist analysis is non-existent. Hence no blueprint of a socialist society is possible and none is proposed.

On the other hand productive forces, which can be expected to form part of a future socialist mode of production, to a certain extent mature within the context of capitalist production relations. (Otherwise the fettering thesis, together with its complement that a new mode of production gives full scope to previously 'fettered' forces, would lose its meaning.)

Forces of production which tend to transcend their capitalist limitations are definitely one part of the material preconditions of socialism. They do not exhaust the set. Another part is represented by social organisational forms which also take shape in capitalist conditions. Such forms express a certain adaptation of the relations of production to the requirements of the new forces. This last point calls for some elaboration.

So far in the book production relations have been presented either as leading the forces of production forward (in an early capitalist epoch) or acting as fetters upon them (in the era of capitalist decline). A third possibility, not mentioned so far, is that fettering can be combined with a certain measure of adaptation of production relations to the new character of production forces. In Chapter 1 fettering was explained as the consequence of action on the part of the ruling class, which defends the instrumentalities of its privileged position even though they become obstacles to further economic progress.

One method of defence, however, is to allow institutions a measure of flexible adaptation of their form to the dictates of progress, as long as the substance of class privilege continues to be served. In this way the ruling class will try to benefit from reforms and from social mutations under its regime. Being, however, the result of adaptation to the emergent forces of production that tend to transcend capitalist limitations, the new organisational forms will, in the nature of things, prefigure to some extent the social regime of the future.

With that future being oriented towards control of the production process by the whole of society and towards social ownership, adaptive changes in the form of capitalist institutions must be expected to display a collectivist character. Collectivism springs up in the very midst of the allegedly individualistic bourgeoisie. As Marx has noticed:[1]

> [T]he stock company business . . . represents the abolition of capitalist private industry on the basis of the capitalist system itself.

Of course, what is abolished is not industry, but the individualistically private character of its ownership. The joint stock company is not owned by any particular individual, but by a group of shareholders. Certainly, their ownership is not joint but separable, since each one of them remains free to dispose of his shares at will without consulting the others. To that extent the joint stock company remains an institution of private ownership. Its private character is also evident, although less explicitly, in the fact that the bigger shareholder or shareholders are in a *de facto* position to dictate the policy of the company virtually as much as if they were private owners. On the other hand, shareholders have, in some respects, to act collectively: the company is subject to a periodic general assembly of its shareholders, to which management has to submit reports and stand for re-election, the rights of the minority of shareholders enjoy a certain protection, etc.

Thus mutations in the form of bourgeois institutions are fraught with deep ambiguities. This makes it possible for the revolutionary class to detach certain institutions from their capitalist paraphernalia and use them in the process of transition to socialism. In that sense mutations of institutional forms share with the forces of production 'fettered' by capitalism the characteristic of being material preconditions of a socialist transformation. ('Material' is here understood as 'pertaining to an objective order of things, independently of the consciousness of the observer'. In that sense the emergence of joint-stock companies must be seen to be quite as 'material' as the introduction of a new method of making steel.)

Together with the new organisational forms which they prompt, new forces of production provide both positive and negative indications of the character of socialist change. If forces of production can be seen to be 'fettered' by existing capitalist relations, a programme of removing the 'fetters' (the negative aspect), will also lay down the first elements of the positive content of socialist institutions. In a very broad sense what 'fetters' the further development of the forces of production in late capitalism is (a) the exploitative and (b) the anarchic character of capitalist production. By contrast socialism would abolish exploitation and institute conscious control by society over its economic activity. The remaining sections of this chapter turn to a closer examination of these matters.

The nature and functions of class privilege

Looked at from the vantage point of capitalism, the economic development of mankind represents one striking feature: an enormous rise in the productivity of human labour. Most of this was achieved over the last two or three centuries of our present capitalist era. Capitalist relations played here a crucial role in two respects: (a) by enforcing a complete separation of the producer from his means of production. Transforming labour power into a commodity, capitalist relations made it possible for mankind to confront production in a totally objective manner. The production process was organised strictly according to its own internal logic, in disregard of any idiosyncrasies of particular individual producers or, indeed, of the subjective needs of man-at-work in general (barring, and even that not always, direct physical damage to the worker's health). (b) By making exploitation compatible with personally free labour, it achieved continuous accumulation of capital on an increasingly large scale, invested in increasingly powerful means of production.

The overall result was that, in the performance, as distinct from the setting, of tasks, production acquired the character of a process of nature, at the command of human society (the latter, however, had to lose control over itself, in the context of the anarchy of capitalist accumulation). These were the specifically capitalist effects of capitalist relations of production.

In addition, capitalism's exploitative regime served a purpose common to all antagonistic, class-divided, exploitative societies hitherto – it created and preserved the material privileges of a ruling class. In the past and, up to a point, also under capitalism, these privileges had served a social function of their own. They enabled a section of society (a minority, no doubt) to engage in activities from which the prevailing degree of scarcity precluded the large majority of the population. These activities were of two kinds: (a) management of the general affairs of society, like government, administration, jurisprudence, (b) activities the only aim of which was a free enjoyment of human faculties, of senses, of intellect, sensitivity, knowledge or wisdom; in general, the development of the human personality as an aim in itself. Art, including the art of enjoying everyday life, theoretical science, philosophy, literature are the examples usually quoted.

It should be obvious that activities of type (a), although not directly productive, in the sense of being physically self-sustaining, are nevertheless often essential to the maintenance of social life. With regard to them, the functional character of class privilege can hardly be called into question. A problem, however, does seem to arise in connection with activities of type (b). As long as they are restricted to an elite can they be said to have any wider social significance? What is the value of the Parthenon to the slave cutting marble for it in the quarry?

One part of the answer might be that such activities serve to consolidate, in the minds of those oppressed, by spectacular display of overpowering beauty, or intellectual or physical brilliance, a conviction of natural superiority of the ruling class; that they constitute, in other words, tools of ideological domination. There may be cases where this has been so, but surely this function would explain only a very small part of the story. Building the Parthenon would be an astoundingly tortuous way of keeping slaves in submission, and probably a very ineffective way too. The Spartans never created anything even remotely like the civilisation of classical Athens, yet their psychological stranglehold over their slave population, based on brutish, naked terrorism, was at least as effective as Athenian rule (also based essentially on violence).

Another part of the answer may be that some of the activities undertaken in the liberal spirit of free intellectual adventure turn out to be beneficial for production in the long run – the outstanding example being, of course, natural philosophy or mathematics in its evolution into applied natural science. This again is correct, but it only covers one part of human self-development: it would totally leave out art, for example.

A complete answer has to be far more general than suggested so far. The social function of class privilege with respect to activities of type (b) is that it creates a human way of life in the midst of inhumanity, so that aspiration to some form of better life is kept alive (usually in the teeth of deep and justified class-resentment). This would seem to be the most general, unintended function of the class-privileged, 'for these are', to quote Keynes,[2] 'so to speak, our advance guard – those who are spying out the promised land for the rest of us and pitching their camp there'.

Various reservations to the above are obviously in order. First, describing a function of a certain section of society does not imply that this section exercises the function as a conscious aim. If that were the implication, the suggested explanation of class-privilege would merit no better than Marx's sarcastic comment on bourgeois protestations about their services to the people, that the bourgeois is a bourgeois for the benefit of the working class!

Second, it should not be concluded that each and every member of the privileged class is actively engaged in exploring the higher reaches of human spirituality. Ruling classes do most emphatically not consist of Platonic philosopher-kings. Nor do they produce natural geniuses at any higher rate than the rest of the population. Hence, when they act with at least some intelligence, they try to recruit talent from the lower ranks of society, and pay it miserably little in the bargain. Not even in creating worthwhile standards for the enjoyment of everyday life have they been seen as an unqualified success. Keynes's remarks on the repercussions of affluence on everyday life are again very appropriate:[3]

> must we expect a general 'nervous breakdown'? We already have a little experience of what I mean – a nervous breakdown of the sort which is already common enough in England and the United States amongst the wives of the well-to-do classes, unfortunate women, many of them, who have been deprived by their wealth of their traditional tasks and occupation – who cannot find it sufficiently amusing, when deprived of economic necessity, to cook and clean and mend, yet are quite unable to find anything more amusing . . . To judge from the behaviour and the achievements of the wealthy classes today in any quarter of the world, the outlook is very depressing! . . . For they have most of them failed disastrously, so it seems to me . . . to solve the problem which has been set them.
>
> I feel sure that with a little more experience we shall use the new-found bounty of nature quite differently from the way in which the rich use it today, and will map out for ourselves a plan of life quite otherwise than theirs.

The conclusion is that privileged social classes do serve a function, but they serve it badly and very wastefully. From this it should not be inferred that a purely meritocratic ruling class would necessarily be much less exploitative. Individuals or groups placed in positions of power and authority in antagonistic societies will always tend to appropriate the lion's share for themselves. Even though their ideological conditioning was very different from that of the average bourgeois, Lenin's noble intention to limit the material rewards of the Communist Party ruling elite to the average worker's wages could not last very long in practice. (In the author's opinion this has been one of the saddest and most signal failures of a Marxist party in power.)

Given its function, class privilege is sustained by three conditions: (1) Availability of free time, i.e. free from the day-to-day drudgery of having to work for a living. (2) Material support without the contribution of productive labour. (3) Continuity in the enjoyment of privilege. The reasons for the first two are obvious. The third has been introduced here to foreclose the suggestion that one way of maintaining the social function of privilege, while avoiding the hardening of the split of society into hostile classes, might be to institute rotation in the exercise of the higher social functions and the enjoyment of the privileges attached to them. This might work in those cases where specialisation was not essential (e.g. jury service) but it would be pointless in anything that required the accumulation of practical experience. If, in addition to talent, it takes a lifetime of systematic practice for a musician to train himself and maintain his form, it is futile to allow everyone to take a turn at the violin once every year.

The problem acquires a different character from the moment that the rise in productivity makes it possible drastically to curtail hours of work without loss of output, when enough is produced to guarantee to everybody standards, not indeed of excessive luxury, but of reasonable adequacy or even affluence. Social privilege then loses its function. It becomes possible to allow a meaningful measure of free personal development to all members of society. The possibility and, assuming one acknowledges a basic goodness in man, the desirability of non-exploitative institutions becomes inscribed in the order of things, where an objective observer can 'read' it. It is significant, from that point of view, to notice that, with all the difference of mentality and general social outlook that separated him from Marx, Keynes could derive, from the premise of a new, high level of productivity achieved under capitalism, predictions about the ending of exploitation very reminiscent of the Marxist ones:[4]

> There are changes in other spheres too which we must expect to come. When the accumulation of wealth is no longer of high social importance, there will be great changes in our code of morals. We shall be able to rid ourselves of many of the pseudo-moral principles which have hog-ridden us for two hundred years, by which we have exalted some of the most distasteful of human qualities into the position of the highest virtues. We shall be able to afford to dare to assess the money motive for what it is, a somewhat disgusting morbidity, one of those semi-criminal, semi-pathological propensities which one hands over with a shudder to the specialists in mental disease. All kinds of social customs and economic practices, effecting the distribution of wealth and of economic rewards and penalties, which we now maintain at all costs, however distasteful and unjust they may be in themselves, because they are tremendously useful in promoting the accumulation of capital, we shall then be free, at last, to discard.

The only thing one would add, from a Marxist point of view, is that after a certain point the antagonisms inherent in exploitation become not only pointless but positively harmful to production itself, in so far as they stand in the way of the means of production achieving their full potential. A non-antagonistic society becomes a precondition of normal economic activity.

Functional capitalism

The possibility of universal sufficiency, if not affluence, and of free time for all, marks the passing away of the social purpose of capitalist exploitation. It does not establish the need for co-operative social relations. Non-antagonism does not necessarily imply co-operation. It is possible to imagine a kind of technological development, different from what has actually taken place, where the means of production evolve into machines of increasingly powerful types, but always retain the scale appropriate for use by the individual artisan. Simple commodity production plus automation of the artisan's workshop might produce affluence, but it would lead neither to social ownership nor to central planning, some measure of which is, undeniably, an element of the Marxist prediction about the future mode of production. (Indeed, if one concentrated on the few predictive remarks by Marx himself rather than on subsequent elaborations, not 'some measure' but complete, all-encompassing central planning is the way of the future. Production is to be integrated on a social scale and be administered as if the whole economy constituted one gigantic factory.) For the collectivist aspects of the socialist prediction, the integrated, large-scale character of the production process is crucially significant. The development of forms of economic organisation in capitalism itself also points in the same direction.

Mutations of form of capitalist relations of production under capitalism itself are in general typified by the rise of collective capitalist ownership, complemented by the separation of ownership and control. Functions which in early and middle capitalism were attached to capitalist ownership change into professional posts open to persons of competence. The very first elements of this kind of change appear as soon as money capital becomes separated from productive or, more broadly, from active business capital (industrial or commercial). The circuit of capital itself may, in a very broad sense, be seen as presupposing some kind of joint ownership. For capital to become productive of surplus-value in a meaningful, continuous manner, it must complete, and go on completing, a sequence of successive circuits. Without this sequence, the unit of which is the individual circuit, capital ownership is pointless. What the capitalist should own economically is the process itself, measured by a certain number of its units, i.e. a certain number of circuits.

For economic ownership also to become formal ownership, one legal subject, one capitalist must unite in his person ownership rights over capital in each and every phase of the circuit. From the moment that money capital becomes separated from productive and from commercial capital, formal ownership over a whole circuit by one person becomes less and less common. Given the indispensable unity of the circuit, various capitalists become its joint owners, not in the sense that they own shares in each and every one of its separate phases, but rather in the sense that each one succeeds the other in ownership, while capital describes its unique orbit. This idea may be illustrated with the help of a scheme of circuit-ownership displayed side-by-side with the scheme of the circuit of capital as follows:

$$\text{I. } M - C \overset{LP}{\underset{MP}{\diagdown}} \dots P \dots C' - M'$$

| II. Money capitalist | Wholesaler of materials | Industrialist | Wholesaler of product | Money Capitalist |

It must be noticed that, from the table of successive owners, workers, who own and sell labour power, have been omitted. As they do not participate in the sharing of surplus value, they cannot be considered as joint owners of *capital*. A second point is that the industrialist may be in business without any capital of his own, working with totally borrowed funds. If so he would be a pure entrepreneur. One aspect of the separation of money capitalists and entrepreneurs is the separation of saving and investment, with its well-known importance in Keynesian theory. Finally the separation of ownership and control is already present, in an elementary form in the circuit of ownership. Although, at each phase of the circuit, particular capitalists can be presumed to be running their own business themselves, the most crucial part of the circuit, the production phase, is exclusively commanded by the industrialist. By virtue of being the direct expropriator of surplus value from the workers he can be seen as the real 'manager', the real person in command, as against all others who are mere owners.

As the capitalist system matures, all these functional separations – potentially contained in the capitalist class-relationship itself, as represented in the circuit scheme – become an actual division of tasks. One aspect of this transformation – the emergence of the complementary roles of 'rentiers-by-necessity' and entrepreneurs, through the medium of the credit system – has already been surveyed in Chapter 7. The increase in the minimum amount of capital needed to cross the threshold into independent business was identified there as the main force behind the appearance of the enforced-rentier stratum. Here a different line of development, affecting, again through the credit system, the position of active owner-managers will be explored.

The professionalisation of the managerial function of capitalists should not be imagined as an invariably non-conflictual, freely and rationally chosen course of action. Intra-class antagonisms play a significant role in these developments. Certain remarks in *Capital* provide an interesting lead into this topic. In the credit system Marx perceived that:[5]

> On the one hand, the capital of the industrial capitalist is not 'saved' by himself, but he has command of the savings of others in proportion to the magnitude of his capital; on the other hand, the money-capitalist makes of the savings of others his own capital, and of the credit, which the reproductive capitalists give to one another and which the public gives to them, a private source for enriching himself. The last illusion of the capitalist system, that capital is the fruit of one's own savings, is thereby destroyed. Not only does profit consist in the appropriation of other people's labour, but the capital, with which this labour of others is set in motion and exploited, consists of other people's property, which the money capitalist places at the disposal of the industrial capitalist and for which he in turn exploits the latter.

This allusion (unique as far as the author knows in Marx) to exploitation among capitalists, raises interesting questions. How can capitalists, being all exploiters, exploit one another. Is there any concept of fairness valid for the sharing of the loot (the surplus-value) among them? Technical rules certainly exist (e.g. distribution in proportion to the size of each one's capital) but, in Marx's perception, there is nothing particularly fair about such rules to make their breach merit the name of 'exploitation'.

It may be that Marx is using language loosely on this particular occasion. In the present author's opinion, however, he is groping towards more basic problems. To the extent that he acts as a production manager the industrial capitalist is, in Marx's eyes, a producer, a supplier of skilled labour, whose labour power is reproduced at a certain cost. The industrial capitalist pays himself for the value of his labour power out of the surplus value that falls to his share. Ordinarily his surplus value surpasses the value of his labour power many times over. It is, however, conceivable that financial capital may snatch the balance from him, reducing him, under the appearance of his maintaining a certain entrepreneurial independence, to the status of a mere salaried employee. At that limit the industrialist would indeed be exploited by the money capitalists.

Even before that point, however, and even if he is never squeezed quite so hard, the industrial capitalist, to the extent that he is losing ground to the financiers in the distribution of surplus value, is in the process of being expropriated as a capitalist. His capacity for independent accumulation, and hence for independent entrepreneurial action, is eroded. This may be a phase preparatory to his explicit expropriation via bankruptcy or takeover, or a step to his indirect transformation into a mere functionary, entrusted with running a certain branch of business, by his financiers. The two methods may obviously be combined.

In the author's opinion, it was such processes of expropriation or subjection of the industrial to the financial interest that Marx had in mind when he raised the possibility of one section of capital exploiting another. He was beginning to perceive that the antagonism between savers and finance capitalists – the first which caught his attention – had a parallel in the conflict between financiers and business managers. The professionalisation of the managerial aspect of capitalist activity was not merely, or not any longer, a method of enlisting talent from other classes of the population in the service of the bourgeoisie. It was becoming the supplement of a process of partial expropriation of capitalist factory owners. Having, as a result of the rise of collective forms of capital ownership, lost their financial hold over business, individual capitalists were also losing their managerial independence. Collective, depersonalised capital sought its natural complement in a body of professional managers. There would, of course, be nothing to stop a small or medium capitalist from offering his services as a manager, if he had the ability. But he would then have to integrate himself into the hierarchical, centralised structure of bureaucratic command, developed by large companies and groups of companies. This he would have to do even in those cases where he would rise to the leadership of the hierarchy (even more so when he would not rise). He would always remain a member of a team, subject to certain collective disciplines, rather than an individual boss.

The role of the individual capitalist, either as a 'rentier-by-necessity' or as a professional manager is, therefore, the result of a process of partial expropriation. The individual passes under the antagonistic control of collective capital. Who represents collective capital? Marx, impressed by the strength of the credit system, laid emphasis on the financiers. It may, however, be more correct to adopt a wider approach, identifying the controlling element of the modern capitalist structure with those groups of capitalists who are able to put together and manipulate amounts of capital funds, not necessarily belonging to them in ownership but sufficiently under their control and sufficient in amount to be invested in independent new ventures. Such capitalists may be financiers or they may constitute boards of directors in large corporations. In the latter case ownership (of productive assets, not of shares) and control coincide in the legal personality of the corporation, but control does not rest on ownership; rather it rests on the capacity of the corporation to take the initiative in raising its own finance.

With collective capitalism a tripartite division of roles and of sections among the bourgeoisie emerges: ownership, management and control. Ownership corresponds to the function of saving, management to the function of administration, control to the function of active capital accumulation (speculation and investment). Owners (savers) and managers are subject to financial manipulators who, being in a position to take the initiative in business, reserve for themselves the role also of the chief beneficiary of the system. The two subject groups, at their lower echelons, cease to be purely bourgeois. They merge with the working class who, on their side, have also become savers, while some of them begin to staff the lower rungs of the managerial hierarchy.

Keynes, Schumpeter and the socialisation of saving and investment

As discussed in the previous two chapters and in the section above, modern collective capitalism tends to socialise both private saving, by pushing it onto 'rentiers-by-necessity', and management, by delegating it to professionals. In both cases an element of expropriation of the original individual capitalist (the owner-manager-saver-investor type) is present. In the case of management, however, the process of expropriation, at the level of the typical manager, has arguably been completed. This does not mean that owner-managers have totally vanished from the scene, but that society typically expects the manager to be a professional, to whom ownership is, for purposes of management, incidental.

With saving, expropriation has not reached the same point. Saving is still, to an important, although possibly no longer predominantly important extent, performed by rentiers, individuals who derive their incomes from some kind of ownership. (The element of expropriation here is that typically such ownership does not give them command over business.) Theory, however, has run ahead of actual developments, pointing to the capacity of collective capitalism to eliminate the individual saver altogether. Schumpeter, in his *Theory of Capitalist Development*, explained the power of the credit system, not merely to induce savings throughout the whole population, workers included, not only to place such savings at the disposal of capitalist entrepreneurs, but essentially to force the population to make savings. Briefly, the method envisaged by Schumpeter consisted of banks using their capacity to create additional, new purchasing power and to make it available, in the first place to entrepreneurs. By using newly created purchasing power, entrepreneurs buy from a fixed stock of available production resources. They raise prices against the holders of existing, as distinct from new, purchasing power, to whom bank support is not available, and oblige them to cut back on their consumption of resources. In real terms it is such people who are forced to bear the brunt of saving. Rentiers are totally irrelevant in this process; all investment can be financed by the forced savings of the whole of the community.

Keynes, writing in the context of his basic assumption that more saving is generated in modern capitalism than can be absorbed by investment in conditions of full employment, took the rather more realistic line that all usefully utilisable saving is, in fact, currently generated by retained earnings and the sinking funds of joint stock companies. To these any amounts accumulated by pension funds must be added. Whatever is saved by individuals over and above that amount merely represents an attempt by rentiers to hang on to a share of surplus value which accrues to them in the form of interest. To the extent that they are successful they achieve this not by virtue of contributing to the increase of productive capital but by the very opposite. Their attempt to over-save forces the economy to operate at some point below full employment; this discourages investment so that the capital stock does not expand as fast as possible. Capital scarcity is thereby eternalised and interest – in the eyes of non-Marxist economists a scarcity price for capital – is maintained as a source of income for rentiers.

Keynes's recommendation was that the State should take on the responsibility of regulating the flow of investment, both in order to maintain full employment and in order to build up the capital stock, at some rate acceptable to the community, to the point where capital scarcity would vanish. Progress towards this goal would evidently be accompanied by a systematic reduction of interest rates to the point where no rentier class would any longer be sustainable. This was Keynes's famous 'euthanasia of the rentier'.

In their theoretical perception of the tendencies and potentialities of modern capitalism both Schumpeter and Keynes envisaged the total abolition of any function for individual owners of capital, i.e. the consummation of the process of expropriation of the small and even of the medium-sized capitalist. For them saving becomes the task not of owners, by virtue of their ownership, but of professionals, by virtue of their expertise and position in the decision-making hierarchy of the economy. Expropriation transforms saving, as it has already transformed management, into a social function rather than an attribute of private property.

The implications for the future of capitalism of the collectivisation of the savings process differ as between the two authors. Schumpeter eliminates the need for a rentier class, but maintains both the financier (the banker) and the entrepreneur (the innovator). In his vision of modern capitalism, control remains firmly in the hands of those whom Marx described as a new financial aristocracy. Schumpeter does not himself derive any emerging need for state involvement from his analysis. It seems only natural, however, to observe that, in a situation where saving is essentially created by the credit system through a process of inflation, the state will very quickly step in to place the process under its control. Keynes, on the other hand, positively invites state control over investment as the only means of taming an activity which, in the hands of individuals, becomes dangerously anarchic.

The significance of what is implicit in Schumpeter about the role of the state as well as of what is explicitly recommended by Keynes, lies in the fact that, in contrast to the case of partial nationalisation, comprehensive control, at the level of the economy as a whole, over central aspects of the aggregate process of capital accumulation is here being considered. This is a result formally very close to the comprehensive economic planning envisaged by Marx as one of the main features of a socialist mode of production. The approximation by Keynes to the idea of planning, in those moments when he goes beyond the regulation by the state of the aggregate level of investment to determining its specific structure sector by sector, is indeed striking:[6]

> For my own part I am now somewhat sceptical, of a merely monetary policy directed at reducing the rate of interest. I expect to see the State, which is in a position *to calculate the marginal efficiency of capital-goods* on long views and on the basis of the general social advantages taking an ever greater responsibility for *directly organising* investment; since it seems likely that the fluctuations in the market estimation of the marginal efficiency of *different types* of capital, calculated on the principles I have described above, will be too great to be offset by any practicable changes in the rate of interest.
>
> [Italics added]

Nationalisation has been seen as a consequence of the increasing scale of production, hence as a direct instance of the relations of production responding to the changed character of production forces. In the case of state-managed investment the link is not as direct or as obvious, but it nevertheless exists. The need to accumulate and, in particular, to centralise vast amounts of capital funds, which provides the impetus to the credit system, is dictated by the increasing scale which technology imposes on the individual capitalist firm. The mediation of the credit system marginalises and, in theory, is expected totally to expropriate the rentiers. The way is, then, cleared for state control. If entrepreneurs are not the owners of the capital which they use, they have no more claim on it than the state which intervenes to maintain full employment. The road from growing forces of production to comprehensive investment regulation is not direct, but it is clearly signposted. Marx's analysis of credit is pregnant with investment control; investment control is pregnant with the socialisation of the economy.

The ambiguity of collective capitalism

The professionalisation of many capitalist functions together with the de-personalisation of capitalist relationships erodes the obviousness of the class character of bourgeois society. It is maintained by various sociologists that class divisions tend to fade away in modern capitalism. The great testing ground of this thesis is the alleged change in the economic and social position of the working class. To the extent that they acquire skills and their incomes tend to rise, workers are supposed to become themselves some kind of professionals, a low-grade version of the middle classes who, on their side, are themselves also said to be taking up productive work. Mostly, however, the argument focuses on the apparently altered position of the working class regarding capital ownership. It is argued that, with the rise of pension funds which enter, as institutional investors, in the Stock Exchange, the ownership position of the working class is wholly transformed. Pension funds have no exclusive ownership over individual companies but they own large packets of shares, large portfolios, which give them an ownership stake in the capital collectively owned by the community. Since pension funds belong to the workers, and shares belong to pension funds, the loop is closed. Workers have become capitalists.

The argument appears, at first sight, appealing but it is not really very solid, for two reasons. The first regards the concept of ownership. The chain: workers → pension funds → share ownership may seem to make sense, until one asks what ownership rights over shares the alleged ultimate 'owners', the workers, can exercise. It will then be found that they have no rights of disposal at all over the immediate object of their supposed ownership, the shares controlled by their fund, let alone the enterprises which originally issued the shares. Not merely as individuals are they deprived of such rights, they have no power collectively either. Their unions either cannot intervene in the management of the funds or, if they can, they are bound by the legal rules of trusteeship, since the typical form of pension funds is that of a trust for the benefit of those insured. This legal form places professional financiers, who are presumed to know best how to invest wisely the members' contributions, in a position of automatic strength regarding control of the funds. Even in the case of ordinary shareholders, it will be argued in a moment, separation of ownership and control renders problematical the sense in which they can still be seen as substantive (not purely formal) owners. In the case of pension funds the concept of workers' 'ownership' is even more thinly diluted. A two-tier separation of ownership and control intervenes between the ultimate beneficiaries and active business, one at the level of company management, a second at the level of share-management by the officials of the pension fund.

Those who hold the view that workers become capitalists through pension funds will not deny these facts but will still insist that workers, via the pension fund's investment, receive a share of surplus value from capital as their pension. It may at first sound paradoxical but, on closer examination, is quite true that the pensions which workers receive are not surplus value, even if their origin is in the profits of enterprises. They are deferred wages, part of variable capital, or of the value of labour power. Properly understood, the commodity labour power is evaluated at the cost of the worker's sustaining a normal natural life. This includes not merely reproduction but also provision for one's old age. Only if wages cover these, not apparently connected with production, costs can they function as proper incentives for a legally free worker, rather than a slave. Formally it would be possible to provide for workers' retirement by keeping them on the payroll of firms that they had served during their working lives even beyond the age of useful employment, until their death. Their working-life wages could then be reduced to the level of current necessity, allowing no margin for saving (from which, as things stand now, pension funds derive their capital).[7]

With the buying and selling of labour-power a basic institution of economic life, collective capitalism remains at its basis a class-divided exploitative system. The impersonal capitalist of a joint-stock company can obviously exploit workers quite as much as the personal factory owner of earlier times. In addition to such fundamental exploitation, collective capitalism has developed a second tier of exploitative society by subjecting the whole of society, all social classes, to the burden of saving, of which proportionally more is cast onto the shoulders of those least able to carry it. The resulting funds are then made available to financial manipulators, who retain for themselves the privilege of disposing over social wealth autocratically, without any genuine public or private accountability.

The exploitative character of collective capitalism is complemented, re-inforced and completed by the intervention in the economy of the modern state. In the previous section of the present chapter Keynes's hopes of a socialisation of the investment process through the state were briefly surveyed. In addition, the state may be portrayed as standing at the pinnacle of the socialisation of capitalist ownership, through the institution of the nationalised industry.

It does not follow, however, that the policy of the actually functioning bourgeois state corresponds either to Keynes's high idealism or to any benevolent version of state socialism. From the discoveries of Keynes and his followers governments have slowly picked up the techniques of functional finance (of controlling the aggregate level of spending in the economy); they have, on the other hand, also learnt that they can use this technique, either to raise the level of economic activity, if private profitability prospects appear promising, or to lower it, generating unemployment, if the need to curb working-class militancy and restore discipline becomes paramount.[8]

With public ownership a similar alternation of phases can be observed. Governments use both their capacity to raise revenue and their legislative and administrative powers to take in hand industrial sectors, the reorganisation of which can no longer be left exclusively to market forces if prohibitive levels of economic and social dislocation are to be avoided. Equally governments restore to the private sector whole sections of formerly national-ised industries, when they perceive that they can do so with (economic, political and social) impunity.

By all these means, private and public, the ruling class manages to place and keep the inevitable collectivist tendencies of modern capitalism in the service of its private interests. Yet the ambiguity of collective capitalism can never be totally exorcised. On the ideological front first – an aspect of social life particularly important in epochs of transition from one mode of production to the next – the increasing and on the whole irreversible trend towards collectivist forms of bourgeois ownership familiarises the public mind with the idea that the natural subject of ownership is the group, the collectivity, rather than the individual. From there the next step, passing from ownership at the level of the group to ownership at the level of society as a whole, is much easier for public consciousness to take, since conceptually it involves a change in quantity rather than quality.

Second, in the practical sphere, it is true that the most collectivist institution of all, the modern bourgeois state, uses its powers of taxation to appropriate a share of surplus value, not only from property but also from labour incomes. By reducing the take-home pay of the working population to support its functions, the state emerges as a partner in exploitation with the bourgeois class.

Even so the identification can never be total, at least not in a democracy. For one thing, public consciousness has not been conditioned to accept it as self-evident that revenues from taxation pass into the hands of government officials in the same, publicly unaccountable, manner that the accumulated capital of society passes into the hands of financiers. The use of the share of surplus-value appropriated by the state must in principle remain under the glare of public scrutiny, through institutions which, in democratic states, aspire to a universal representative character.

For another, the modern democratic state has to respond to the demand, arising mainly from the lower income strata and, indeed, from the working class, of providing collectively a number of services (health, national insurance, education) which capitalist markets never supplied in an anywhere near satisfactory manner to the working majority. In organising such services, the bourgeois state is certainly acting mainly in the interests of the bourgeoisie, in a triple sense: (a) it takes on certain of the costs of reproduction and maintenance of an efficient labour force (health, education, unemployment pay). Such costs would either not be undertaken at all, with a resulting deterioration in the quality of industrial labour, or they would be included in the value of labour power. Given that there appear to be very significant economies of scale in the centralised supply of such services, to pay for them through the worker's wage packet would probably reduce profitability more than by the corresponding amount of taxation allocated to their finance. (b) By supplying free of direct charge certain services at those moments of the person's or the society's economic life when the working man is feeling at his most vulnerable as an individual (illness, unemployment, old age), the state reduces the level of social tension, and makes the burden of propertylessness, of exploitation more tolerable for proletarians. Consequently, it defuses to some extent the explosiveness of class division. (c) In adopting an attitude of economic paternalism, the state adds to the maintenance of law and order a second reason legitimising its own existence and power over society.

At the same time the welfare aspect of bourgeois states, apart from constituting a real improvement of the material position of the workers, represents also a concession in the long-term strategic confrontation between socialism, capitalism and their respective supporters. It gives an everyday demonstration of the possibility of successful provision for individual needs via collective channels in areas where private provision had, on the whole, failed for the majority of the population. Objectively, the welfare state is a bridgehead of socialist institutions involuntarily conceded in the midst of bourgeois territory. Whether it become a launching pad for the socialisation of further aspects of life is a matter of the determination and political strength of the working class. Thirdly, Keynesian-inspired policies, without ever having approached, even at a distance, some of the more daring social visions of Keynes himself, have achieved at least this much: by leading certain governments at certain times to accept responsibility for full employment they have opened a serious breach in the bourgeois ideological defences of the social *status quo*. It has become very hard convincingly to maintain any longer that an unbridgeable gap exists between economics and politics, between the private and the general interest. In Chapter 2 of this book the fundamental nature of this assumption for the bourgeois mode of production has been explained. By denying it, Keynesian-inspired theorists and politicians have taken a road which – with or without them or even against them – may lead to socialism.

The anguished efforts of the monetarists, with their insistence on the inevitability of a certain 'natural' rate of unemployment which the government can do nothing about, are an attempt to regain the ground lost in this respect through the spread of Keynesianism. Such efforts are a piece of additional evidence for the thesis of the genuine ambiguity of collective capitalism. It would seem obvious that, if the state, the most centralised collective institution of all in bourgeois society, were in a position to regulate aggregate unemployment at will, the whole economy, at least in some of its more important aspects, could be run as one unit from one centre in a conscious, deliberate manner. This is exactly the kind of economy which Marx foresaw as maturing inside the integument of capitalist relations of production.

It does not follow that collective capitalism is already socialism. Far from it. However, in the areas of ownership (joint-stock companies), in the areas of capital accumulation (socialisation of saving, theoretical possibility for socially managed investment) and in the area of overall economic manage-ment, it has created institutions which a determined working class, or indeed a more widely – from the class point of view – based socialist movement can put under control and use without having to start from scratch, for the construction of a socialist mode of production. In a sense rather broader than Lenin meant it, the institutions of collective capitalism are indeed 'ripe for expropriation'.

CHAPTER 10

The working class

In 1859 Marx wrote:[1]

> [M]ankind always sets itself only such problems as it can solve, since, looking at the matter more closely, it will always be found that the task itself arises only when the material conditions for its solution already exist or are at least in the process of formulation.

This statement has serious methodological implications about task-setting in society in general, which will be looked at below. Any methodological discussion, however, must be conducted in the light of the obvious fact that the task uppermost in Marx's mind was the transition to a socialist society.

The quotation above contains one of the most ambitious, rich, complex but also most intriguing formulations of historical materialism. Partly it restates the basic thesis that perception and consciousness follow upon change in the material conditions of production rather than precede it, but it goes considerably beyond this thesis. From the formation of consciousness as understanding, it advanced to consciousness as perception and adoption of tasks, adding that the setting of the task in itself includes some guarantee of successful resolution. Had the potential of success not existed, mankind would not have set the task for itself, because it would not have perceived or sensed the need for it.

From the existence of a potential for success no certainty of success can be inferred. It is conceivable that the task will be mishandled, the potential wasted, the result of the effort catastrophic. Marx's indomitable optimism would allow for this possibility only very reluctantly, but allow for it he did.[2] Even with this qualification, however, his *Preface* statement is not unproblematic. To talk about tasks is not the same as talking about ideas or perceptions. That the latter are reflections in the mind of an anterior material reality (although admittedly there never is such a thing as purely passive reflection) is much easier to accept than that on the basis of such perception only, tasks will be set. The setting of a task implies much more strongly the need for human initiative and action. Human beings are not neutral to whatever action they initiate or are called upon to take. They proceed only after they have become convinced of its worthwhileness, after they have made a positive value judgement about it (or such a judgement has been imposed on them). The reference to tasks in the *Preface* raises the whole difficult question of value judgements.

One aspect of this question is whether mankind can proceed to value judgements about action, set itself tasks, on a non-existent or inadequate material basis: whether, in other words, it is possible to imagine societies binding themselves to utopian tasks. To this the answer can only be that *sections* of mankind are known, and acknowledged by Marx, to have adopted utopian aims, for example, the socialist colonies founded by Robert Owen[3] in Britain or in America. Marx also knew the possibility of, and advised strongly against, premature working-class revolutions. Therefore, the dictum of the *Preface* that mankind *always* sets itself *only* such tasks as it can solve must be interpreted as compressing a special meaning in the phrase 'setting a task'. The task would have to be undertaken in such a way as to involve the whole of society in a sustained effort of long perspective and duration, before it can be accepted as having been seriously 'set'. (Even the term 'the whole of society' cannot be taken literally.

But more problems remain. Even if the need for a task and the potential for its fulfilment exist, will mankind necessarily adopt it? In what form? If, given a certain material reality, a whole range of responses is possible, how will selection be made among them, so that just one of them becomes a task?

The formulation of the *Preface* does not touch on these issues. Resolving them is prior to setting a task and relating it to the potential of its fulfilment. It might be argued that the *Preface* takes as its starting point the moment that a task has been 'set' (in the sense mentioned above), that it assumes the prior problems of choice and value judgements to be solved somehow, and that it limits the analysis to ascertaining the necessity of correspondence between a task already 'set' and the preconditions of its resolution.

An interpretation along these lines might be defensible, but it would conflict with and impoverish the rest of Marx's work. The author of the *Preface* was quite conscious of the existence of the problem of some open-endedness in the choice and adoption of a course of action in society. It will be argued, in the present chapter, that he constructed his analysis of the economic development of capitalism in such a way as to show, not only the objective possibility of socialism or its desirability from a wider, human, point of view, but also the virtual inevitability for the relevant social agency, the working class, to adopt it as an aim. In this he was not distorting the data to fit them to his own preconceptions. Recognising implicitly, sometimes even explicitly, various alternatives of capitalist development, he selected the one that seemed to him both plausible and pregnant with possibilities for the most radical break with a past of class-division and exploitation. To unravel and assess this part of Marxism is the objective of the present chapter.

'Mankind' and social class

Change in material conditions has been accepted above as prior to the adoption of a new task by society. Even so, it has to be acknowledged that material conditions in their non-human aspects (and even human activity, in so far as it operates as a mere mechanical rather than intellectual force of production, e.g. the labour of a galley slave or of an alienated wage-earner at the factory conveyor belt) do not speak for themselves to disclose their social potential. This is either directly and exactly assessed or indirectly and intuitively sensed by conscious human agents, who take action to implement social change. Corresponding to the distinction between diagnosis and 'sensing', the setting of the goal of socialism by society for itself may be either scientific or ideological (with 'ideology' taken to have the meaning attributed to it in the 1859 *Preface*).

A scientific perception of the goal of socialism does not invent new relations of production arbitrarily; it 'reads' them out of the structure of changed material conditions. The relevant changes have been summarised in the previous chapter. Using a broad, suggestive analogy – nothing more than that – new relations of production are like shadow-prices; they are not extant but implicit in the material structure of production. Prices actually charged on the market reflect distortions and deviations from the optimality of perfect competition. Similarly, existing production relations in the phase of decline of a mode of production are sub-optimal, in the sense of fettering the forces of production. In the case of prices, material constraints and the economy's objective function determine between them a set of optimal exchange ratios which nowadays can be accurately found by modern mathematical techniques. Though not actual, such prices do exist as a potential corrective of distortions caused by market rigidities. By analogy, 'shadow relations of production' already exist conceptually and can be scientifically discovered in those cases where material conditions have already changed sufficiently, but relations of production have not yet, or not yet completely, adapted to them.

Human agents, however, may not be in a position to proceed scientifically. They do not necessarily have direct consciousness of the source of their inspiration or of the real repercussions of their contemplated action. Accordingly 'a distinction should always be made between the material transformation of the economic conditions of production, which can be determined with the precision of natural science, and the legal, political, religious aesthetic or philosophic – in short, ideological forms in which men become conscious of the conflict and fight it out'.[4]

The two kinds of perception are not unconnected; they have a common starting point in the development of material reality. Nor are they necessarily in conflict, one representing true, the other false consciousness. Such conflicts do arise. It is also possible, however, for the difference between ideology and science to be one of degree of clarity, thoroughness and rigour, rather than of basic concept. The relationship between Marxism and socialism is a good case in point. The latter antedates the former historically, representing the spontaneous ideological aspirations of a large section of the working class. Marxism offers a structured, closely-argued approach to the socialist ideal; but, this apart, the socialism which it champions is an article recognisably similar, in its broad lines, to what instinctive working-class socialists would claim, have in fact claimed, as their own.

The presence of the two kinds of perception mentioned above is connected with the wider problem of the subject of new social consciousness. The thesis of the *Preface* is that 'mankind' sets to itself and resolves tasks. But who is 'mankind'? In a class-divided society the term obviously cannot refer to 'everybody' because one section of the population, the old ruling class, will inevitably resist change. Feudal lords, as a class, will not embrace bourgeois relations of production, capitalists, as a class will not adopt socialism. In the context of the *Preface* 'mankind' can only mean the class which, at the critical juncture, has become the standard-bearer of human progress, in the sense of leading the change into a more advanced mode of production. If successful, this class will probably form and lead a very wide coalition, with other discontented groups of the population outside its own ranks, isolating the hitherto ruling class politically. A near-consensus may, at such moments, arise, giving the impression that it is, indeed, 'mankind' who have adopted a certain course of action.

In a class-divided society such an impression can never correspond totally with reality. The emergence of new social consciousness must be studied first and foremost as the consciousness of that class which seeks to assert its collective interests by replacing existing relations of production with new ones. In the case of the transition to socialism, the class in question is the working class. Both because its class-consciousness must, in the context of historical materialism, be rooted in the economy and because the formation of such consciousness is a necessary link in the change of the mode of production, a rudimentary study of class-consciousness is a legitimate topic of Marxist economics.

A new kind of class-consciousness, the kind that dictates the adoption of a new task for society, presupposes a certain detachment from ideas and modes of thinking dominated by existing relations of production. Given the distinction between a scientific and an ideological way of apprehending the need for and character of social change, scientists, although not exempt from the influence of the ruling class, should, in principle, be in a position to display such detachment.[5] But the working-class does not consist of scientists. What is it that makes workers detach themselves from the dominant ideas and turn either to a socialist message originating amongst Marxist intellectuals or to socialist ideas spontaneously springing up, by a process of ideological mutation, amidst their own ranks?

The stranglehold of market ideology

The very first step in such detachment must be the perception that economic goals can be pursued by means different from and even opposed to those available under the bourgeois mode of production. The typical way of pursuing such goals in capitalism is via the market. The great ideological strength of the market is that it appears as a totally objective mechanism which enables a collectivity of individuals to function in a mutually supportive manner but without pre-arranged agreement. It does this, however, only on condition that individuals or their conscious collective agencies remain for ever precluded from attempting any direct intervention in the extra-sensitive mechanism of their own coordination. They are too crude, too narrow, too blinkered by self-seeking egoism to be entrusted with making any conscious decision concerning the collectivity. Each one must remain imprisoned within the bounds of his/her own egotism, so that the invisible hand of competition is left undisturbed to shape an economy beneficial as far as possible to all. Individual or collective self-determination appears very severely curtailed by the semi-mystical elevation of the coordinating mechanism of the economy into something untouchable, irreplaceable and as inevitable as some kind of destiny. Briefly, the ideological message of the market is that socialism, if not totally impossible, is certainly a very inefficient way of organising economic life. Hence the voluminous effort deployed in bourgeois economics, both to extol the virtues and to demonstrate the timeless, ahistorical character of what it defines as the laws of the market.

By contrast the Marxist analysis explains the ideological power of the market not by extolling merely its impersonal character but by strongly projecting the reified (the objectified) form which economic relations assume. The economy is seen as operating by means of an interaction of commodities, money, value, capital and labour power, relating among themselves as if they were forces of nature, independent of human volition. Human consciousness stands opposite to them mystified, under the spell of the fetishism of commodities. Human agents act as executives of the dictates of their own objectified relations; they enact roles (often self-destructive ones) in a scenario written for them by economic forces beyond their control. The capitalist is capital personified, the worker is reduced to a supplier of muscle-power.

In playing out their social roles individuals have little choice but to vary their behaviour. However, the conditions of its very existence sometimes push the working class to a direct confrontation with the laws of the market.

One such instance of some importance is the determination of the rate of absolute surplus value. It has been seen (Chapter 4) that this is not so much determined by the interplay of objectified economic relations as by direct political and social class struggle between capitalists and workers. Class struggle implies the development of a certain degree of collective consciousness in individuals. They discover that they do not have to be the playthings of their objectified relations. They may exploit degrees of freedom which the economic structure allows; they may try to oppose the domain of such forces, as in the case of the conflict over the length of the working day. Such subjective reactions, reaching the limits of rebellion of economic agents against the objectified rationality of the economy which they are supposed to implement, obviously become one of the forces which shape the concrete configuration of economic reality. In this way the detachment of working class consciousness from the thrall of bourgeois ideology begins.

The further and really crucial problem is whether, in the final resolution of any historical enterprise, the subjective aims of individuals or classes who attempt to take conscious action in the context of capitalist relations are attained or frustrated. The attitude of Marxist economics is that, on the whole, attempts at manipulating the objectified economic forces or at opposing them in the context of capitalist institutions may have some limited success but are, in the long run, doomed to failure. The logic of capital has to prevail in the end or the capitalist economy ceases to function, plunging society into a destructive economic crisis. When this becomes a real prospect, the working class has either to consummate its process of detachment from bourgeois ideology by opting for a fully-fledged programme of revolutionary change, or slide back into an unresolvable semi-dependence on the institutions of collective capitalism. Which of the two possibilities materialises depends on the image the working class makes of itself and of its place in the world.

Class in itself and class for itself

From the moment in the historical development of capitalism when the number of proletarian workers reaches significant proportions, they acquire certain group-features that set them apart, as a separate social class. They share in common their propertylessness and their exploited economic conditions, two basic ills which, in the context of capitalist institutions are irredeemable. This establishes for them an objectively definable collective interest in the achievement of a regime based on the social ownership of the means of production to end the exploitation of the working man. But it does not follow that the workers recognise their class interest in historical change immediately as it becomes objectively definable. For as long as they have not arrived at such recognition Marx sometimes describes them, adopting and modifying the 'in itself' or 'for itself' philosophical distinction from Hegel,

as a 'class-in-itself', or a class-for-others. After they have acquired consciousness of their long-term class interest Marx describes them as a class-for-itself.
It is the class-for-itself that constitutes the agency of the transition to socialism.
It forges its own ideology, its independent political party, and proceeds to
confront the bourgeoisie on the basic question of the nature of production
relations. Before it can proceed to a confrontation along the whole front, it
is essential for the working class to acquire consciousness of its situation
through practical experience of partial issues. It is important for its political
formation to achieve even limited success in opposing the objective force of
capitalist economic relations. It is also, however, important, if workers are
to eventually turn to socialism as the solution, that the efforts of the workers
with respect to partial reforms be ultimately frustrated. The working class is
then made to realise that piecemeal improvements of its position have no
lasting value, as long as the fundamental feature of capitalistic organisation,
the propertylessness of the producers, is left intact. Action against the very
institution of capitalist ownership follows upon such a realisation.

Is this realisation conditional on the prior emergence in capitalism of the
collectivist elements which make the transition to socialism a practical
possibility? The distinction made in the *Preface* between two epochs in each
mode of production, characterised by the transition of the relations of
production from catalysts into fetters of the forces of production, can be
closely paralleled by two epochs in the consciousness of the working class:
one in which they accept the objectified rationality of capitalist economic
relations, and a second during which they begin to reject and oppose such
rationality, moving from the state of a class-in-itself to that of a class-for-
itself. Engels, Marx's lifelong friend and collaborator, formulated this thesis
in a rather striking manner:[6]

The connection between distribution and the material conditions of existence of
society at any period lies so much in the nature of things that it is always reflected
in popular instinct. So long as a mode of production still describes an ascending
curve of development, it is enthusiastically welcomed even by those who come off
worst from its corresponding mode of distribution. This was the case with the
English workers in the beginnings of modern industry. And even while this mode
of production remains normal for society, there is, in general, contentment with
the distribution, and if objections to it begin to be raised, these come from within
the ruling class itself (Saint-Simon, Fourrier, Owen) and find no response whatever
among the exploited masses. Only when the mode of production in question has
described a good part of its descending curve, when it has half outlived its day,
when the conditions of its existence have to a large extent disappeared and its
successor is already knocking at the door – it is only at this stage that the constantly
increasing inequality of distribution appears as unjust, it is only then that appeal is
made from the facts which have had their day to so-called eternal justice.

Interestingly, the question of reversal of attitudes among the working class constituted one of the early preoccupations also of Keynes, whose thesis on the matter displayed striking similarities to that by Engels. Having explained that the pre-First World War mechanism of capital accumulation depended on what Keynes saw as a 'double bluff or deception' (or, perhaps, false consciousness as Marxists might be tempted to say) that 'on the one hand the labouring classes accepted from ignorance or powerlessness or were compelled, persuaded or cajoled . . . into accepting a situation in which they could call their own very little of the cake . . . and on the other hand the capitalist classes were allowed to call the best part of the cake theirs . . . on the tacit underlying condition that they consumed very little of it in practice', the author of the *Economic Consequences of the Peace* went on to add:[7]

> In the unconscious recesses of its being society knew what it was about. The cake was really very small in proportion to the appetites of consumption, and no one, if it were shared all round, would be much the better off by the cutting of it. Society was working not for the small pleasures of today but for the future security and improvement of the race – in fact for 'progress' . . . [However] the war has disclosed the possibility of consumption to all and the vanity of abstinence to many. Thus the bluff is discovered; the labouring classes may be no longer willing to forgo so largely, and the capitalist classes, no longer confident of the future, may seek to enjoy more fully their liberties of consumption so long as they last, and thus precipitate their own confiscation.

There is an uncanny (certainly unintended) Marxist resonance in all this. Keynes perceives two epochs in modern capitalism: an early one, where economic progress is being achieved, and as a result the most deprived class of society, the working class, remains quiescent; and a late one, where the shattering by the War of the idea of progress provokes hostility and an incipient revolt on the part of the workers. The grounds on which the sequence of consent and rebellion is explained run parallel in Engels and in Keynes. It must also be noticed that in both authors the emphasis is laid on the negative rather than the positive elements of working-class consciousness; on the growing sense of injustice, on rebelliousness rather than on any adoption on the workers' part of an enlightened grand design for socialist change.

Leaving aside Keynes, who never had much to say about the working class, it is the negative effects of the economy on the situation and consciousness of the working class that has received most attention in Marxist theory.

In parallel the maturing in capitalism of *objective* conditions propitious to the transition to socialism has been emphasised as a scientific discovery by Marxists. But no spontaneously working mechanism has been discovered in bourgeois society, whereby these positive conditions can be registered in the minds of the working class, and translated into a conscious strategy directly conceived by the workers. Whether and how the positive socialist potential, accumulated inside a bourgeois society, can be made actual by the working class without mediation by intellectuals remains the most important and most imperfectly resolved question of Marxist political theory and practice. This issue is raised again in a later section, which concentrates on the process of formation of negative consciousness.

The laws of motion of capitalism

Following upon Marx's declaration in the *Preface* to the first German edition of *Capital* that 'it is the ultimate aim of this work to lay bare the economic law of motion of modern society', Marxist scholars[8] have identified a complex of four laws of motion that can be said to fulfil Marx's purpose. These are: (1) the law of the falling rate of profit, (2) the law of increasing concentration and centralisation of capital, (3) the law of increasing severity of the trade cycle, and (4) the law of increasing impoverishment of the working class. The main economic aspects of laws (1), (2) and (3) have already been discussed in Chapters 6, 7 and 8. What remains is: (a) to state the law of increasing impoverishment; (b) to consider the joint impact of all four laws on the condition, the consciousness and the prospects of the working class; (c) to consider the modification of the effects listed in (b) following from a relaxation of the law of the falling rate of profit; and (d) to compare the original Marxist forecast with the state of the working class, as it developed historically.

(a) Increasing impoverishment – a tendency which Marx thought he could deduce from his analysis of capitalism – appears in two forms: absolute and relative. The former makes sense only if it is defined as consisting of a progressive decline in the real income of the working class, the latter as a decline of the relative share of labour in the distribution of income. Some authors have argued that Marx subscribed to a prediction of impoverishment in both forms, but, at least in the texts of his maturity there is no support for a theory of absolute impoverishment. Relative impoverishment, on the other hand, is an almost natural consequence of increases in productivity which cheapen wage-goods, reducing the value of labour power. This result may indeed be neutralised by workers achieving, through struggle on the wages front, appropriate money wage levels (i.e. levels that will maintain, for a given rate of inflation and rate of growth of the national product, a constant share for labour in the distribution of income).

With the burden of unemployment becoming heavier in periods of rapid technological progress, and with the militancy of the working class being consequently affected adversely, it is doubtful whether workers' defensive action can check the erosion of the value of labour power completely. Marx, at least, was persuaded that struggle on the wages front could work only as a palliative. He also expected long-term unemployment to increase with the development of capitalist production. Both considerations led him to endorse the prediction of a relative impoverishment of the proletariat to accompany capital accumulation.

(b) In what has been described in the Introduction as 'the early Marxist model', the four 'laws of motion' constitute one coherent mechanism, endowed with a hierarchical causal structure. At the top of the hierarchy (or at the very centre of the structure) stands the law of the falling rate of profit. As already discussed in Chapter 8, this law pulls together the main socio-economic strands which shape the development of the capitalist mode of production: competition among capitalists, class struggle between labour and capital, technical progress as a weapon in both inter-capitalist competition and in the struggle between capital and labour. The character of technical progress (increased mechanisation reducing the rate of profit), prompts the expansion of the scale of operations of individual capitals as these strive to make up through the size of output what they have lost in profitability per unit.

Increased mechanisation may reduce the rate of profit, but it makes the competitive capacity of capitalist industry for small commodity production vastly more devastating. The capacity of capitalism to enlist increasing numbers of formerly independent producers into the proletariat is one of the consequences of the law of the falling rate of profit. At the same time individual capitalists, in their effort to expand the scale of their operations, have resort to either voluntary or compulsory mergers (described by Marx as a process of concentration and centralisation of capital). Such measures reduce the numbers of active capitalists, relegating a certain number of formerly independent employers to the ranks of rentiers-by-necessity or even to the higher echelons of the working class. The fall in the rate of profit leads both to capitalist ownership acquiring the impersonal form which makes it ripe for expropriation and to the polarisation of society into two opposite, numerically very unequal, social classes. The law of concentration and centralisation of capital is thus a second consequence of the law of the falling rate of profit.

Large, centralised capital is in a better position to raise the capacity of the production process up to but also beyond what existing markets can absorb. The greater the centralisation of capital the greater its degree of mechanisation, the greater the mechanisation the wider the gulf between productive potential and the absorptive capacity of the markets. Therefore the greater the overproduction and the severity of the economic crises are likely to be. In the context of weakening profit margins such crises became more difficult to overcome, since the ability of firms to sustain and finance losses out of prior accumulation of reserves has been eroded. Hence the law of increasing severity of the crisis can be deduced as one further consequence of the tendency of the rate of profit to fall. Increasingly severe crises, in their turn, lead to more prolonged unemployment and further efforts to raise the rate of exploitation, either by reducing the cost of labour power (of the wage-goods) or even by an outright squeeze on existing real wage levels. Increasing impoverishment is thus linked with the other three laws.

The manner of operation of the laws of motion is not rigidly fixed but any variety in the ways whereby they combine does not bring their coherence in question. As discussed in Chapter 8, it is possible for the fall in the rate of profit to be moderated or arrested, but only at the expense of a greater centralisation of capital – which affects the ownership texture of bourgeois society – or with an increased rate of exploitation which, particularly if achieved through increased pressure of unemployment, forms the basis for more severe realisation crises. If, in order to forestall realisation crises, a decline in the rate of profit is allowed to continue, a point is reached where the crisis is precipitated through an investment strike by capitalists.

In any case the working class is likely to suffer. If the rate of profit falls, crises and unemployment are likely to be the result. If its fall is arrested, the rate of exploitation will rise while a crisis need not necessarily be avoided. Increased centralisation of capital, accompanied by increased mechanisation, will lead to a strengthening of the ability of employers to introduce techniques of scientific management that subjugate and dehumanise labouring activity even further. The coherence of the laws of motion has the effect that any development of the mechanism of the capitalist economy, if left to its natural course, acquires a negative aspect for the working class. No economic event is distant enough to become dissociated from the exploitation of labour. A takeover battle among tycoons in the Stock Exchange will eventually lead to some 'rationalisation' of the companies involved, allowing them to shed some labour and exploit those remaining more thoroughly. A development in company law will facilitate the formation of more integrated, technically more advanced firms which are less dependent on labour. The same will ultimately be the case with a string of scientific discoveries coming out of universities. No important economic event leaves the position of the working class unaffected, no variation in the manner of operation of the laws of motion offers it much reprieve. Harassed on all sides, exploited, increasingly excluded from the fruits of civilisation, with only temporary relaxations of its harsh regime during phases of extraordinary prosperity, perceiving no way out of its condition in the context of capitalist institutions, the working class responds with a rejection of the capitalistic system in its totality. The workings of the economic mechanism, the 'laws of motion of capitalism', virtually press-gang it into the service of a socialist revolution. Marx has summarised all this in one unforgettable piece of revolutionary rhetoric.[9]

Hand in hand with this centralisation of capital . . . develop on an ever extending scale, the cooperative form of the labour-process, . . . the transformation of the instruments of labour into instruments of labour only usable in common . . . Along with the constantly diminishing number of the magnates of capital, who usurp and monopolise all advantages of this process of transformation, grows the mass of misery, oppression, slavery, degradation, exploitation; but with this too grows the revolt of the working class, a class always increasing in numbers, and disciplined, united, organised by the very mechanism of the process of capitalist production itself. The monopoly of capital becomes a fetter upon the mode of production . . . Centralisation of the means of production and socialisation of labour at last reach a point where they become incompatible with their capitalist integument. The knell of private property sounds. The expropriators are expropriated.

It has already been argued that the very mechanism which drives the working class to exasperation paves the way for the success of its revolutionary enterprise. It brings forth types of ownership easily amenable to nationalisation; it weakens the ruling bourgeoisie numerically (increasing centralisation of capital) and financially (diminishing profitability). By pushing the economy to one crisis after another it discloses the inability of capitalists to keep the productive mechanism ticking over with reasonable order and discredits the bourgeoisie as a ruling class. Its influence on the intermediate strata of society, the buffers of the class struggle, declines. It even loses the support of its own intellectuals, some of whom decamp to the revolutionary proletariat.

If its assumptions are granted, the early Marxist model is very convincing in predicting both the inevitability of a proletarian revolution and the great likelihood of its success. It is, therefore, itself a very effective means of influence towards shaping the consciousness of the working class in its desired manner. This certainly reflects Marx's intention, since he was first and foremost a revolutionary.

Does this imply that the early Marxist model is not a positive but a purely normative one which does not so much predict as decree revolution for the capitalist mode of production? This is far from being the case. The model rests on assumptions which have undoubtedly been selected on the basis of a pre-theoretical overall perception of the likely development of the capitalist system. These assumptions function as simplifying devices for separating what Marx perceived as a basic pattern in reality from secondary, non-essential, characteristics which confuse the picture. They lay the foundations of a clearcut model which makes confrontation with the evidence and with events clear and instructive.

The early Marxist model thus contains a nucleus as positive as any in economics. At the same time it proposes a course of action (a 'task for mankind') to the working class which is justified on the basis not only of their current position but also of an anticipation of their prospects, as predicted by the positive part of the model.

The prediction is not arbitrary, tailor-made to suit the normative recommendation. In the socio-economic reality that confronted the builders and the users of the early Marxist model, there was sufficient support to make such predictions objectively plausible. However, theory predicted not simply current or repetitive but also anticipated future events. An element of irreducible uncertainty is always associated with such anticipations (see Chapter 1).

Few concessions to such uncertainty were made in the early Marxist model. For the purposes of inviting the working class to a certain course of action, the future part of the model's predictions was granted equal certainty-status with the analysis of current reality. The working class could, of course, choose a different future, that of the socialist transformation of society. Barring such change, the worsening of the workers' position, as predicted in the positive part of the model, was treated as inevitable.

This interplay between two possible images of the future was part of the didactic strategy of the model. In that sense it might be seen as proposing a normative rather than a positive kind of analysis. Originally the intention behind the construction of the model was to play down the normative aspect. The purely positive predictions of material developments under capitalism were such as to drive the working class into revolt, whether or not they adhered to the scientific analysis of Marxism. It is arguable, however, that the normative aspect, which in the original model remains, so to speak, in reserve, must acquire increased relevance, in case the deterministic prediction of a working-class revolution fail to materialise.

The modified Marxist model

In section (b) above (p. 216) the central place of the falling tendency of the rate of profit among the laws of motion of capitalism has been emphasised. The emphasis reflects Marx's own evaluation of the relative importance of this law. In it he saw the affirmation of his historical-materialist thesis that the bourgeois mode of production is led to its demise not be agencies external to it but by the very development of the forces of production under its own auspices. It is no exaggeration to say that the law of the falling tendency of the rate of profit lies at the very heart of Marxist economics, as defined in the first chapter of the present book. This explains the persistence which many Marxist theorists have shown in its defence.

Given, however, the shakiness of the logical necessity of a decline of profitability caused by increased mechanisation; given also the inconclusive character of the statistical trends so far; the falling tendency of the rate of profit, while it may still assert itself as quite important in special cases over certain periods, cannot maintain the status of the most central of the laws of motion of capitalism. What are the consequences of its removal for the coherence and the functioning of the early Marxist model? This question leads the discussion to points (c) and (d) listed at the beginning of the previous section.

The Marxist model does not fall apart, but some of its more drastic predictions have to be modified. It does not fall apart, because one of the premisses of the original rate of profit law, the rise in the technical composition of capital remains valid, as explained in Chapter 8, and has proven empirically very robust. Even if it is not translated into a rising value composition (i.e. if either technical progress or the effect of the choice of techniques restrain the costs of constant capital), rising technical composition is in itself sufficient to lead to increases in the scale of production, to greater integration among productive units and, in general, to a higher degree of socialisation of the production process. These developments are sufficient for strengthening the tendency towards concentration and centralisation which is, in any event, inherent in capital accumulation as a result of its orientation towards exchange value (money). The interdependence between the development of the forces of production and the evolution of the form of ownership is thus maintained. Furthermore, the removal of a persistent tendency for the rate of profit to fall in no way reverses the tendency of the productive potential to outrun the absorption capacity of the market. The link between the development of the forces of production and the recurrence of periodic crises remains. What changes is the capacity of capitalist firms to withstand economic tempests. Under the modified operation of the model, they no longer suffer from a systematic, long-term erosion of the source of their financial health. One of the causes of a progressive deepening of the trade cycle is thus removed. The increased resilience of the economic mechanism is bound also to affect for the better the position of the working class. Fewer bankruptcies mean less unemployment, while a stronger financial position implies a more relaxed attitude by capitalists on the issue of the rate of exploitation. Relative impoverishment has to follow the law of the falling rate of profit in demotion from their original pre-eminence in the model.

The remaining two out of the original four laws of motion of capitalism – the tendency to increasing concentration and centralisation of capital, and the tendency to periodic crises – retain their full significance. Based directly on the tendency of the technical composition of capital to rise, they manifest both the negative and the positive aspects of the tension between the growth of the forces of production and production relations: negative in the destructiveness of economic crises, positive in the adaptation of bourgeois property relations to more impersonal, collectivist capitalist forms, amenable to the transition to genuine socialist property relations.

The modified Marxist model undoubtedly lacks something of the drive, the coherence and the force of the original. In terms of causality it is more pluralistic. Certain disruptive economic phenomena, like periods of falling profit rates, of persistently rising unemployment, of worsening living standards among the working population, are no longer as indissolubly linked with the central, irreversible, long-term trends of development of the capitalist mode of production. Such phenomena may still occur. Rates of profit, for example, may keep on falling for long periods, if the working class finds itself in so strong a political and economic position as to force continuous wage concessions from their employers. Or they may fall for the totally different reason that a certain capitalist nation loses out in the course of international competition against other capitalist nations on world markets; or because the balance of power between entrepreneurs and rentiers has shifted in favour of the latter, so that interest rates start devouring profits; or because the state in its expanding role absorbs an inordinate part of surplus-value into taxation. Relative and even absolute impoverishment may reappear because a certain government decides to throw the full weight of the power of the state on the side of the capitalists in the distributional class struggle. Or unemployment in a certain capitalist nation may increase, because capitalists find it more profitable to invest abroad. Just as the causes of such negative phenomena become plural and less-than-essential to capitalism, so their cures may be various and less-than-revolutionary. The modified Marxist model allows considerably greater room than the original for policies of a reformist character.

Working-class numbers and automation

The position of the working class is correspondingly modified. In the original Marxist conception it is given the role of agent of social change, both because of its position in the system of social relations and of its increasing relative weight, numerical and strategic, among other social forces in bourgeois society. Some of this does not change. In the course of capitalist development the numbers of the working class do increase relative to those of self-employed small commodity producers, on the basis both of the original and of the modified Marxist model. On the well-grounded empirical generalisations that capitalist production: (1) is inherently expansive (as a result of its orientation to exchange value in independent form, i.e. to money); (2) enjoys decisive cost advantages over pre-capitalist commodity producers (as a result of the socialisation of the labour process, involving large scale production, division of labour and mechanisation); (3) is centralised (the law of concentration and centralisation of capital remains valid); (4) appears historically first as an enclave in territory dominated by small independent commodity producers and expands by out-competing and absorbing them into capitalist factories; the prediction of the proletarianisation of the vast majority of producers appears very plausible.

To this prediction three objections have been raised: (1) that capitalism, while destroying the independence of old-style small commodity producers, gives birth to new kinds of independent producers (e.g. garage owners and maintenance mechanics servicing consumer durables on location); (2) that it creates among the work force a stratum of highly salaried managerial and technical employees who, both in terms of remuneration and of responsibility, cannot be equated to proletarians despite their formally dependent employment status. To these two objections a third one, of rather different character has been added recently: (3) that mechanisation, in its latest automation phase, has inaugurated a process of virtually complete elimination of labour from the area of immediate production and even from clerical activities in business. The consequence is not that the growth in numbers of the working-class is counterbalanced by the emergence of a new middle-class (as under (4) and (2)), but that the working class will dwindle into an unemployable sub-class, described sometimes as the social, to distinguish it from the economically active, proletariat.

In the course of the historical evolution of the capitalist mode of production developments like those described under both (1) and (2) can be traced and statistically documented. Nor were they totally unanticipated by Marx. Even so, the restructuring of the labour force of society in the direction of a shift of the great majority of producers to proletarian status has by and large been realised. From being numerically predominant, independent small commodity producers, either of the old or of the new type, have been reduced to a very secondary role. In advanced capitalist societies between two-thirds and three-quarters of the population conforms to the description of the propertyless (in terms of means of production) wage or salaried employee.

This transformation, beginning in the individualistic phase of capitalism, has been completed in its collectivist phase. During the former, big transfers from peasant agriculture into industry were made, but independent entrepreneurs still remained 50 per cent or more of the population.[10] In the latter, the number of self-employed small commodity producers sank at best to 10 per cent, and considerably less than that in the most advanced capitalist economies. Percentages like these indicate that Marx's prediction of the working class becoming the main class of society must be considered as fulfilled. From the point of view of sheer numbers, capitalism has indeed given rise to the social force seen as capable and peculiarly suited to usher in socialism, putting an end to the capitalist mode of production.

Compared to the genuinely self-employed small commodity producers, the salary earners, who, like the wage-earners, obtain employment by offering their services on the market for jobs, but who differ from ordinary workers in terms of education, professional and social status, job security, level of remuneration and overall attitude towards the bourgeois organisation of society, are numerically considerably more important. Amounting to about 15–20 per cent of the population, they are those to whom the description of 'the new middle class' most properly applies. Even so, their numbers have not reversed the trend to the numerical superiority of the working class proper; nor do they reach anywhere near the 50 per cent figure of independent entrepreneurs in early capitalism. They cannot be considered as having reconstituted that class in a new guise.

Their importance lies elsewhere. They are numerous enough to constitute a buffer stratum between labour and capital, to function as a medium for the transmission of policy from the high levels of bourgeois hierarchy to shop-floor operatives in industry and commerce. Being directly involved with the working class, they may be more effective in exercising a conservative influence upon workers than the former self-employed or small masters who also, in their heyday, constituted a formidable bulwark of private property in society. On the other hand, being themselves also, in principle at least and very often in practice, detached from any meaningful ownership of the means of production, they might, if threatened by developments affecting their position and income, find it easier to side with the working class, assuming that the latter adopted a confrontational attitude towards capitalist institutions.

The third objection to the prediction of the proletarianisation of the producers differs radically from the other two. Even from the standpoint of the present time it refers more to the future than to the present. It focuses not simply on increasing mechanisation (which is a fact) but on complete mechanisation of the direct process of production, combined with automation and computerisation of office work associated with production and trade. Such technical developments, equivalent to the abolition of productive work, are still more a matter of forecast and, to some extent, of speculation, than of hard statistical evidence. No comprehensive investigation of the effects of automation on industrial employment appears, so far, to have been published in any capitalist (or, for that matter non-capitalist) country. Qualitative or selective evidence, however, makes it plausible that industrial economies may be at the beginnings of a process leading to the elimination of the wage-worker as a factor of production in substantial sectors of industry or of clerical work. For medium-sized industrial economies (like France or Japan) losses of jobs resulting from this kind of technical progress during the period of the 1970s have been estimated at around one million places. Regarding the future, selective forecasts of reduction of employment until the end of the current decade range from 25 per cent of clerical jobs in retailing to 50 per cent (or even 100 per cent) of the unskilled labour force in the motor industry.[11]

To these drastic unemployment projections it may be retorted that automation is nothing but a more advanced kind of mechanisation. In the past, the latter certainly did displace workers, whenever it was first introduced in any branch, but it more than compensated for this by creating larger numbers of jobs through the increase in industrial activity which it stimulated. The final outcome was that rising numbers of workers kept on being employed in industry, at higher capital–labour ratios than before each wave of mechanisation.

Statistics in advanced industrial economies support this picture only up to a point. United States figures show that the percentage of the labour force employed in industry kept on increasing until round about 1920.[12] After that year the trend started moving in the opposite direction, so that by now the percentage of the total workforce employed in industry is smaller than it was in the early years of this century. This contraction has so far been balanced by the compensating expansion of the tertiary sector. It is doubtful whether, in the United States or elsewhere, such compensation can continue in the future. Computerisation is particularly suited to office work; the prospects are that in the coming decade millions of clerical jobs will be eliminated as a result of its introduction. Services are not identical with clerical work, but they often comprise a strong office component.

With jobs eliminated at high rates, both in the industrial heartland of the economy and in the tertiary sector, it is hard to see where a compensating expansion of jobs could come from. The abolition of work through technology is becoming a real prospect. It will, of course, never be a 100 per cent affair, nor will it occur suddenly. It will probably begin by reshaping the existing division of the working class into an industrial hard core and a 'softer peripheral working population. A certain number of engineers, scientists and highly skilled technicians will remain necessary in industry, while on their side a semi-unemployed reserve army, a sub-class or rather a non-class of social proletarians, recruited both from industry and from the tertiary sector, unable to look forward to any settled period of employment over their whole lifetime, will begin to form.

The reasons for such drastic mutations in the character of the working class concern the basic aspects of the relationship of the worker and the machine, the very microeconomics of capital-labour substitution, and are, in consequence, fundamental. They were stated with total clarity many decades ago by one of the most distinguished pioneers of automation, Norbert Wiener. Despite the date of his pronouncements (1948) they can still be read with profit.[13]

The automatic factory and the assembly line without human agents are only so far ahead of us as is limited by our willingness to put such a degree of effort into their engineering as was spent, for example, in the development of the technique of radar in the Second World War.

I have said that this new development has unbounded possibilities for good and for evil. For one thing, it makes the metaphorical dominance of the machines, as imagined by Samuel Butler, a most immediate and non-metaphorical problem. It gives the human race a new and most effective collection of mechanical slaves to perform its labor. Such mechanical labor has most of the economic properties of slave labor, although, unlike slave labor, it does not involve the direct demoralizing effects of human cruelty. However, any labor that accepts the conditions of competition with slave labor accepts the conditions of slave labor, and is essentially slave labor. . . .

Perhaps I may clarify the historical background of the present situation if I say that the first industrial revolution, the revolution of the 'dark, satanic mills', was the devaluation of the human arm by the competition of machinery. There is no rate of pay on which a United States pick-and-shovel laborer can live which is low enough to compete with the work of a steam shovel or an excavator. The modern industrial revolution is similarly bound to devalue the human brain, at least in its simpler and more routine decisions. Of course, just as the skilled carpenter, the skilled mechanic, the skilled dressmaker have in some degree survived the first industrial revolution, so the skilled scientist and the skilled administrator will survive the second. However, taking the second revolution as accomplished, the average human being of mediocre attainments or less has nothing to sell that it is worth anyone's money to buy.

To the extent that forecasts like these manage to capture the main lines of development in the near future, automation is likely to bring about what the rise of the 'new middle classes' never came anywhere near realising: to marginalise the working class numerically. Even before that point is reached, mechanisation, by restructuring the workforce in the direction of the tertiary sector, has already undermined the social weight of the working class. If the main weapon of the workers in normal times is the strike, industrial workers are in a much better position to exercise pressure on their employers (sometimes by exercising pressure also on society as a whole) than are services employees. The effects of a strike by workers employed in the electricity industry would be quick and drastic; university lecturers may go on strike for a year before anyone takes any notice. (There are, of course, exceptions: a strike by bank employees would be much more disruptive and immediately noticeable.)

Automation of the kind described remained beyond the contemplation of the authors who refined the early Marxist model. Marx himself was one of the early visionaries of fully automated production, but he would have never believed this sort of technical progress possible under capitalism.[14] Long before the abolition of work became a practical proposition – indeed, in order that it should so become – socialist transformation would have overtaken capitalism. The weakening of bourgeois rule, as a result of the worsening spasms of economic crises and the increasing resentment of the working class following upon their increasing impoverishment, would have seen to that.

In actual historical experience, however, economic crises did not become invariably worse; on the contrary, in some important respects, they became more manageable. As to impoverishment, even casual observation of the conditions of the working class in advanced capitalist countries, compared to say their condition in 1844, when Engels described it so eloquently in his *Condition of the Working Classes in England*, should be sufficient to make any suggestion of absolute impoverishment look ludicrous. Relative impoverishment is a more delicate matter, particularly if one were to take into account the increasingly tenuous hold by workers over the production process as a result of mechanisation and automation. From the point of view of distribution, on the other hand, the stylised statistical facts are that relative shares between land, labour and capital have remained roughly constant over the last one hundred years or so. Depending on definitions, an increasing labour share can be identified for Britain and the USA. Even if one were not to take such evidence at face value, the least one would have to admit is that no strong downward trend of the share of labour seems to have asserted itself, as one would expect if the hypothesis of relative impoverishment were to be valid.

Where do these remarks lead the discussion of the relationship between the early Marxist model and its modified sequel, both of them seen as forecasts of a transition to socialism? Under the impact of theoretical analysis and of practical experience, a dichotomy would seem to have developed in the early model. One of its laws and part of another – increasing concentration and centralisation of capital and a rising technical composition of capital – have split off and constituted themselves into a self-contained valid sub-model. Its predictions are both crucial for the development of the capitalist mode of production and, as far as one can see, correct. Capitalism does become more collectivist in its property relations; production does become more efficient, increasingly less dependent on direct human labour but increasingly more dependent on science and, through it, on the collective intellectual effort of humanity. The positive elements that, in Marx's original conception, were to underpin the transition to socialism (production based on the collectivity rather than on specific individuals; large-scale, collectively owned capitalist firms, ripe for socialisation; high productivity making possible an adequate share of material means and of leisure for every member of society) have in fact been assembled by the very development of the capitalist system.

The negative developments, on the other hand, that were both to weaken the hold of the bourgeoisie over society and to drive the working class into rebellion (falling rate of profit, increasing severity of crises, increasing impoverishment) either did not materialise at all or their occurrence did not keep pace with the accumulation of the positive elements. The objective conditions for socialism did mature within capitalist society, but the subjective agency in advanced capitalist countries did not enlist itself in the task of social transformation with the degree of decisiveness, either theoretically predicted for it or expected on the basis of its early nineteenth-century stirrings. A kind of paralysis of the mechanism of social evolution seems to have overtaken advanced capitalism; the need for change has become anaesthetised while the creativity of the old mode of production in bringing about the adaptive renewal of its institutions has long become exhausted.

A critique of negativity

Even if the early Marxist model of capitalism had worked to the letter, it is doubtful whether the working class, in the shape in which the capitalist labour process has moulded it, would be capable of fulfilling any other role than that of providing the big battalions of the revolutionary struggle. In particular it is hard to see how it could act as the subjective agency of construction of socialism. For Marx, working-class intervention in the course of history depended heavily on the purely negative position of workers in bourgeois society described by the early Marxist model. His famous slogan in the Communist Manifesto issues from exactly this spirit 'the proletarians have nothing to lose but their chains; they have a world to win'. It is possible that a whole dialectic of inversion of negativity into positivity might be attempted around this theme. It might be the task of a book on political philosophy. In economics only the bare minimum of such considerations can be introduced.

The basis of the negativity of the working class is its propertylessness. This prevents workers from taking any initiative in the sphere of production. To survive, they have to adapt passively to the projects dictated to them by capital; they have to become part of capital. If capital excludes them from its realm, they are cut off from the network of social relations, and, eventually, from the very means of subsistence. Their negativity, which is only latent while they are employed, bursts forth in an acute form when they are unemployed. Even when they assume the active stance of opposition against their exploiters, their action can only take the negative form of a strike, never (unless they tackle the capitalist system as a whole) the form of adopting an alternative way of producing.

The exclusion of the working class from the means of production is total. No niche of ownership is allowed them; no participation in the conduct of business or control over results achieved. Share ownership does not change anything in this respect. The typical working-class person owns no shares; even for those who do own some, a controlling role in the company would be beyond their wildest imagination. Pension funds do own significant packets of shares, but the funds themselves are not under workers' control.

The response of the working class to the totally negative condition it finds itself relegated to by bourgeois society is a symmetrically total rejection of all forms of private property in the means of production. To shed some more light on this point it is useful to compare the condition of the working class with that of the bourgeoisie, during the epoch of the latter's emergence from the cocoon of feudal relations. The bourgeoisie did not come forth as a propertyless class. It represented a different kind of private property – commercial private property versus feudal private property. By contrast, the working class has no particular kind of property of its own to assert versus other classes. The only way open for it to redress its exclusion from propertied society is to regain property for its members. This cannot be done on an individual basis, e.g. by parcelling and redistributing the means of production, because it would eventually lead to the restoration of capitalism or to totally inefficient forms of simple commodity production. In view of the technically integrated character of production, capital ownership can either be centralised in the hands of a few individuals (i.e. of a section of society, a privileged class) to the exclusion of the rest, or else collectivised at the level of society as a whole (with collectivist capitalism, discussed in Chapter 9, as an intermediate stage). What is ruled out, by the character of the means of production, is their parcellisation and equal redistribution to individual producers, in the manner of an old-style land reform.

Total exclusion of the working class from any kind of ownership over the means of production, combined with the character which the production process assumes in capitalism, produces the result that the working class can regain ownership only if ownership becomes communal.

Ownership, however, is only the legal form of relations of production, not these relations themselves. Socialist ownership cannot be identified with socialist production relations, which are not a matter of form but of substantive operation of the production process. This will have to assume a co-operative character, not simply in the execution of tasks (this has already taken place in capitalism) but also at the stages of decision-making and of administration.

Whatever one may think about the feasibility of such schemes under the best of circumstances, it is certain that the labour process in capitalism is as far removed as anything from preparing the workers to perform functions of direction in a cooperative manner. Some writers have seen in this evaluation of the current position of the working class a certain inconsistency with Marx. In the opinion of the present author this is not so. A certain part of the analysis in *Capital* does indeed suggest that the labour process gives rise to conditions conducive to the forging of the proletariat into the collective social subject, required for genuine socialist relations of production. In the workshops of the manufacturing epoch of capitalism, where labour was technically still the main force of production, division of labour, specialisation of each worker to one particular task has led to a situation where specific individuals produced only parts, sections, in themselves unutilisable, of commodities while only the working team as a whole, the collective worker, turned out a finished product. Based on their production experience individuals could, therefore, perceive themselves as members of an organic whole and, given a chance to act as decision makers, shape their behaviour accordingly. They might adopt an attitude of cooperation, in the knowledge that as parts of a whole they had to cater as well as possible for the totality as a means of catering for the parts, which were themselves.

With the advent of modern industry, the character of the collective worker alters decisively. Individuals no longer complement one another, in a system of division of labour; they become mere minders of a system of machines, which now itself embodies the principle of the division of labour, translated into a principle of division of tasks among specialised machines. The human machine-minders no longer constitute the members of a collective productive organism. A mechanical organism has replaced the collective worker, while workers revert to a state of simple cooperation, serving their machines each side by side without meaningfully relating to each other during their working hours. This, plus the fact that the job of tending a machine can become simplified to the point where it can be learnt with a few weeks of training, makes individuals easily interchangeable, easily replaceable by other individuals. Common work in a factory, under these conditions, can no longer constitute the material basis for working-class solidarity. It does not bind people together; it isolates them, it induces them to look upon one another with indifference rather than with involvement. Factory production constitutes no objective lesson towards the formation of a collective subject for economic and social decision making. (Common mass opposition against employers, on the other hand, undoubtedly creates a certain measure of solidarity, but this is a different matter. It concerns the negative rather than any positive aspect of working class consciousness.)

Marx was well aware of these limitations imposed upon the workers' outlook by their conditions of work. He commented on them as follows:[15]

> So far as division of labour re-appears in the factory, it is primarily a distribution of the workmen among the specialized machines; and of masses of workmen, *not however organized into groups*, among the various departments of the factory, in each of which they work at a number of similar machines placed together; *their co-operation*, therefore, *is only simple*. The organized group, peculiar to manufacture, is replaced by the connexion between the head workman and his few assistants. [Italics added]

Possibly it is even less than simple, if by this term the direct harnessing of a number of human forces to a common task (e.g. the lifting of a heavy weight, rowing a ship) is understood. Workers in a factory do not cooperate in that sense; they merely work side by side.

Marx extended his remarks to include the effects of their material conditions on working class consciousness:[16]

> Dr Ure, the Pindar of the automatic factory, describes it, on the one hand as 'combined co-operation of many orders of work-people, adult and young, in tending with assiduous skill, a system of productive machines, continuously impelled by a central power' . . . ; on the other hand, as 'a vast automaton, composed of various mechanical and intellectual organs . . . all of them being subordinate to a self-regulating moving force.' These two descriptions are far from being identical. In one, the collective labourer, or social body of labour, appears as the dominant subject, and the mechanical automaton as the object; in the other, the automaton itself is the subject, and the workmen are merely conscious organs, co-ordinate with the unconscious organs of the automaton, and together with them, subordinated to the central moving-power. The first description is applicable to every possible employment of machinery on a large scale, the second is characteristic of its use by capital, and therefore of the modern factory system.

Finally, not only is the working class atomised by the conditions of its productive activity, it also becomes progressively deskilled. Deskilling has two important consequences. On the one hand it devalues labour power, undermining the bargaining position of labour. On the other, more relevant to the present discussion, it erects a barrier between the technical methods of production and the understanding of the worker. Already in the early epoch of manufacturing workers start losing their grip over the mental aspect of the labour process, since the pattern of the division of labour which distributes them to tasks is devised not by them but by the capitalist employer and his engineers.

Even so, at that stage, production techniques must be presumed to be still rather transparent to ordinary understanding. The real separation of the workers from the meaning of their productive activity comes, for obvious reasons, with mechanisation. Finally scientific management, with its time and motion studies, deprives the worker of mental control even over his very movements. For anyone aspiring to understand the production process as a whole, so as to undertake decision making, the least promising way forward would be through the experience of a modern factory worker.

The position of the working class, prior to socialism, may once again be compared with the position of the bourgeoisie in feudal society. Although dominated by the nobility, the bourgeoisie in its practical life held positions of command, in finance, commerce, shipping and in early forms of manufacture. This provided the bourgeois as individuals with training for the posts of social leadership assumed by them after their victorious clash with their feudal superiors. In the case of the workers their practical life operates in an exactly opposite manner; as individuals, it debilitates them for the role of decision makers.

These remarks are not intended to lead to the conclusion that the working class is inherently unsuitable as a subjective social force for the socialist transformation of society. They are intended to point out the limitations of the economy in generating such a force. Even if the pure negativity of the working class in the matter of ownership does implant in the minds of the proletariat the desire to abolish their propertyless condition, thereby turning their negativity into the positive state of socialist ownership, the matter does not rest there. There are other aspects of working-class negativity besides that of ownership. The disintegration of the collective worker caused by machinery, the atomisation of the working class in its role of an active labour force and its deskilling, render it incapable of visualising itself practically as a collective manager of the actual production process. As a rule the source of motivation in their attempting to take initiative in the economic sphere remains negative, the collective confrontation with the employers over wages and conditions of work. The exceptional cases in which workers proposed that they could actually take over firms and run them more successfully than their employers are so few and so unconvincing as to strengthen the rule. Even trade unionism cannot be seen as invariably favoured by the actual experience of the working class. The need for solidarity against employers is frequently counterbalanced by the individualism inherent in the atomised conditions of existence among labouring men. To take the necessary broader view of their own interests and of society, workers have to step outside their day-to-day work experience or their competition in the market for jobs. Mere trade unionism presupposes that; any more ambitious organisation, aiming at the socialist transformation of society, makes it imperative.

Despite Marx's percipient remarks on the state of helplessness and intellectual bafflement to which modern technology reduces the worker, the early Marxist model depended heavily on their direct experience in the production process to instil in them a revolutionary consciousness. This is because it laid most emphasis on negative consciousness. Increasing impoverishment was expected to act as an inexhaustible source of negativity.

Here lay the fatal flaw of the model. Not simply because the direct predictions of the theory of impoverishment have not been borne out in the experience of advanced capitalism. The problem was more fundamental. Even had they been they would, at most, have fuelled a working-class revolt. There is no reason why, of their own, they would have oriented such revolt towards socialist aims. In class societies no great social transformations are ever consummated without the concurrence of two elements: a revolt of the majority against the ruling class and a positive orientation to a new order of things. It has been argued that the direct experience of the working class cannot be depended on to supply the positive orientation. It does not form the working class as a practically capable subject of socialist relations of production. The difficulties that this creates are not limited to the building of a genuine socialist society, after the overthrow itself is inhibited by the debilitating influence of the economy on the social perspectives of working people.

For all his fundamental theoretical commitment to production as the main determinant of social activity, Marx was not blind to the need for an extra-economic formation of the working class. In the *Communist Manifesto* he even turns to the bourgeoisie as the first political educator of the workers whom bourgeois politicians mobilise for their own purposes but, in so doing, initiate in the broader aspects of social action. For his own part, Lenin's way out of this dilemma was through his famous thesis that socialist consciousness has to be imported into the working class from the outside, from social science which has discovered the laws of motion of society, independently of workers' experience. In practice, this meant that Marxist intellectuals had to take the lead and educate the working class towards the task of socialist construction. 'Mankind' would thus ultimately arrive at the proper 'setting of its tasks', not through working-class spontaneity but through the leadership of revolutionary intellectuals. In Lenin the methodological distinction, latent in the *Preface*, between a scientific and an ideological-instinctive perception of the task of socialist change, acquired institutional implementation.

Leninist parties have scored remarkable successes in rallying significant sections of the working class, in conquering state-power and in introducing state-ownership of the main means of production in various countries of the world. They have also suffered their well-known degeneration into mechanisms of authoritarian and even dictatorial domination over the supposedly ruling class in a socialist society, the working class. Even so, one element in Lenin's thesis remains unshakeable: his decisive acceptance of the fact that, for the formation of its socialist consciousness, the working class has to seek a socio-political experience beyond the debilitating limits of its narrow role in the production process. The non-operation of the law of increasing impoverishment of the proletariat in advanced capitalist countries can only reinforce this thesis.

In conditions of modern democratic regimes, on the other hand, there seems to be no reason why the political formation of the working class should invariably be taken in hand by a tightly-knit group of Marxist revolutionary intellectuals. The working class takes part in political life as a matter of course. It is even conceivable that, to the extent where developments in robotics and automation tend to marginalise the participation of workers in the production process, their participation in the political process will acquire increased relative weight.

A greater variety of intellectual influences in the direction of socialism also seems likely to develop. Based on their contribution to the advancement of science or technology, scientists of all disciplines may start perceiving the incompatibility of capitalist institutions with further progress (or even with mere survival) and may wish to pass the message on to the working class. An early sample of this kind, justifying both optimism and pessimism can be found in the already-quoted writings of Norbert Wiener, who commented on the likely social consequences of automation as follows:[17]

It may very well be a good thing for humanity to have the machine remove from it the need of menial and disagreeable tasks, or it may not. I do not know. It cannot be good for these new potentialities to be assessed in the terms of the market, of the money they save; and it is precisely in the terms of the market, the 'fifth freedom', they have become the shibboleth of the sector of American opinion represented by the National Association of Manufacturers and the *Saturday Evening Post*. I say American opinion for as an American, I know it best, but the hucksters recognize no national boundary . . .

The answer, of course, is to have a society based on human values other than buying or selling. To arrive at this society, we need a good deal of planning and a good deal of struggle, which, if the best comes to the best, may be on the plane of ideas, and otherwise – who knows? I thus felt it my duty to pass on my information and understanding of the position to those who have an active interest in the conditions and future of labor, that is, to the labor unions. I did manage to make contact with one or two persons high up in the C.I.O., and from them I received a very intelligent and sympathetic hearing. Further than these individuals, neither I nor any of them was able to go. It was their opinion, as it had been my previous observation and information, both in the United States and in England, that the labor unions and the labor movement are in the hands of a highly limited personnel, thoroughly well trained in the specialized problems of shop stewardship and disputes concerning wages and conditions of work, and totally unprepared to enter into the larger political, technical, sociological, and economic questions which concern the very existence of labor. The reasons for this are easy enough to see: the labor union official generally comes from the exacting life of an administrator without any opportunity for a broader training; and for those who have this training, a union career is not generally inviting; nor, quite naturally, are the unions receptive to such people.

This was written some forty years ago. Technology did not progress as rapidly as Wiener expected, which may partly explain the lack of response to his message. Recent developments appear to give this message renewed urgency. If the technologically unemployed, or at best occasionally employed, section of the working class becomes as numerous as some forecasts suggest, the main focus of class struggle will have to shift permanently from production, over which the unemployed have no grip, to the political arena, where, at least in democratic states, they are equipped with an automatic right of participation. It is conceivable, unMarxist though it may sound, that in the future the working class will increasingly seek to forge its unity and its socialist project (without which it is condemned to remain propertyless) in the sphere of democratic politics rather than in trade union agitation. Marx, who constructed and held on tenaciously to the early Marxist model, knew that, even under that model, economics have eventually to graduate into politics, if social change is to occur. The same message, only strengthened, emerges also from the demise of his early model.

Notes and references

Preface

1. 'Normal science' in this Preface has the meaning given to it by the inventor of the term, Thomas Kuhn, in *The Structure of Scientific Revolutions* (2nd edn, enlarged), Chicago 1970, p. 10. 'In this essay,' writes Kuhn, '"normal science" means research firmly based upon one or more past scientific achievements, achievements that some particular scientific community acknowledges for a time as supplying the foundation for its further practice'.
2. 'Marx's "Doctrine of Increasing Misery"' in Ronald L. Meek, *Economics and Ideology and Other Essays* (London, 1967) p. 126.
3. Joseph M. Gillman, *The Falling Rate of Profit* (New York, 1958) p. 1.
4. V. I. Lenin, 'The Three Sources and Three Constituent Parts of Marxism', *Selected Works*, Vol. I (Moscow, 1970) p. 66. As a less dithyrambic but basically concurrent assessment of the unity of Marx's thought, the following passage from Thornstein Veblen is to the point: 'Except as a whole . . . , the Marxian system is not only not tenable, it is not even intelligible . . . No member of the system, no single article of doctrine, is fairly to be understood, criticised, or defended except as an articulate member of the whole and in the light of the preconceptions and postulates which afford the point of departure and the controlling norm of the whole'. Thornstein Veblen, 'The Socialist Economics of Karl Marx and his Followers', *Quarterly Journal of Economics*, August 1906.
5. On the philosophical difficulty of rejecting a scientific theory as soon as it is contradicted by certain evidence see I. Lakatos, 'Falsification and the methodology of scientific research programmes', in *The methodology of scientific research programmes*, Vol. I (Cambridge, 1978) pp. 8 ff.
6. For some anomalies in Newtonian physics see Paul Feyerabend, *Against Method* (London, 1975) p. 35 and passim.
7. See his 'Marxian Value Theory and Crises' in Ian Steedman and others, *The Value Controversy* (London, 1981) pp. 20 ff.
8. Karl Marx, *Capital*, Vol. I (New York, 1967) p. 9.
9. P. A. Samuelson, 'Marxian Economics as Economics', *American Economic Review*, Papers and Proceedings, 57, 1967, p. 623.

1 Economics and historical materialism

1. Karl Marx, 'Theses on Feuerbach', in Karl Marx and Frederick Engels, *Collected Works*, Vol. 5 (London, 1976) p. 8.
2. J. M. Keynes, *A Treatise on Money*, Vol. II in his *Collected Works*.
3. A vast number of reprintings of this famous text exists. The author is quoting from K. Marx and F. Engels, *Selected Works*, Vol. 1 (Moscow, 1969) p. 502.
4. It is important to notice that even in physics there exist propositions which are fundamental in the construction of theories while being, at the same time, very difficult, if not in principle impossible, to confront with empirical evidence. Some very striking examples of this have been mentioned in Pierre Duhem's classic *The Aim and Structure of Physical Theory* (New York, 1962). Thus Duhem writes: '[T]hese principles cannot be refuted by experiment . . . because *the operation which would claim to compare them with the facts would have no meaning*' (pp. 212–13). Duhem goes on to offer the example of the principle of inertia: 'The principle of inertia teaches us that a material point removed from the action of any other body moves in a straight line with uniform motion. Now, we can observe only relative motions; we cannot, therefore, give an experimental meaning to this principle unless we assume a certain point chosen . . . as a fixed reference point to which the motion of the material point is related . . . There are as many different laws as there are frames of reference' (p. 213). More striking is the example of the principle that the centre of gravity of an isolated system can have only a uniform rectilinear motion (given on pp. 213–14). Concerning the possibility of experimental verification of this Duhem quotes the comments of M. Poincaré, his great contemporary physicist. 'Can we make this verification? For that it would be necessary for isolated systems to exist. Now, these systems do not exist, the only isolated system is the whole universe. But we can observe only relative motions; the absolute motion of the centre of the universe will therefore be forever unknown' (since the existence of a fixed point of reference outside the universe to which the motion of the universe would be related is logically impossible). Are such principles, therefore, totally exempt from experimental verification or falsification? Not at all. According to Duhem, 'taken in isolation these different hypotheses have no experimental meaning; there can be no question of either confirming or contradicting them by experiment. But these hypotheses enter as essential foundations into the construction of certain theories of rational mechanics' and are therefore testable in one block, together with the theories of which they form a part (p. 215). This may well be the case also of Marx's principle of correspondence between the forces and the relations of production. In itself very difficult, if not impossible, to test empirically, it is testable together with the whole of Marxist economics as the latter is confronted with the accumulating evidence. (See also Preface, notes 5 and 6.)
5. Karl Marx: *The Eighteenth Brumaire of Louis Bonaparte* in Karl Marx and Frederick Engels, *Collected Works*, Vol. 11 (London, 1979) p. 103. Strictly speaking, this text is not directly relevant to the argument because, in *The Eighteenth Brumaire* Marx refers to spiritual rather than to material constraints. About material constraints, and the margins of choice these allow, he spoke clearly in the *German Ideology*: 'History does not end by being resolved into "self-consciousness" as "spirit of the spirit", but that each stage contains a material

result, a sum of productive forces, a historically created relation to nature and of individuals to one another, which is handed down to each generation from its predecessor; a mass of productive forces, capital funds and circumstances, which on the one hand is indeed modified by the new generation, but on the other also prescribes for it its conditions of life and gives it a definite development, a special character. It shows that circumstances make men just as much men make circumstances' (*Collected Works*, Vol. 5, p. 54. Similar ideas are expressed also in the *Poverty of Philosophy*, in *Collected Works*, Vol. 6, p. 173). Despite the existence of so much direct support in the sources for the idea under discussion, the quotation in the main text was preferred because of the crispness of its literary form, even though its context in *The Eighteenth Brumaire* is somewhat different here. Readers owe this cataclysm of Marxological explanations to the fastidiousness of Professor G. A. Cohen, who made it a point of honour for the author to clarify fully the textual (and contextual) position.

2 Commodity production and capitalism

1. Pierro Sraffa, *Production of Commodities by Means of Commodities* (Cambridge, 1960).
2. J. M. Keynes, *The General Theory of Employment, Interest, and Money* (London, 1961) p. 235.
3. Robert Nozick, *Anarchy, State and Utopia* (Oxford, 1974) p. 160.
4. Karl Marx, *Capital*, Vol. I (New York, 1967) p. 176.

3 The labour theory of value

1. Karl Marx, *Grundrisse* (London, 1973) pp. 157–8.
2. J. B. Say, *Traité d'économie politique; 5me édition* (Paris, 1826) Vol. I, pp. 130–1. Quotation translated from the original by the present author.
3. J. M. Keynes, *The Economic Consequences of the Peace* in his *Collected Works*, Vol. II (London, 1971) p. 11.
4. J. M. Keynes, *The General Theory of Employment, Interest and Money* (London, 1961) p. 159.

4 Value, labour power and exploitation

1. This thesis has been christened 'the Walras–Lange–Lerner theory of exploitation' by Arun Bose in *Marxian and Post-Marxian Political Economy – An Introduction* (London, 1975) p. 52.
2. A classical statement of this thesis is contained in Joan Robinson, *The Economics of Imperfect Competition*, 2nd edn (London, 1969) pp. 281ff., in particular p. 288.
3. Karl Marx, *Theories of Surplus Value*, Part III (Moscow, 1971) pp. 105–6.
4. Karl Marx, *Capital*, Vol I (New York, 1967) p. 279.
5. Ibid., p. 233.

6. Bob Rowthorn, 'Marx's Theory of Wages' in his *Capitalism, Conflict and Inflation* (London, 1980) pp. 205ff. Section 9, in the main text of the book follows, up to a point, Rowthorn's excellent analysis.
7. Karl Marx, *Capital*, Vol. I (New York, 1967) p. 171.
8. The concept of 'social formation' was first introduced, as far as the author is aware, by Louis Althusser in his well-known book *Reading Capital* (London, 1968). It is contrasted to the more basic idea of a mode of production by being historically specific – whereas the mode of production is a more abstract generalisation. Capitalism is a mode of production, British capitalist society in the 19th century is a social formation. It is typical of a social formation that it represents a hybrid of more than one mode of production with the characteristics of one of them predominant, however.
9. Karl Marx, 'Wages, Price and Profit' in *Selected Works*, Vol. 2 (Moscow, 1969) p. 73.
10. Karl Marx, *Poverty of Philosophy*, in Karl Marx and Frederick Engels: *Collected Works*, Vol. 6, p. 125.
11. Karl Marx, *Theories of Surplus Value*, Part II (Moscow, 1969) p. 119.
12. Karl Marx, *Capital*, Vol. I (New York, 1967) pp. 234–5.
13. Ibid., pp. 522–3.
14. John Hicks, *A Theory of Economic History* (Oxford, 1969).
15. Joseph A. Schumpeter, *The Theory of Economic Development* (Oxford, 1961).
16. John Hicks, *A Theory of Economic History* (Oxford, 1969), p. 28 and p. 141.
17. Ibid., p. 58.
18. Ibid., p. 163.
19. Joseph A. Schumpeter, *The Theory of Economic Development* (Oxford, 1961) p. 154.
20. Ibid., p. 147.
21. Ibid., p. 147, note.

4 Appendix

1. The interested reader may look up a brief summary of that early history in Michio Morishima and George Catephores, *Value, Exploitation and Growth* (London, 1978) pp. 147–8.
2. Karl Marx, *Capital*, Vol. III (Moscow, 1971) p. 45.
3. Ibid., p. 158.
4. Eugen Böhm-Bawerk, *Karl Marx and the Close of his System*, (editor, P. M. Sweezy) (London, 1949).
5. Ladislaus von Bortkiewicz, 'Value and Price in the Marxian System', *International Economic Papers*, 2, 1952, pp. 5–60 and 'On the Correction of Marx's Fundamental Theoretical Construction' in the Third Volume of *Capital*, in Sweezy, P. M. (ed.) *Karl Marx and the Close of his System* (London, 1949).
6. Ladislaus von Bortkiewicz, 'Value and Price in the Marxian System' (see note 5), p. 52.
7. Karl Marx, *Capital*, Vol. III (Moscow, 1971) p. 164.
8. This generalisation was achieved by J. Winternitz in a note entitled 'Values and

prices: A solution of the so-called transformation problem', *Economic Journal*, June 1948, pp. 276–80.

9. For an interesting attempt in this direction see David Laibman, 'Values and Prices of Production: The Political Economy of the Transformation Problem', *Science and Society*, 1974.

10. See Michio Morishima and George Catephores, *Value, Exploitation and Growth* (London, 1978) pp. 160–6.

11. F. Seton, 'The "Transformation Problem"', *Review of Economic Studies*, 25, 1957, pp. 149–60.

12. These theorems have been conveniently collected in G. Debreu and I. N. Herstein, 'Non-negative Square Matrices', *Econometrica*, 21, 1953, pp. 597–606.

13. Paul A. Samuelson, 'Understanding the Marxian Notion of Exploitation: A Summary of the So-Called Transformation Problem Between Marxian Values and Competitive Prices', *Journal of Economic Literature*, 9 June 1971, pp. 399–431.

14. Michio Morishima and George Catephores, *Value, Exploitation and Growth* (London, 1978) p. 45ff.

15. For a worthy but, ultimately, unsuccessful attempt see Samuel Bowles and Herbert Gintis, 'The Marxian Theory of Value and Heterogeneous Labour: A Critique and Reformulation', *Cambridge Journal of Economics*, 1977, 1, pp. 173–92, but also the reply by Michio Morishima in the 1978, 2, issue of the same Journal, and George Catephores, 'On Heterogeneous Labour and the Labour Theory of Value', in the 1979, 1 issue.

16. J. M. Keynes made a similar assumption for his wage unit in the *General Theory* (London, 1961) pp. 41–4.

5 Money and growth

1. Recall the phrase from the 1859 *Preface*: 'It is not the consciousness of man that determines his existence – rather, it is his social existence that determines his consciousness'. This aspect of Marxism has earned high praise even from an opponent as determined as Popper, who has proclaimed himself a disciple of that point of view; see his *The Open Society and its Enemies*, Vol. II (London, 1957) pp. 89 ff.

2. Karl Marx, *Capital*, Vol. I (New York, 1967) p. 133.

3. Ibid., pp. 151–2.

4. The distinction hinted at here is the same as W. W. Rostow makes in *The Stages of Economic Growth* (Cambridge, 1971) Chapter 2.

5. Karl Marx, *Capital*, Vol. I (New York, 1967) p. 592.

6. J. M. Keynes, 'Economic Possibilities for our Grandchildren' in *Collected Works*, Vol. IX, *Essays in Persuasion* (London, 1972) p. 326.

7. Ibid., p. 329.

8. Ibid., p. 328.

9. Ibid.

10. See Maurice Dobb, *Studies in the development of capitalism* (London, 1963) chapter three, particularly pp. 120ff.

11. Karl Marx, letter to Paul Annenkov, 28 December 1846 in Karl Marx and Frederick Engels, *Collected Works* (London, 1982) p. 99.

6 Capitalism and crisis

1. Karl Marx and Frederick Engels, *Manifesto of the Communist Party* in Karl Marx and Frederick Engels, *Collected Works*, Vol. 6 (London, 1976) p. 489.
2. See Chapter 5, note 11.
3. See for example *Capital*, Vol. III (Moscow, 1971) p. 482.
4. Karl Marx, *Capital*, Vol. III (Moscow, 1971) p. 264.
5. See Karl Marx, *Capital*, Vol. I (New York, 1967) p. 6.
6. V. I. Lenin, *Imperialism, the highest stage of capitalism*, in *Selected Works*, Vol. I (Moscow, 1963) p. 667.
7. In this respect it is worth quoting Lenin at some extent. In comparing slow-growing Britain with fast-growing but market-deficient Germany, he wrote: 'Thanks to her colonies, Great Britain has increased the length of "her" railways by 100 000 kilometers, four times as much as Germany. And yet, it is well known that the development of productive forces in Germany, and especially the development of the coal and iron industries, has been incomparably more rapid this period than in Britain – not to speak of France and Russia', *Collected Works* (Moscow, 1970) p. 744.
8. In his analysis of imperialism Lenin was very much influenced by the unorthodox British economist J. A. Hobson, whose book, *Imperialism* he used extensively and frequently quoted in his own *Imperialism*.
9. For a broad discussion of this idea the reader might consult Engels's *Origins of the family of private property and of the State*, in Marx–Engels, *Selected Works* (Moscow, 1968) pp. 461ff.
10. Mainly Paul A. Baran and Paul M. Sweezy in *Monopoly Capital*, chapter 3 and *passim*.
11. J. A. Schumpeter, *Capitalism, Socialism and Democracy* (London, 1952) chapter VII.
12. J. M. Keynes, *The General Theory of Employment, Interest, and Money* (London, 1961) p. 373.
13. Ibid., p. 220.
14. See Karl Marx, *Capital*, Vol. II (Moscow, 1967) p. 401. Marx did attempt to introduce fixed capital in one of the refinements of his basic scheme, ibid., pp. 453ff. This led him to some very interesting considerations about what in modern macroeconomic terminology could be described as 'leakages' and 'injections'. These are examined in this chapter, p. 143 of the present book.
15. Michio Morishima, *Marx's Economics* (Cambridge, 1973) p. 120.
16. See, for example, Bernice Shoul, 'Karl Marx and Say's Law', *Quarterly Journal of Economics*, November 1957, pp. 611–29.
17. This is the view implicit in Duncan K. Foley's path-breaking paper, 'Realization and Accumulation in a Marxian Model of the Circuit of Capital', *Journal of Economic Theory*, 28, 2 (December).
18. Karl Marx, *Capital*, Vol II (Moscow, 1967) p. 50.
19. See note 17.

20. This felicitous distinction is made in W. J. Baumol, and B. S. Becker, 'The Classical Monetary Theory', *Economica*, Vol. XIX (Nov. 1952), pp. 355–96.
21. Karl Marx, *Capital*, Vol. II (Moscow, 1967) pp. 494, 496, 498, 502–4.
22. Ibid., p. 495.
23. Ibid., pp. 498–9.
24. Ibid., p. 472.
25. Ibid., pp. 472–3.
26. Rosa Luxemburg has claimed that expanded reproduction, hence the accumulation of capital, is totally impossible in the absence of a non-capitalist environment. (See her book, *The Accumulation of Capital*, particularly chapters XXVI to XXIX). In this extreme form her argument has been successfully refuted. (For a good summing up of that discussion see P. M. Sweezy, *Theory of capitalist development* (London, 1962) chapter XI.) But as a source of increasing difficulties for the capitalist system the exhaustion of a dominated non-capitalist environment is certainly worthy of the greatest attention.

7 Growth, acceleration and credit

1. Marx uses both the term and the concept of entrepreneur, although he does not explicitly associate the one with the other. For the term see *Capital*, Vol. III (Moscow, 1971) p. 374; for the substance, ibid., pp. 600, 607–8.
2. Ibid., p. 383.
3. Ibid., p. 380.
4. Ibid., p. 506.
5. Ibid., p. 439.
6. Ibid., p. 438.
7. Ibid., p. 259.
8. J. M. Keynes, *The General Theory of Employment, Interest and Money* (London, 1961) p. 150.
9. Ibid., p. 161.
10. Karl Marx, *Capital*, Vol. I (New York, 1967) pp. 383–4.
11. Ibid., p. 632.
12. Ibid., p. 138.
13. Karl Marx, *Capital*, Vol. II (Moscow, 1967) p. 474.
14. Karl Marx, *Capital*, Vol. III (Moscow, 1971) p. 237.
15. Karl Marx, *Capital*, Vol. II (Moscow, 1967) p. 77.
16. Karl Marx, *Capital*, Vol. III (Moscow, 1971) p. 304.
17. Karl Marx, *Capital*, Vol. II (Moscow, 1967) p. 75.
18. Karl Marx, *Capital*, Vol. III (Moscow, 1971) p. 304.
19. Ibid., p. 250.

8 The falling tendency of the rate of profit

1. The two basic early studies are: Joseph M. Gillman, *The Falling Rate of Profit* (New York, 1958) and Shane Mage, 'The Law of the Falling Rate of Profit', unpublished PhD thesis, Columbia, 1963. For a more recent attempt see Thomas

E. Weiskopf, 'Marxian crisis theory and the rate of profit in the postwar US economy', *Cambridge Journal of Economics*, 1979, 3, pp. 341–78.

2. For an excellent, although tendentious, summing up of the case against Marx's 'laws' see Philippe von Parijs, 'The Falling Rate-of-Profit Theory of Crisis: A Rational Reconstruction by Way of Obituary', *The Review of Radical Political Economics*, 12, 1 (Spring, 1980).

3. Karl Marx, *Capital*, Vol. III (Moscow, 1971) pp. 211ff.

4. Ben Fine and Lawrence Harris in their *Rereading Capital* (London, 1979) pp. 58ff., give a good discussion of this point.

5. This kind of neutrality of technical progress is rigorously defined in M. Morishima, *Marx's Economics* (Cambridge, 1973) pp. 142–3.

6. See P. M. Sweezy, *Theory of capitalist development* (London, 1962) pp. 100ff.

7. Karl Marx in *Grundrisse* (London, 1973) pp. 338–40 gives such arithmetical examples. For a more general mathematical treatment see David Yaffe: 'The Marxian Theory of Crisis, Capital and the State' in the *Bulletin of the Conference of Socialist Economists*, Winter 1972, p. 26.

8. Karl Marx, *Capital*, Vol. III (Moscow, 1971) p. 247.

9. Karl Marx, *Theories of Surplus Value*, Part III (Moscow, 1972) p. 368.

10. It may, of course, still be argued that, even if capitalism is capable of pushing productivity to its natural limits, that kind of productivity is more consistent with socialist than with capitalist social relations of production. Socialism would then appear as socially desirable but not as technically – in the sense of giving further scope to the development of the forces of production – indispensable. It might be interesting to reconsider the principles of historical materialism in the light of these remarks (the idea for which I derived from a very stimulating discussion of the main text with Professor Meghnad Desai) but they are not pursued further in the present book.

11. Anwar Shaikh, 'Political economy and capitalism: notes on Dobb's theory of crisis', *Cambridge Journal of Economics*, 1978, 2, pp. 233–51 and the discussion in the 1979, 1980 and 1981 issues of the journal.

12. See John E. Roemer, 'Continuing controversy on the falling rate of profit: fixed capital and other issues', *Cambridge Journal of Economics*, 1979, 3, pp. 379–98; Ian Steedman, 'A note on the "choice of technique" under capitalism', *Cambridge Journal of Economics*, 1980, 4, pp. 61–4; and the reply by Shaikh, 'Marxian competition versus perfect competition' in the same issue.

13. J. M. Keynes, *The General Theory of Employment, Interest and Money* (London, 1961) pp. 149–50.

14. Julius Sensat, Jr, *Habermas and Marxism* (Sage, Beverly Hills, 1979) pp. 125ff., particularly p. 149.

15. Philip Armstrong and Andrew Glynn, 'The law of the falling rate of profit and oligopoly', *Cambridge Journal of Economics*, 1980, 4, pp. 69–70.

16. This remarkable suggestion has been made by J. Persky and J. Abberro, whose 1978 paper, 'Technical innovation and the dynamics of the profit rate' is summarised in J. E. Roemer, 'Continuing controversy on the falling rate of profit: fixed capital and other issues', *Cambridge Journal of Economics*, 1979, 3, pp. 387–8.

9 The rise of collective capitalism

1. Karl Marx, *Capital*, Vol. III (Moscow, 1971) p. 438.
2. J. M. Keynes, 'Economic possibilities for our grandchildren', in his *Collected Works*, Vol. IX (London, 1972) p. 328.
3. Ibid., p. 327.
4. Ibid., p. 329.
5. Karl Marx, *Capital*, Vol. III (Moscow, 1971) p. 508.
6. J. M. Keynes, *The General Theory of Employment, Interest and Money* (London, 1961) p. 164.
7. This paragraph and the previous one have been based on the excellent article by Lawrence Harris: 'On Interest, Credit and Capital', *Economy and Society*, Vol. 5.2 (May).
8. Modern capitalism has thus fulfilled the prediction of M. Kalecki, in his pathbreaking wartime article: 'Political Aspects of Full Employment', *Political Quarterly*, 1943, No. 4, pp. 322–31.

10 The working class

1. *Preface* to the *Contribution to the Critique of Political Economy*.
2. See Karl Marx and Frederick Engels, *Manifesto of the Communist Party*, in *Collected Works*, Vol. 6 (London, 1976) p. 484: 'oppressor and oppressed . . . carried on an uninterrupted . . . fight that each time ended either in the revolutionary reconstruction of society at large, or in the common ruin of the contending classes.'
3. Robert Owen (1771–1858) was a pre-Marx socialist, described by Marx as 'utopian'.
4. See above, note 1.
5. Marx's assessment of Ricardo illustrates the former's belief in the capacity of original thinkers to lift themselves above their class limitations. See *Theories of Surplus Value*, part II (Moscow, 1969) p. 118.
6. Frederick Engels, *Anti-Dühring* (Moscow, 1969) p. 180.
7. J. M. Keynes, *The Economic Consequences of the Peace*, in his *Collected Works*, Vol. II (London, 1971) p. 12.
8. See Preface, notes 2 and 3.
9. Karl Marx, *Capital*, Vol. I (New York, 1967) p. 763.
10. Harry Braverman, *Labor and Monopoly Capital* (New York, 1974) p. 404.
11. André Gorz, *Farewell to the Working Class* (London, 1982) p. 126ff.
12. Harry Braverman, *Labor and Monopoly Capital* (New York, 1974) p. 394.
13. Norbert Wiener, *Cybernetics* (Cambridge, Mass., 1948 and 1961) p. 27.
14. In his 'Critique of the Gotha Programme', for example, he clearly envisages socialism as a regime more productive than capitalism. See also his comments on the impact of sciences as a direct force of production, on the demise of capitalism, in *Grundrisse* (London, 1973) pp. 705–6.
15. Karl Marx, *Capital*, Vol. I (New York, 1967) p. 420.
16. Ibid., pp. 418–19.
17. Norbert Wiener, *Cybernetics* (Cambridge, Mass., 1948 and 1961) pp. 27–8.

Further reading

1 Economics and historical materialism

Anderson, Perry, *In the Tracks of Historical Materialism* (London, 1983).
Cohen, G. A., *Karl Marx's theory of history, a defence* (Oxford, 1978).
Levine, Andrew and Wright, Eric Olin, 'Rationality and Class Struggle', *New Left Review*, 123 (London, September–October, 1980) pp. 47–68.
Popper, Sir Karl, *The Poverty of Historicism*, 2nd edn (London, 1961).

2 Commodity production and capitalism

Marx, Karl, *Capital*, Vol. I, chapter 1, sections 1, 2 and 4; chapter 6 and chapter 24.
Meek, R., *Economics and Ideology and Other Essays* (Chapman & Hall Ltd, London, 1967) Part Two.
Morishima, M. and G. Catephores (1975), 'Is there an "historical transformation problem"?' The *Economic Journal*, Vol. 85, pp. 309ff.
Renner, K., (1949), *The Institutions of Private Law and their Social Functions* (Routledge & Kegan Paul, London) chapters 1, 2 sections I, II and III.

3 The labour theory of value

Böhm-Bawerk, Eugen, *Karl Marx and the Close of his System*, ed. P. M. Sweezy (Merlin Press, London, 1949).
Rubin, I. I., *Essays in Marx's Theory of Value* (Black & Red, Detroit, 1972).
Steedman, I. *et al.*, *The Value Controversy* (Verso, London, 1981).
Steedman, I., *Marx After Sraffa* (NLB, London, 1977).

4 Value, labour power and exploitation

Bose, A., *Marxian and Post-Marxian Political Economy: An Introduction* (London, 1975).

Cohen, G. A., 'The Labour Theory of Value and the Concept of Exploitation' in Steedman, I. *et al.*, *The Value Controversy* (Verso, London, 1981).

Gintis, Herbert and Bowles, Samuel, 'Structure and Practice in the Labour Theory of Value', *Review of Radical Political Economics*, 12:4. (Winter, 1981).

Rowthorn, Bob, *Capitalism, Conflict and Inflation: Essays in Political Economy* (Lawrence & Wishart, London, 1980).

5 Money and growth

Braverman, H., *Labor and Monopoly Capital; the degradation of work in the twentieth century* (Monthly Review Press, New York, 1974) chapters 4 and 5.

Brenner, R., 'On Sweezy, Frank and Wallerstein', in *New Left Review*, 104 (London, July–August, 1977).

Desai, M., *Marxian Economics*, 2nd edn (Basil Blackwell, Oxford, 1979).

Friedman, A., *Industry and Labour* (Macmillan, London, 1977) chapter 6 and passim.

Keynes, J. M., 'Economic Possibilities for our Grandchildren' in his *Collected Works*, Vol. IX, *Essays in Persuasion* (Macmillan, London, 1972).

6 Capitalism and crisis

Desai, M., *Marxian Economics*, 2nd edn (Basil Blackwell, Oxford, 1979) chapters V and XIII.

Foley, D., 'Realization and accumulation in a Marxian Model of the Circuit of Capital', *Journal of Economic Theory*, 28,2 (December).

Itoh, M., *Value and Crisis: essays on Marxian Economics in Japan* (Pluto Press, London, 1980) chapter 4.

Lenin, V. I., *Imperialism, the highest stage of capitalism*, in *Selected Works*, Vol. I (Moscow, 1963).

Morishima, M., *Marx's Economics, a dual theory of value and growth* (Cambridge, 1973).

Union for Radical Political Economics, *US Capitalism in Crisis* (New York, 1978) (particularly the contributions by Anwar Shaikh and Thomas E. Weisskopf).

7 Growth, acceleration and credit

Dobb, M., *Political Economy and Capitalism* (Routledge & Kegan Paul, London, 1940). (Second edition. First published, 1937) chapter IV.

Fan-Hung, 'Keynes and Marx on the Theory of Capital Accumulation, Money and Interest', *Review of Economic Studies*, October 1939.

Itoh, M., *Value and Crisis, essays on Marxian Economics in Japan* (Pluto Press, London, 1980) chapter 5.

8 The falling tendency at the rate of profit

Fine, B. and Harris, L., *Rereading Capital* (Macmillan, London, 1979).

Gillman, J. M., *The Falling Rate of Profit* (New York, 1958).

Morishima, M., *Marx's Economics, a dual theory of value and growth* (Cambridge, 1973) chapter 6.

van Parijs, P., 'The Falling Rate of Profit Theory of Crisis: A Rational Reconstruction by Way of Obituary', in the *Review of Radical Political Economics*, 12, 1 (Spring 1980).

Sensat, J. Jr, *Habermas and Marxism, an Appraisal* (Sage, Beverly Hills, 1979).

Shaikh, A., 'Marxian Competition versus Perfect Competition: further comments on the so-called choice of technique', *Cambridge Journal of Economics*, 1980, 4, pp. 75–83.

Sweezy, P., *Theory of Capitalist Development* (Dennis Dobson Ltd, London, 1962) chapter 4.

Appendix to Chapter 8

Sensat, Julius, Jr, *Habermas and Marxism* (Sage, Beverly Hills, 1979) chapter 7 (the proofs given follow this text.

9 The rise of collective capitalism

Baran, P. A. and Sweezy, P. M., *Monopoly of Capital* (Penguin, Harmondsworth, 1966).

Fine, B. and Harris, L., *Rereading Capital* (Macmillan, London, 1979) chapters 7, 8 and 9.

Galbraith, J. K., *The New Industrial State*, revised edn (André Deutsch, London, 1972).

Green, F., 'Occupational Pension Schemes and British Capitalism' in *Cambridge Journal of Economics*, 6 (Academic Press, London, 1982) pp. 267–84.

Keynes, J. M., *The General Theory of Employment, Interest and Money* (Macmillan, London, 1961).

Minns, Richard, *Pension Funds and British Capitalism* (Heinemann, London, 1980).

Schumpeter, J. A., *The Theory of Capitalist Development* (Oxford University Press, Oxford, 1961).

10 The working class

Braverman, H., *Labor and Monopoly Capital: the degradation of work in the twentieth century* (Monthly Review Press, New York, 1974) chapters 17–20.

Gorz, A., *Farewell to the Working Class* (Pluto Press, London, 1982).

Wiener, N., *Cybernetics* (Harvard University Press, Cambridge, Mass., 1948 and 1961).

Index